THIRD EDITION

MORE READING POWER 3

Extensive Reading • Vocabulary Building • Comprehension Skills • Reading Fluency

D0140670

Linda Jeffries

Beatrice S. Mikulecky

PEARSON
Longman

More Reading Power 3, Third Edition

Copyright © 2012 by Pearson Education, Inc.

Pearson Education, 10 Bank Street, White Plains, NY 10606

Staff credits: The people who made up the *More Reading Power 3, Third Edition* team, representing editorial, production, design, and manufacturing, are Pietro Alongi, Dave Dickey, Oliva Fernandez, Massimo Rubini, Jaimie Scanlon, Jane Townsend, Paula Van Ells, and Pat Wosczyk.

Text composition: Rainbow Graphics
Text font: 11.5/13 Adobe Caslon
Illustrations and tech art: Bergandy Beam and Rainbow Graphics
Credits: See page 298.

Library of Congress Cataloging-in-Publication Data
Jeffries, Linda.
  More reading power / Linda Jeffries, Beatrice S. Mikulecky.—3rd ed.
    p. cm.—(Reading power)
  Previous ed. published: N.Y. : Pearson Longman, 2003; More reading power / Beatrice S. Mikulecky, 2nd ed.
  ISBN 0-13-208903-3
  1. English language—Textbooks for foreign speakers. 2. Reading—Problems, exercises, etc. 3. Reading comprehension—Problems, exercises, etc. I. Mikulecky, Beatrice S. II. Title.
  PE1128.J3475 2011
  428.6′4—dc23

                                                    2011028501

ISBN-10: 0-13-208903-3
ISBN-13: 978-0-13-208903-6

Printed in the United States of America
1 2 3 4 5 6 7 8 9 10—V011—15 14 13 12 11

Contents

Acknowledgments

First of all, I thank my husband for his patience and support while I was working on *More Reading Power 3*. I am also grateful to my friend and colleague in Modena, Anna Masetti, for her helpful feedback; and to John Rodgers at Cambridge Tutor's College, UK, for his very useful input on skimming. Last, but not least, I am indebted to the development editor, Jaimie Scanlon, for her key role in putting together the book. Many thanks once again for encouraging me and keeping me on track.

More Reading Power 3 Reviewers:

The publisher would like to extend special thanks to the following individuals who reviewed *More Reading Power*, and whose comments were instrumental in developing this edition.

Barbara Inerfeld, Rutgers, The State University of New Jersey, New Brunswick, NJ; **Barbara Morris**, University of Delaware, Newark, DE; **Suzanne Medina**, California State University, Long Beach, CA.

Thanks,
Linda

About the Authors

Linda Jeffries holds a master's degree in TESOL from Boston University. She has taught reading, writing, and ESL/EFL at Boston College; Boston University; the Harvard University Summer ESL Program; the University of Opole, Poland; and the University of Bologna, Italy. She lives in Italy, near Bologna, and teaches academic reading and writing at the University of Modena.

Bea Mikulecky holds a master's degree in TESOL and a doctorate in applied psycholinguistics from Boston University. In addition to teaching reading, writing, and ESL, she has worked as a teacher trainer in the Harvard University Summer ESL Program, in the Simmons College MATESL Program, and in Moscow, Russia. Bea Mikulecky is the author of *A Short Course in Teaching Reading Skills*.

Introduction to *More Reading Power 3*

To the Teacher

More Reading Power 3 is unlike most other reading textbooks. First, the book is organized in a different way. It has four separate parts that correspond to four important aspects of proficient reading, and therefore it is like four books in one.

Teachers should assign work in all four parts of the book every week.

The four parts of *More Reading Power* are:

- **Part 1: Extensive Reading**
- **Part 2: Vocabulary Building**
- **Part 3: Comprehension Skills**
- **Part 4: Reading Fluency**

The focus of *More Reading Power* is also different. While most books focus on content, this book directs students' attention to their own reading processes. The aim is for students to develop a strategic approach to reading at an early stage, so that they learn to view reading in English as a problem-solving activity rather than a translation exercise. This will enable them to acquire good reading habits and skills and will help them build confidence in their abilities. This way they will gain access more quickly to English-language material for study, work, or pleasure.

For a successful outcome, teachers should follow the indications in the *Teacher's Guide* for working with the book. It is especially important to have students work as much as possible in pairs or small groups. Talking about their work will help them formulate ideas and consolidate vocabulary learning.

More Reading Power 3 is intended for students at the intermediate level (Common European Framework of Reference for Languages Level B2). It is assumed that students who use this book will have an English vocabulary of about 1,000 words.

In this third edition of *More Reading Power 3*, the approach remains the same as in the earlier editions, though in response to recent research as well as feedback from teachers, there is more emphasis on vocabulary learning. All the units have been updated, and more guidance has been added for students in learning the skills. The new and improved features of this edition include:

Part 1: Extensive Reading—new nonfiction and fiction passages, as well as more guidance for dealing with new vocabulary in extensive reading

Part 2: Vocabulary Building—guidance in vocabulary learning methods: selecting useful vocabulary, dictionary work, guessing meaning from context, analyzing word parts and word families, noticing and learning collocations, and understanding referents

Part 3: Comprehension Skills—new activities for study-reading, including outlining and text marking, new unit on reading longer passages, and new "Focus on Vocabulary" section in each unit with a reading passage containing 16 target words and exercises to teach these words

Part 4: Reading Fluency—new units with longer passages, new content, and a variety of question types

Note: The separate *Teacher's Guide* contains the answer key, a rationale for the approach taken in *More Reading Power 3*, specific suggestions for using it in the classroom, and a sample syllabus.

To the Student

Reading is an important part of most language courses and also an essential skill for study at an English-language school or university.

Improving your reading will allow you to read more in English. This can help you expand your vocabulary, learn to think in English, and improve your writing skills in English.

In *More Reading Power 3*, you will work on reading in four ways in the four parts of the book:

Part 1: Extensive Reading—reading a lot in books that you choose
Part 2: Vocabulary Building—learning how to study vocabulary
Part 3: Comprehension Skills—understanding and following ideas in English
Part 4: Reading Fluency—learning to read faster and with understanding

Work in **all four parts** of the book every week to become a good reader in English.

Extensive Reading

Introduction

What Does Reading Mean to You?

A. *Complete this questionnaire about reading in your life.*

Reading Questionnaire

Name: _____

First language: _____

Do you enjoy reading in your first language? _____

Do your parents enjoy reading? _____ Your friends? _____

What do you read in your language? (Circle.)

    books   magazines   web pages/Internet articles

    newspapers   other (explain) _____

If you enjoy reading books, what types of books do you like best? (Circle.)

    novels   mysteries   thrillers   fantasy   history   biography

    graphic novels   science/technology   other: _____

Write your favorite book and/or writer (in your language), if you have one:

    Book title: _____

    Writer's name: _____

If you read in English, what do you read? (Circle.)

    books   magazines   web pages/Internet articles

    newspapers   other (explain) _____

Have you read any books in English? _____

If so, what book(s) have you read? _____

B. *Talk with other students about your answers to the questionnaire. Do you enjoy reading the same things?*

What Is Extensive Reading?

- reading **a lot**—several whole books
- choosing books that *you* want to read
- reading as fast or as slow as you want
- not having tests on your reading

According to research, the best way to improve your reading is by reading extensively; that is, by reading a lot. In fact, the best readers are people who **love to read** and who **read extensively.**

Extensive reading can also help improve your English in various ways. It can help you

. . . learn new words.
. . . learn how words are used.
. . . understand sentences more quickly.
. . . become a better writer.

How is this possible? It is possible because you get a lot of practice with the language when you read extensively. While you are reading, your brain processes words and sentences in English. Not surprisingly, you get better at this kind of processing. You may get so good at it that you begin to *think* in English. (But this only happens if you read *a lot*.)

New Vocabulary in Your Reading

When you read extensively, you will find many new words. What should you do about the words you don't know?

> **Rule 1** Do not look up all the new words in the dictionary. If you stop often to look up words, you will forget the story and you will not enjoy reading.

It is usually not necessary to know the exact meaning of every word. You can often follow the story without knowing some words. Try these exercises with missing words. This is like reading a passage with words you don't know.

EXERCISE 1

A. *This passage is from the beginning of a short story. Read the passage and answer the questions. Do not try to guess the missing words.*

Once there was a young woman who came from a good family. She had all the xxxxxx of money and a good education, and she was xxxxxx. She fell in love and married, but then her luck ended. Her love for her husband soon xxxxxx. She had two lovely children, a boy and a girl, but she did not enjoy them; she could not love them. She told herself that she hadn't been quite xxxxxx for children, but in her heart she knew she would never have been ready. She wasn't really interested in children. Deep down she felt they were xxxxxx her time. There were other, more important things she wanted to do with her life.

The children seemed to know what she was thinking and looked at her coldly. She xxxxxx to be a gentle, loving mother to them, but inside she felt only impatience. She knew she was not xxxxxx to love, not her children or anyone else. Still, everybody said she was a wonderful mother. When they said this, she smiled and the children smiled, but they all knew it was not xxxxxx.

The mother, the father, and the children lived in a large house outside the city, with a xxxxxx yard, a big car for the father, and a station wagon for the mother and children. They had a nanny to help with the children and the house, and gardeners to cut the xxxxxx and trim the shrubbery.

    a. Who are the characters (people) in this story so far? _____

    b. How does the woman feel about her children? _____

    c. How do the children feel about her? _____

d. What happens when the mother and children are together? _____

e. What do other people think about the family? _____

B. ***Talk about your answers with another student. Give examples from the text to explain and support your answers.***

EXERCISE 2

A. ***The story continues below. Read the passage and answer the questions. Do not try to guess the missing words.***

Everything in the house and the yard was as it should be. The children had rooms full of toys, xxxxxx, and the latest electronics. The parents dressed well, xxxxxx friends for dinner, went out for concerts and to the opera. But all the xxxxxx, a question hung in the air. The mother worked part time in a real-estate office, but she didn't make many sales. The father had a job in a bank. His salary was good, but what he and the mother xxxxxx was not enough for the way they were living.

The mother began to xxxxxx. The children were growing up and needed new things for school, for sports, for their xxxxxx. All these things were expensive. She went online and looked for ways to xxxxxx money. But she'd heard stories about people who had lost everything to those sites, so she turned off her computer. With all her worrying, her face became xxxxxx. She needed more money, *more money*.

And so the children always heard the unspoken xxxxxx. Nobody said it out loud, but it could be felt all the time. They heard it at Christmas, when packages with expensive toys and sports equipment were xxxxxx under the tree. They heard it at dinner when their parents talked about friends going to Vail for a long ski weekend, or flying to Paris for spring vacation. The children would look up from their games for a moment and listen. Then they would see in each other's eyes that they both had heard.

a. What kind of feeling is there in the house? _____

b. Does the father work? Is he successful? _____

c. Does the mother work? Is she successful? _____

d. What does the mother try to do? _____

e. What seems most important to the parents? _____

f. What do you think will happen to the family? _____

B. ***Talk about your answers with another student. Give examples from the text to explain and support your answers.***

C. ***Talk with your class. How many of the questions could you answer, even with a lot of missing words? How well do you think you understood the passages?***

> **Rule 2** Try to guess the general meaning of a new word from the other words and sentences around it (the context). This general meaning may be enough for you to continue reading and follow the story. (See Part 2, Unit 3 for more practice with guessing meaning.

EXERCISE 3

A. *Read the passage from Exercise 1 again. This time, try to guess the missing words or phrases and write them in the blanks.*

Once there was a young woman who came from a good family. She had all the

_____ of money and a good education, and she was _____.
     1   2

She fell in love and married, but then her luck ended. Her love for her husband

soon _____. She had two lovely children, a boy and a girl, but she did
        3

not enjoy them; she could not love them. She told herself that she hadn't been quite

_____ for children, but in her heart she knew she would never have
     4

been ready. She wasn't really interested in children. Deep down she felt they were

_____ her time. There were other, more important things she wanted to do
     5

with her life.

The children seemed to know what she was thinking and looked at her coldly. She

_____ to be a gentle, loving mother to them, but she felt only impatience.
     6

She knew she was not _____ to love, not her children or anyone else. Still,
        7

everybody said she was a wonderful mother. When they said this, she smiled and the

children smiled, but they all knew it was not _____.
        8

The mother, the father, and the children lived in a large house outside the city,

with a _____ yard, a big car for the father, and a station wagon for the
     9

mother and children. They had a nanny to help with the children and the house, and

gardeners to cut the _____ and trim the shrubbery.
       10

B. *Talk about your answers with another student. Are they the same?*

A. *Read the passage from Exercise 2 again. Try to guess the missing words or phrases and write them in the blanks.*

Everything in the house and the yard was as it should be. The children had rooms full of toys, _____(1), and the latest electronics. The parents dressed well, _____(2) friends for dinner, went out for concerts and to the opera. But all the _____(3), a question hung in the air. The mother worked part time in a real-estate office, but she didn't make many sales. The father had a job in a bank. His salary was good, but what he and the mother _____(4) was not enough for the way they were living.

The mother began to _____(5). The children were growing up and needed new things for school, for sports, for their _____(6). All these things were expensive. She went online and looked for ways to _____(7) money. But she'd heard stories about people who had lost everything to those sites, so she turned off her computer. With all her worrying, her face became _____(8). She needed more money, *more money.*

And so the children always heard the unspoken _____(9). Nobody said it out loud, but it could be felt all the time. They heard it at Christmas, when packages with expensive toys and sports equipment were _____(10) under the tree. They heard it at dinner when their parents talked about friends going to Vail for a long ski weekend, or flying to Paris for spring vacation. The children would look up from their games for a moment and listen. Then they would see in each other's eyes that they both had heard.

B. *Talk about your answers with another student. Are they the same?*

Rule 3 If a word appears several times and it seems important to the story, circle it (with a pencil if it is not your book). When you finish reading, you can look it up in the dictionary. If it is a useful word, write it in the margin (the side of the page) or in your vocabulary notebook.

Note: For this class, you will need a vocabulary notebook. You will learn more about how to keep a vocabulary notebook in Part 2, Unit 2.

In this unit, you will learn about two types of reading material: fiction and nonfiction. You will practice steps for reading and understanding both fiction and nonfiction.

> **Note:** The definitions for some words are given at the bottom of each page to help you follow the fiction and nonfiction passages. These are not common words, so you do not need to learn them.

Fiction

Fictional stories or books are about people and events that are not real. The author makes up the people, the events, and sometimes the place. Fiction often includes a "message"—an idea or opinion about life in general.

Kinds of fiction: short stories, novels, historical novels, romances, thrillers, crime, science fiction. The passage in the first exercise is a short story by Mark Hager.

EXERCISE 1

A. *Preview: Read the title and look very quickly through the story below (for not more than 30 seconds). Ask yourself, Who and what is it about?*

B. *Now read the story to the end. Do not stop to look up new words.*

Good Morning
by Mark Hager

When I was a boy, I walked through two miles of woods to get to our schoolhouse, and I would take my father's twenty-two rifle[1] with me and hide it in a hollow tree before I got to the schoolhouse, and get it as I came home in the evening.

One evening, coming from school, I ran into a community uprising at Mr. Epperly's house. Mr. Epperly's cow had gone mad[2] and was bawling[3] lonesome bawls and twisting the young apple trees out of the ground with her horns, and the whole community was demanding that Mr. Epperly's dog, Old Ranger, be shot, as Old Ranger had fought and killed the mad dog that bit the cow.

---

[1]**twenty-two rifle** a gun used for hunting
[2]**go mad** become wild and dangerous because of rabies, a disease
[3]**bawl** cry loudly

Mr. Epperly wanted to know if it wouldn't be safe to put Old Ranger in the stable[4] or someplace and keep him penned up until the danger period was over, but the neighbors said no; that Mr. Epperly's children might slip out and feed him through the cracks and get bit.

Mr. Epperly said he could not do it himself, and wanted to know who would volunteer to do it, but none of the men would.

Mr. Epperly came to me, and said, "Joe, why can't you take him with you through the woods on your way home and do it?"

I told Mr. Epperly I did not want to shoot Old Ranger. I saw Mr. Epperly's three kids were already keeping close to the old dog.

Mr. Epperly then pulled a one-dollar bill from his pocket.

"I will give you this dollar bill if you'll do it," he said.

I considered. I had never yet had a one-dollar bill all my own and while the idea of shooting Old Ranger did not appeal to me, it did seem like a thing that was demanded by the whole community, and they all put at me[5] to do it, trying to make me feel like a kind of hero, and pointed to the danger to Mr. Epperly's children. Then Mr. Epperly put a piece of clothesline around Old Ranger's neck, and I started with him. The Epperly kids began to cry.

As I walked through the woods by the little path, I started looking for a place suitable to shoot a dog and leave him lay. I saw a heavy clump[6] of wild grapevines, and I led him down under there and then got back up in the path. Old Ranger looked at me and whined[7] and wagged his tail. He wanted to come to me. I recollected[8] always seeing him wherever there was a splash of sunshine in Mr. Epperly's yard when I would pass there and Mr. Epperly's kids would join me for school.

I went down and untied Old Ranger and walked on. I came to a place where there was a hickory grove[9] in a little flat area where the underbrush[10] was thin. I recollected how Old Ranger liked to go to the hickory groves and tree squirrels[11]. I led Old Ranger down and tied him close to the trunk of a big hickory tree.

I started to take aim, but Old Ranger started prancing[12] and looking up the tree. I remembered then hearing Mr. Epperly tell how Old Ranger would do that when he'd tree a squirrel and Mr. Epperly would raise the gun to shoot, and I could not fool Old Ranger like that.

Besides, there was too much light and Old Ranger could see me take aim. I decided to wait for the gloom.[13] Soon as the sun dropped a few more feet behind the Wilson Ridge, there would be gloom, and maybe Old Ranger would not see so plainly how I pointed the gun.

While I waited for the gloom, the burning started in my pocket. I took the one-dollar bill out. I had a feeling there was something nasty about it.

While I thought of that, Old Ranger reared and barked and surged[14] at the cord leash,[15] and when I looked back out the path I saw Mr. Epperly's three kids, but they

(continued)

---

[4]**stable** building where horses or cows are kept

[5]**put at me** encourage

[6]**clump** a group of bushes or trees growing close together

[7]**whined** made a soft noise

[8]**recollect** to remember

[9]**hickory grove** a group of hickory trees

[10]**underbrush** bushes

[11]**tree squirrels** to make squirrels run up a tree

[12]**prancing** jumping

[13]**gloom** dark

[14]**surge** pull

[15]**cord leash** rope

were running away. They had turned to run when Old Ranger barked. I guessed they had slipped off from their house and followed just to see where I left Old Ranger.

The thought struck me that they would run back to their house and tell I had not shot Old Ranger yet, and that would set the folks to worrying again, and I took aim. I thought I had better fire in their hearing. I took aim at Old Ranger, but I could not touch the trigger the way he looked at me and tried to speak, so I fired in the air so the Epperly kids could say they heard the shot.

I stuck the dollar back in my pocket, went down and hugged Old Ranger around the neck. I knew I would never shoot Old Ranger. I took him and walked on. I got to the edge of our field. I climbed on the gate and sat a long time and considered. I tried to think up how I could explain to my mother why I had brought Old Ranger home with me so that she would not be scared. I could not decide how I could explain with a good face that I had a one-dollar bill in my pocket I had been given to shoot Old Ranger.

I remembered where I had seen an empty castor-oil bottle at the edge of the path. It was still there, and I got it, and stuck the one-dollar bill in it, and buried the bottle in some soft dirt under the corner of the fence.

My mother decided that since I had fired the shot, she would let me keep Old Ranger for a month, with the community thinking he was dead, but it was the hardest month I ever spent.

The Epperly kids would not walk with me to school. They would pucker up[16] to cry when they saw me, and the kids down at the schoolhouse, they would say with a sneer,[17] "What did you buy with your dollar bill?"

I could not answer. I could not tell them about the castor-oil bottle under the fence corner or Old Ranger in our stable; the Epperly kids searched the woods on both sides of the path to our house, hunting for the body of Old Ranger, but they would not ask me where I had left him, and other neighbors spoke of how Old Ranger's great booming[18] voice was missed.

Mrs. Epperly was kind to me. I met her in the road one day, and she told me how she had scolded[19] the kids for treating me like that. "But," she added, "if it was to do over, I would not allow it done. The children…Mr. Epperly, too; they're half crazy."

Then came the happy morning. "You can take Old Ranger home now, Joe," my mother said. "Been over a month. No danger now."

I went to the stable, got Old Ranger, and he reared and licked my face. I shouldered my book strap, and led Old Ranger down the path. I stopped at the fence corner and got the castor-oil bottle with the one-dollar bill in it. I had a time trying to hold Old Ranger's mouth shut so I could get in sight of the Epperly house before he barked.

At the right place where they could see us when they came running to the front porch, I let Old Ranger have his voice. Old Ranger let go with a great howl that rolled and rocked across the ridges, and the Epperlys came bounding.[20] Mr. and Mrs. Epperly and the three kids. They alternated between my neck and Old Ranger's, and I don't know to this day which of us got the most hugging.

(continued)

---

[16]**pucker up** the expression on a face (especially of a child) before he/she starts crying

[17]**sneer** an unkind expression or tone of voice that shows no respect

[18]**booming** very loud

[19]**scold** to criticize someone, especially a child, about something they have done

[20]**bounding** running

90   I handed Mr. Epperly the castor-oil bottle.

"Why did you do that?" he said.

"It felt nasty in my pocket," I said.

He tried to make me keep it and when I wouldn't, he just pitched[21] it toward me and his three kids, and we started for the schoolhouse, feeling rich, with a whole dollar to
95 spend.

---

[21]**pitch** throw

C. *Read the story again. If there are words you don't know, skip over them or guess the general meaning. The important thing is to follow the story.*

D. *Discuss these questions with another student:*

- Where does the story take place?
- When do you think it takes place: in the 21st century or earlier?
- What do you learn about the narrator (the person who tells the story)?
- Who are the other characters (people) in the story?
- Why do people in the community think that Old Ranger should be shot?
- Why doesn't the narrator shoot Old Ranger?
- Why doesn't he take Mr. Epperly's dollar in the last paragraph?
- Did you like this story? Why or why not?

E. *Work with another pair. Retell the story from beginning to end. Try to use your own words. (You can look back at the text.)*

Nonfiction

Nonfiction is writing—articles or books—about real people, places, events, or things. The writer gives information that he or she says is true. (Other people may disagree with the writer.)

Kinds of nonfiction: history, biography, science, technology, politics, psychology, health, travel, nature, "how-to" (cooking, gardening, etc.).

The passage in Exercise 2 tells about a historical period—the Second World War—and a particular group of people—the Navajo Indians. What do you know about this period and these people?

Discuss these questions with another student.

- When was the Second World War? Who was involved?
- Did your country or hometown suffer from this war?
- Did anyone in your family fight in it?
- Where do the Navajo Indians live?
- What do you know about them?

A. *Preview the passage: Read the title and look very quickly through the passage (for not more than 30 seconds). Ask yourself,* **Who and what is it about?**

B. *Now read the passage to the end. Do not stop to look up new words.*

The Code Talkers

June 1942, Camp Elliott military base, San Diego, California: 29 men sat in a locked classroom. The men were all Navajo Indians who had been recruited[1] to the Marines for a "special assignment." They had already completed the basic training course and proven that they were in excellent physical condition (better than most Americans) and could
5   shoot a rifle[2] expertly. Now they were waiting to find out why they had been recruited.

As these men waited, some of them were probably remembering other classrooms with locked doors and barred windows. Most of them had been sent off the Navajo reservation[3] (in Arizona and New Mexico), to government-run boarding schools[4] for Indians. The aim of these schools was to turn the Navajo children into "Americans."
10   Their hair was cut short, their Navajo clothes and jewelry were taken away, and they were dressed like other American children. They were not allowed to celebrate Navajo religious traditions, and had to follow the school's strict Christian teaching. Above all, they were not allowed to speak their language—not even among themselves. The punishments for breaking the rules were severe. The first time a child was heard speaking in Navajo, his
15   mouth was washed out with soap. The second time, he was beaten or shut up alone in the dark for days.

The Navajos had also been treated cruelly by Americans in the more distant past. When the Navajo homeland became part of the United States in 1848, American settlers moved into the area and soon came into conflict with the Navajos. The government
20   decided to resolve this conflict by moving all the Navajos off their homeland and into a camp in the middle of the desert. Many Navajos died of hunger and cold while walking the three hundred miles to the camp, and more died during their four years there. Later, they were allowed to return to their land, which became the Navajo Reservation. For a proud and independent people, this experience was a great shock.
25   Over the years, the story of the Long Walk was told and retold to each generation. It may seem surprising then that many Navajo men rushed to join the U.S. Army in December 1941 after the Japanese attacked Pearl Harbor. Their reasoning was very simple: In spite of the injustice they had suffered in the past, their homeland was part of the United States, so they were ready to defend it.

---

[1]**recruit** to get people to join
[2]**rifle** gun
[3]**reservation** an area of land in the U.S. kept separate for Native Americans to live on
[4]**boarding school** a school where students live

30   Then, a few months after the United States joined the war two U.S. Marine officers came to the Navajo reservation and began recruiting young Navajos for a "special assignment." The 29 men now sitting in this room were the result. Whatever they may have imagined about their special assignment, they certainly did not expect what they heard that morning from the Marine officer.

35   He told them first about military codes and how they were used to send important messages in wartime. He explained that the Marine Corps badly needed a new code. They were fighting in the Pacific against the Japanese on many small islands spread out over thousands of miles. In order to develop an effective strategy against the Japanese, the American commanders needed to communicate often and secretly. But so far, the

40   Japanese had always been able to break the American military codes and find out about their plans.

The Navajos' job, therefore, was to create a new military code based on the Navajo language. All the terms had to be short and easy to remember, as the code would not be written down. Above all, the officer told them, everything involving the code was top

45   secret. They were not to discuss their work with anyone inside or outside the Marines.

At first, the Navajos could not believe what they were being asked to do. At school they had been punished for speaking Navajo, but now they were being asked to use it. Was this some kind of joke? However, the Marine officer was totally serious. He wrote his instructions on the blackboard and left the room, once again locking the door.

50   At that point, the men may have wondered why they had been chosen for this task. They were not a well-educated group. Many of them had not finished high school and none had a college degree. How could they succeed where officers in Washington with special machines had failed?

But after their first shock, the 29 men sat right down and got to work. They decided

55   to start with the alphabet. For each English letter, they chose an English word. Then they translated that word into Navajo. For example, for the letter *A*, they chose *ant*, which became *wol-la-chee* in code. For the letter *B*, they chose *bear*, which became *shush* in code, and so on. Most of the words they chose were plants, animals, or other simple things from their lives on the reservation.

60   By the end of the first day, the men had finished the alphabet. The next day they started on military terms. For each term they thought of a related Navajo word. For example, for "hospital" they used the Navajo for "place of medicine," for "bomb" they used the Navajo for "egg," and for "route" they used the Navajo for "rabbit trail."

Once the alphabet and the military terms were completed, everything had to be

65   memorized. This was the easiest part for the Navajos. They all had excellent memories because from an early age, they had learned to listen carefully and remember what they heard. None of the Navajo stories, prayers, or songs they had grown up with were written down.

While at Camp Elliott, the Navajos also received training in the mechanics and

70   operation of radios and field telephones. Then they began to practice sending and receiving coded messages. One Navajo would receive a message in English from an officer. He would translate it into code and send it by radio or telephone to another Navajo code talker, who would translate it back into English and pass it on to another officer.

(continued)

75 Some of the Marine officers doubted that the Navajos would be able to translate messages accurately. But the Navajos soon proved that they were not only accurate, but also very fast. Whereas it took the coding machines about four hours to send and receive a message, it took the Navajos only two to three minutes.

In September 1942, the first group of Navajo Code Talkers was ready for combat.
80 They were sent to the Pacific to take part in the months-long battle for the island of Guadalcanal. It was essential for the Americans to stop the Japanese, who had been rapidly advancing toward Australia.

The job of the Code Talkers on Guadalcanal—and in later battles—was to help the officers communicate so they could organize operations on different parts of the island
85 and at sea. Often the Code Talkers were in extremely dangerous circumstances, under heavy fire and with dead soldiers all around them. But right from the beginning, they showed an extraordinary ability to concentrate and get their job done. Furthermore, the Navajos proved to be valuable soldiers. They were calm, courageous, disciplined, uncomplaining, fast on their feet, and quick to adapt to difficult situations.

90 It took many months for the Americans to liberate Guadalcanal from the Japanese. Then they began to advance slowly toward Japan, island by island. By 1944, it was clear that the Japanese were losing the war, but they continued to fight. Finally, the Americans dropped atomic bombs on Hiroshima and Nagasaki, and on August 14, 1945, Japan surrendered.

95 By the end of the war, four hundred Code Talkers had been trained and sent to the Pacific. When the fighting was over, they made their way back to their homes on the Navajo reservation. In spite of their important contribution to the war, in spite of their courage and discipline, they received no special recognition. If they stayed on the reservation, they were given little help in restarting their lives, unlike other American
100 soldiers. Above all, they still were not allowed to talk about the Navajo code—just in case another war broke out and the code was needed again.

Even without these orders, the Navajos probably would not have talked much about their wartime experiences. They were a modest and peace-loving people, who did not believe in celebrating war. So there were no homecoming parades on the reservation. But
105 many families did hold special Navajo ceremonies for their sons and husbands to help them get over the nightmares and depression that often affect soldiers after combat.

In spite of this, some Code Talkers had difficulties after the war. It was not easy for them to accept the poverty and the limited work opportunities on the reservation, or the racism and discrimination they met off the reservation. The result was sometimes self-
110 destructive behavior, including heavy drinking and suicide.

However, a number of the Navajos went back happily to their old lives, and others moved off the reservation to become successful professionals. Those who moved to the cities could take advantage of the special law that helped returning soldiers pay for college. Carl Gorman, one of the original 29, became a successful artist and teacher in
115 California. Teddy Draper, who had learned Japanese during the war, became a language teacher. Both eventually returned to the reservation to teach young Navajos at the new schools and colleges that they helped start.

The first public recognition for the Code Talkers came after 1969, when the Navajo code was finally declassified (no longer secret). The Marines held a ceremony in Chicago

120

that year to reunite some of the Code Talkers and they formed an association. In 1971, President Nixon presented the Code Talkers with a certificate of appreciation. In 1982, the United States Congress decided that August 14 would be National Navajo Code Talkers Day. Then, finally, in 2001, the 29 original Navajos who had created the code were awarded the Congressional Gold Medal, and the other 370 Code Talkers were

125

awarded the Silver Medal. For many of them, this award arrived too late. Only 5 of the 29 were still alive.

C. *Read the passage again. If there are words you don't know, skip over them or guess the general meaning. The important thing is to follow the story.*

D. *Discuss these questions with another student:*

- What people, places, and events does this passage describe?
- What have you learned about Native Americans from this passage? About Najavo Indians?
- What have you learned about the Second World War from this passage? About military codes?
- Have you ever tried to invent or learn a code?

E. *Work with another pair. Retell the passage from beginning to end. Try to use your own words. (You can look back.)*

Books

Choosing Books for Extensive Reading

Which Books Are Best for You?

Books that interest you   Your teacher and friends can give you ideas, but you should look for books that *you* want to read. Do not choose a book just because you have heard of it or because you think you will learn from it. Choose a book you will *enjoy*.

Books that are not too difficult   A book that has many unknown words is hard to understand. It also is not very enjoyable to read. You should look for a book that is easily enjoyable, so you will actually read it.

Books written for language learners   If you do not feel confident about reading books in English, there are many very good stories and nonfiction books that are written in simpler language especially for learners.

Books written for native speakers   If you are confident reading in English, you will have a wider choice among these books.

On pages 27–30, you will find a list of suggestions, books that students have enjoyed. However, you do not need to choose one of these books. Any book at the right level that interests you is good for extensive reading.

You can probably find something you will enjoy at a bookstore or library. Easier books, which can also be enjoyed by adults, can be found in the young adult or children's sections. Preview books to make sure they are right for you.

Previewing a Book

Follow two steps when previewing books. Here is the first step:

1. Find out about the book.
   - Read the front and back covers, and the first page (often viewable on Internet sites). What is it about? Is it the kind of book you would enjoy?
   - Read reviews by your classmates or on the Internet (Amazon.com or other sites). What do people say about the book? Do they recommend it?

A. Read the back cover and book review of **The Outsiders** by S. E. Hinton. Then discuss the questions with another student.

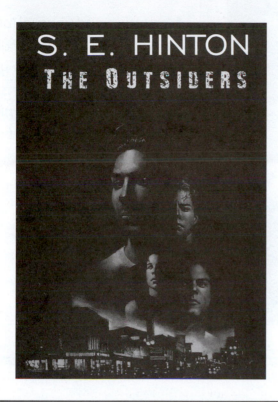

(from the back cover)

A heroic story of friendship and belonging. Ponyboy can count on his brothers. And on his friends. But not on much else besides trouble with the Socs, a vicious gang of rich kids whose idea of a good time is beating up "greasers" like Ponyboy. At least he knows what to expect—until the night when someone takes things too far.

Review:

I read this book last year, in my junior year of high school. I was going through a bad time and I was upset a lot. Then I started this book and I really got involved. The main character, Ponyboy Curtis, goes through a lot of the same problems I was going through. I wasn't part of a gang, like Ponyboy, but there were groups in my school and you had to belong to the right one, or you were in trouble. This is not a very happy book, but it's a lot like real life, maybe because the author was only 16 when she wrote it. It really gives an inside view of the teen experience.

a. What kind of book is this? (mystery, romance, thriller, history, etc.)

b. What or who is it about?

c. Does it seem interesting to you?

B. *Read the back cover and book review of* **The Island of the Blue Dolphins** *by Scott O'Dell. Then discuss the questions with another student.*

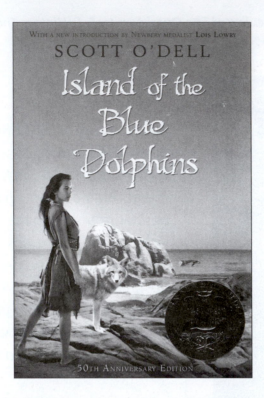

(from the back cover)

A haunting and unusual tale based on the true story of an American Indian girl who spent 18 years alone on a rocky island far off the coast of California. Dramatic and unforgettable.

Review:

A few years ago, I read this book in school. It was one of my favorites. I recently read it again and I'm happy to report that the story is still worth reading by young and older readers. It's told from the point of view of an American Indian girl, who spends many years alone on an island. The book tells of her adventures—how she ends up alone on the island at the age of 12 and how she survives by fishing, hunting, and fighting her enemies. Once you start reading, you won't be able to put it down. Beautiful writing and a moving story.

    a. What kind of book is this?

    b. What or who is it about?

    c. Does it seem interesting to you?

C. *Which of these books is more interesting to you? Compare your opinions to those of other students.*

Here is the second step in previewing a book:

2. **Check the level of difficulty.**
   - If the book is written for English language learners, you should probably start reading at Level 3. If that seems easy, your next book can be at Level 4.
   - If the book is for native speakers (adult, young adult, or children), use the method below to check the difficulty.

Try out this method on a book written in English. (Your teacher will give you a book, or you can use a page from Part 4 of More Reading Power.)

A Quick Method for Measuring Difficulty

1. On a full page, count the number of words you do not know. _____
2. Calculate the number of words on the page. (The number of words in three full lines divided by 3. Multiply that by the number of lines on the page.) _____
3. Calculate the percentage of unknown words on that page. (For example, five unknown words on a 250-word page is 2%.) _____

Guidelines for Reading Your Books

1. Read for at least 30 minutes every day. Find a regular time for reading. Each time you stop, write the date in pencil in the margin. Your teacher will check on your progress.

2. Do not stop to look up new words unless they are necessary to follow the story.

3. If you want to learn vocabulary from your book, you can use a pencil to underline the words you think might be useful. Later, when you have finished reading, or on another day, you can look them up. Then write them in your vocabulary notebook (with the parts of speech, sentences where you found them, and definitions).

4. When you finish a book:
   - Tell your teacher.
   - Write the title of the book on your Reading Log on page 26.
   - If you liked the book, tell your classmates about it.

Learn to Read Faster

You will enjoy extensive reading more if you can read quickly. You will probably also read more. That will help you read better and more quickly. Then you will read more and better.

However, like many students, you may read slowly in English. This is often the result of habit. You read at a certain rate (speed) because your eyes are used to moving across the page at that speed.

The first step in learning to read faster is to find out how fast you read, or your reading rate.

Finding Your Reading Rate

1. Calculate the average number of words per page:

   a. Turn to any full page in the book. Count the total number of words in any three lines on the page. Divide that number by three. This is the average number of words per line.

   b. Count the total number of lines on the page and multiply it by the number of words.

   $$\underline{\hspace{3cm}} \times \underline{\hspace{3cm}} = \underline{\hspace{3cm}}.$$
   (lines)　　　　(average words per line)　　　(words per page)

2. Time your reading: Open your book to the page you are now reading. With a pencil, mark your place on the page. Before you start reading, write the exact time in the margin. Read at a comfortable speed for about 10 or 15 minutes. Write the exact time you finish.

3. Calculate the number of minutes you read:

   $$\underline{\hspace{3cm}} \text{ min.} - \underline{\hspace{3cm}} \text{ min.} = \underline{\hspace{3cm}} \text{ min.}$$
   (finishing time)　　　　(starting time)　　　　(reading time)

4. Calculate the number of words you read:

   a. Count the number of pages you read (including parts of pages): _____

   b. Multiply the number of pages by the number of words per page.

   $$\underline{\hspace{3cm}} \times \underline{\hspace{3cm}} = \underline{\hspace{3cm}}.$$
   (pages read)　　　　(words per page)　　　(words you read)

5. Calculate your reading rate:

   Divide the number of words you read by the number of minutes.

   $$\underline{\hspace{3cm}} \div \underline{\hspace{3cm}} = \underline{\hspace{3cm}}.$$
   (words read)　　　　(minutes)　　　(reading rate—words per minute)

6. Write the date and your reading rate on the Extensive Reading Rate Progress Chart on page 21.

Rate Practice

Follow the steps above to check your reading rate regularly (about once a week). Each time you check it, write the date and your rate in the chart.

When you start a new book, use a new chart. When you have completed the charts below, ask your teacher for new blank charts.

Book Title _____   Book Title _____

Author _____   Author _____

RATE (words per minute—WPM)

| 520 |
| 500 |
| 480 |
| 460 |
| 440 |
| 420 |
| 400 |
| 380 |
| 360 |
| 340 |
| 320 |
| 300 |
| 280 |
| 260 |
| 240 |
| 220 |
| 200 |
| 180 |
| 160 |
| 140 |
| 120 |
| 100 |
| 80 |

Date

RATE (words per minute—WPM)

| 520 |
| 500 |
| 480 |
| 460 |
| 440 |
| 420 |
| 400 |
| 380 |
| 360 |
| 340 |
| 320 |
| 300 |
| 280 |
| 260 |
| 240 |
| 220 |
| 200 |
| 180 |
| 160 |
| 140 |
| 120 |
| 100 |
| 80 |

Date

Reading Sprints

Students sometimes read slowly simply because they are used to reading that way. They learned to read in English by moving their eyes slowly across the page and they continue to move their eyes slowly.

One way you can learn to read faster is by doing reading sprints. These sprints are like the sprints that runners do. They force themselves to run much faster for short periods. Afterward, they can run a little faster all the time. Regular practice with reading sprints (about twice a month) will help you increase your reading rate. It will also help you become a more flexible reader, so you can speed up or slow down as you need.

To do reading sprints, you will need:

- your extensive reading book (preferably a book that you have already started).
- a clock or watch if you are at home. (Your teacher will time you if you are in the classroom.)

Guidelines for Reading Sprints

Read ALL of the directions before you begin.

1. With a pencil, mark the place where you are now in your book. Write the exact starting time in the margin. Then read for *five* minutes. (Your teacher will time you the first time.)

2. Make a mark (X) in the margin where you stopped reading. Count the number of pages you just read: _____.

3. Starting at the X, count ahead the same number of pages you read in step 1. (For example, if you just read two and a quarter pages, count ahead two and a quarter pages.) Make a new mark in the margin (X).

4. Now try to read from the first X to the new X in only *four* minutes. Time yourself, or your teacher will time you. You will need to force your eyes to move faster along the page, skipping words or even whole lines of text.

5. If you do not succeed the first time, try again until you do. Each time you try, start from where you finished the last time and count ahead the same number of pages in new text. Mark the place (X) where you stop reading. (Do not worry about understanding everything you read now.)

6. When you are able to read the pages in four minutes, count ahead and try to read the same number of pages in *three* minutes. (You can read these pages again later if you feel you are missing a lot.)

7. Now try for *two* minutes. Keep trying until you succeed. You may be able to catch just a few words from each page. This does not matter. The important thing is to make your eyes move quickly and understand *something*.

8. When you can "read" the pages in two minutes (or close to that), mark the place where you stopped. You do not need to count ahead this time. Start reading from that place at a comfortable speed for five minutes. Time yourself or your teacher will time you.

9. Count the number of pages you read during these five minutes: _____. How does this compare with the number of pages you read the first time? Many students find that their comfortable reading speed is faster than it was before the sprints.

Discussing Your Books

Talking about your extensive reading books is useful for several reasons. First, it can help you better understand what you read. When you tell someone about a book, you review the story in your mind. This helps you think more clearly about the story and your response to it. Furthermore, reactions and comments from your classmates or teacher may lead to new thoughts and ideas about the book.

Talking about your books will also help you learn to express your thoughts in English about what you read. This is an important skill for school or college. In the activities in this section, you will learn about and practice some of the ways that English readers think and talk about their reading.

Book Conferences

A book conference is a conversation with your teacher. It is not a test. You do not need to study for it. When you finish a book, tell your teacher and make a date for a conference.

Your teacher will ask you questions like these:
- What is the title?
- Who is the author?

For fiction:
- Where does the story take place? When?
- Who are the main characters (people in the story)?
- What happens to them?
- Is there a character you particularly like? Dislike?
- Does the story or the characters relate to your life in any way?
- Did you have any strong feelings about any part of the book?
- Would this book be a good movie? Why or why not?
- What would you have done if you were _____?

For nonfiction:
- What is it about?
- Was it hard or easy to understand? Does the author explain it well?
- What have you learned from reading this book?
- Does this interest you? Why or why not?
- Does it relate to your life in some way?
- Has this book changed your thinking in any way?
- Did you like the book?
- Would you recommend it to others? Explain your opinion.

Reading Circles

A reading circle is a small group of students that meets to talk about the books they are reading.

Your teacher will tell you who will be in your reading circle (four to five students) and when it is time for a meeting (about once a week).

Rules for Reading Circles

At each meeting, the students in the group take turns talking about their books. Each student should speak for not more than two minutes. Suggested talking points:

- where you are in the book
- difficulties: for example, difficult words or a confusing plot (story)
- if fiction: the setting (where and when it takes place), the characters, and the plot
- if nonfiction: the subject, the author's ideas, the content
- your opinion about the book

Students who are not talking must listen and then ask at least one question. The student to the right of the speaker should watch the time and say when two minutes are up.

Book Presentations

A book presentation is a short (four- to five-minute) oral report to the class about a book you have read.

How to Prepare for a Book Presentation

1. On a small piece of paper, write notes (not whole sentences) about:
   - the title and author
   - any difficulties you had in reading the book (vocabulary, dialog, plot)
   - if fiction: the setting, main characters, and a very brief summary of the plot (story)
   - if non-fiction: the subject and a very brief summary of the content
   - your opinion. Would you recommend this book?
2. Practice using your notes to talk about the book. Practice by yourself and with a friend. It can also be very useful to record yourself and listen to the recording.
3. When you practice, don't just read from your notes. Look at them only when you need to. Look up as much as possible. Speak slowly and clearly. Try not to stop or say "um" or "ah" too often. Repeat sentences until you can say them smoothly.
4. Time your talk before you give it in class. If it takes less than four minutes, think of more things to say. If it takes more than five minutes, cut out some parts.

Writing about Your Books

Book Files

When you finish a book, ask your teacher for a file card. Then make a card about the book. This will go into the class book files. You and your classmates can use the files to find books you like.

EXAMPLE

TITLE: _The Outsiders_

AUTHOR: _S. E. Hinton_

NUMBER OF PAGES: _180_ **FICTION:** _x_ **NONFICTION:** ____

SUMMARY: _The story of a teenage boy who lives with his brothers. (His parents died in an accident.) He's part of a gang, but he's very unhappy about his life. The story is very dramatic (someone is killed) and full of strong emotions._

RATE THE BOOK: ☆☆☆☆ _A great book!_

Book Reports

Each time you finish a book, fill in a book report form. Ask your teacher for another form when you have filled in this one.

BOOK REPORT

Title: _____

Author: _____ Fiction: _____ Nonfiction: _____

Number of pages: _____ Difficulty (1 = very easy, 10 = very difficult): _____

Type of book:

    novel   mystery   thriller   fantasy   science fiction

    history   biography   science/technology   other: _____

Setting (fiction) or subject (nonfiction): _____

_____

Characters and plot (fiction) or ideas/explanation (nonfiction): _____

_____

_____

Your general opinion: _____

_____

_____

What did you like best about this book? _____

_____

_____

What did you like least? _____

_____

_____

Rate this book: _____

★ ★ ★ ★ = a great book!   ★ = not very interesting
  ★ ★ ★ = a good book   × = a terrible book
    ★ ★ = some good parts

READING LOG

1. Title: _____

   Author: _____ Date: _____

2. Title: _____

   Author: _____ Date: _____

3. Title: _____

   Author: _____ Date: _____

4. Title: _____

   Author: _____ Date: _____

5. Title: _____

   Author: _____ Date: _____

6. Title: _____

   Author: _____ Date: _____

7. Title: _____

   Author: _____ Date: _____

8. Title: _____

   Author: _____ Date: _____

9. Title: _____

   Author: _____ Date: _____

10. Title: _____

    Author: _____ Date: _____

11. Title: _____

    Author: _____ Date: _____

12. Title: _____

    Author: _____ Date: _____

Suggested Reading

If you are unsure of your ability to read a whole book in English, you might start with a book written for English language learners. The vocabulary and the sentence structure in these are easier than in books written for native speakers.

Most publishers of ESL/EFL textbooks publish these books, which are called "graded readers." Some graded readers are simplified versions of books written for native speakers and some are new stories. Start with a book at level 3 (low-intermediate, with about an 800-word vocabulary). If this seems easy, you can move to a higher level.

Among books for native speakers of English, the easiest to read are often those written for young people and found in the children's or young adult sections of bookstores and libraries. Many of these books are not childish at all, and are in fact also popular with adults. Though they are easier than adult books, they are not all necessarily easy. Check the level as you would with any book for native speakers.

The following list includes books (for native speakers) that have been enjoyed by students, both native speakers and language learners. These are just suggestions, however. You do not have to read books from this list. Any books are good for extensive reading—if they are interesting to you and are at the right level.

For many of the books on the list, an audio CD is available. Listening and reading at the same time is very good practice. After you listen to and read a book, try just reading or just listening another time. It will seem much easier the second time. You will understand the story better and will learn more words.

Book List

Key:

*	This author has written other popular books
🎧	Audio CD available
YA	Young Adult

Fiction

🎧 *Absolutely True Diary of a Part-Time Indian.* Alexie, Sherman. A young American Indian draws cartoons to deal with the family disasters and racism in his life. (288 pages) YA

🎧 *Alchemist, The.* Coelho, Paulo. The story of a Spanish shepherd boy who dreams of treasure, goes on a journey, and meets many people who teach him about life. (208 pages)

🎧 *Art of Racing in the Rain, The.* Stein, Garth. A heart-warming story told by Enzo, a dog, the faithful companion of a race-car driver. (336 pages)

Book Thief, The. Zuzak, Markus. Death itself narrates this story of an orphan girl in Germany during World War II. (576 pages) YA

Bridget Jones' Diary. Fielding, Helen.* A funny and realistic novel (in the form of a diary) about a single young woman in search of self-improvement. (267 pages)

🎧 *Chocolate War, The.* Cormier, Robert. A classic story of a high school student who becomes the hero of the school when he fights a secret society. (191 pages) YA

🎧 *Code Orange.* Cooney, Caroline. When a New York teenager discovers a one-hundred-year-old sample of smallpox, he and his friends are in danger. (208 pages) YA

🎧 *Code Talking.* Bruchac, Joseph. A novel about Navajo Indians in the U.S. Marines in World War II, and how they sent messages in their native language to help America win the war. (240 pages) YA

🎧 *Confessions of a Shopaholic.* Kinsella, Sophie.* International best seller about a young woman who is addicted to shopping. Colorful and funny. (320 pages)

🎧 *Countess below Stairs, A.* Ibbotson, Eva.* After the Russian Revolution, a beautiful young countess has to leave Russia for England, where she takes a job as a servant. (400 pages) YA

🎧 *Curious Incident of the Dog in the Night-Time, The.* Haddon, Mark. Told from the point of view of an autistic teenager. Bitterly funny, original, and moving. (226 pages)

🎧 *Double Helix.* Werlin, Nancy. A suspenseful novel about love and the genetic-engineering experiments of Dr. Wyatt. (252 pages)

🎧 *Eragon.* Paolini, Christopher.* In a fantasy world, a young boy and a dragon have adventures. YA

🎧 *Flush.* Hiaasen, Carl.* Serious personal and environmental issues dealt with in a humorous way and a colorful setting in Florida. (272 pages) YA

🎧 *Giver, The.* Lowry, Lois.* Jonas lives in a perfect society: no pain, no crime, no unhappiness. But then he becomes the receiver of memories, and he learns about some terrible choices. (192 pages) YA

🎧 *Harry Potter and the Sorcerer's Stone* (Original U.K. title: *Harry Potter and the Philosopher's Stone*). Rowling, J. K.* In these famous adventures, Harry discovers that he's a wizard. (312 pages) YA

🎧 *Hatchet.* Paulson, Gary.* Brian is on the way to visit his father when the airplane crashes and Brian finds himself alone in the Canadian wilderness. (195 pages) YA

Hitchhiker's Guide to the Galaxy, A. Adams, Douglas*. This book is science fiction, fantasy, and lots of fun—a best seller for many years. (224 pages)

🎧 *House on Mango Street, The.* Cisneros, Sandra. Growing up in the poor, Hispanic part of Chicago, Esperanza learns to make a happy life in middle of difficulties. (110 pages)

🎧 *Hunger Games, The.* Collins, Susanne. The United States in a not-too-distant future, when young people must compete in a brutal game. (384) YA

🎧 *I Know What You Did Last Summer.* Duncan, Lois. A horror story full of suspense about a group of young people and their secret. (198 pages) YA

🎧 *Interview with the Vampire.* Rice, Anne*. A classic about vampires in 18th-century Louisiana. (352 pages)

🎧 *Island of the Blue Dolphins.* O'Dell, Scott. This beautiful book tells the story of a Native American girl left alone for years on an island. (192 pages) YA

🎧 *Julie of the Wolves.* George, Jean Craig.* Julie, an Eskimo girl, is married against her will at 13 and runs away into the wilderness to live with the wolves. (176 pages) YA

Just Listen. Dessen, Sara.* A teenage girl is unhappy at home and at school, but a friend helps her find herself and cope. (400 pages) YA

🎧 *Lavinia.* LeGuin, Ursula. This famous writer of science fiction has recreated the world before ancient Rome in a dramatic tale of passion and war. (288 pages)

🎧 *Life of Pi.* Martel, Yann. A strange and fascinating story about a boy and a tiger on a boat. (326 pages)

🎧 *Lord of the Flies.* Golding, William. A classic—their plane crashes into the sea and a group of English schoolboys find themselves alone on an island. (208 pages)

🎧 *Lucky One, The.* Sparks, Nicholas.* Near death leads a soldier to the love of his life. (336 pages)

Man from the Other Side, The. Orlev, Uri. In 1943 in Warsaw, Poland, a young man with anti-Jewish feelings discovers that his dead father was Jewish. (192 pages) YA

🎧 *Monster (Amistad).* Myers, Walter Dean.* In this tense story, 16-year-old Steve tells about his trial for murder and his life until then. (288 pages) YA

🎧 *Nine Dragons.* Connelly, Michael.* Detective Harry Bosch once again investigates a murder in Los Angeles. (480 pages)

🎧 *No. 1 Ladies Detective Agency, The.* McCall Smith, Alexander.* Entertaining. Madame Ramotswe decides to open a detective agency in Botswana (Africa). Delightful and revealing. (272 pages)

🎧 *Outsiders, The.* Hinton, S. E. An intensely realistic and dark tale about youth gangs, written when the author was 16 years old. A classic. (208 pages) YA

🎧 *Pigman, The.* Zindel, Paul.* Funny and serious, moving and perceptive, this is a classic story about two young people's search for meaning in life. (192 pages) YA

🎧 *Princess Diaries, The.* Cabot, Meg.* A high-school student in New York City, Mia finds out that her father is really a European prince, and she is a princess. (304 pages)

🎧 *Redheaded Princess, The.* Rinaldi, Anne.* The dramatic story of the beautiful young princess who became Queen Elizabeth I. (224 pages) YA

🎧 *Sisterhood of the Traveling Pants, The.* Brashares, Ann.* A heartening story of four teenage friends who share a pair of jeans over a summer and discover the value of their friendship. (336 pages) YA

🎧 *Speak.* Halse Anderson, Laurie. Why is Melinda no longer speaking to anyone? It's not because of the usual problems at home or at school. (208 pages) YA

🎧 *Stormbreaker: An Alex Rider Adventure.* Horowitz, Anthony. In this spy thriller series, Alex's uncle mysteriously dies, and Alex finds out that he was a spy for the government. (192 pages) YA

🎧 *Summer of My German Soldier, The.* Greene, Bette. During World War II, a Jewish girl in the American Midwest falls in love with a German prisoner of war. (199 pages) YA

🎧 *Twilight.* Meyer, Stephanie.* Though long, this book and the others in the series are hugely popular with young people around the world. Vampires and romance. (544 pages)

🎧 *Uglies, The.* Westerfield, Scott.* This first book in a trilogy tells of a future world where everyone becomes beautiful at the age of 16. (432 pages) YA

🎧 *Witness.* Hesse, Karen. When the Ku Klux Klan arrives in a small town in Vermont, the people in the town react in many different ways. (288 pages) YA

Nonfiction

Alive: The Story of the Andes Survivors. Read, Pier Paul. The dramatic story of 16 people (some of them from a Uruguayan rugby team) who survived a plane crash in the Andes. (398 pages)

🎧 *Boy.* Dahl, Roald. The funny and shocking childhood and school experiences of this famous English writer. (176 pages) YA

Chimpanzees I Love: Saving Their World and Ours, The. Goodall, Jane. The world-famous expert tells of her experiences with chimpanzees. (268 pages)

Diary of a Young Girl, The. Frank, Anne. This well-known book tells the true story of a Jewish girl hiding from the Nazis in World War II Holland. (368 pages) YA

🎧 *Dreams from My Father.* Obama, Barack. The autobiography of the 44th President of the United States, from his childhood until he is 25. (480 pages)

🎧 *Escape: The Story of the Great Houdini.* Fleischman, Sid. The rags-to-riches story of a poor Jewish boy who became a great magician and escape artist. (210 pages) YA

Farewell to Manzanar. Houston, Jeanne Wakatsuki, and Houston, James D. A girl from a Japanese American family grows up behind barbed wire in California. (146 pages) YA

Ghosts of War: The True Story of a 19-Year-Old GI. Smithson, Ryan. An honest and powerful retelling of the author's experience in Iraq. (352 pages)

Go Ask Alice. Anonymous. The real diary of a 15-year-old girl who became addicted to drugs. (188 pages) YA

It Happened to Nancy: By an Anonymous Teenager, A True Story From Her Diary. Sparks, Beatrice. The true story of a teenager who thought she had found love, but instead found AIDS. (238 pages) YA

Leonardo's Horse. Fritz, Jean. The life and times of Leonardo da Vinci, and the story of a sculpture that he never made. (127 pages) YA

🎧 *Letters to a Young Brother: Manifest Your Destiny.* Harper, Hill. The author's personal story as a young black man in America and his responses to letters from other young men. (192 pages) YA

Long Way Gone: Memoirs of a Boy Soldier, A. Beah, Ishmael. The experiences of a boy growing up in Sierra Leone and how he is forced to take part in the civil war. (229 pages)

🎧 *Marley: A Dog Like No Other.* Grogan, John. As a family dog, Marley is 90 lbs. of trouble, fun, and love. (208 pages)

🎧 *Night.* Wiesel, Elie. Taken from his Hungarian village as a boy, the author survived the Nazi death camps. This book asks fundamental questions about life and faith. A masterpiece. (120 pages)

One Kingdom: Our Lives with Animals. Noyes, Deborah. The author, a former zookeeper, looks at the ways animals and humans have connected throughout history. Wonderful photographs. (144 pages) YA

Only the Names Remain: The Cherokees and the Trail of Tears. Bealen, Alex W. The sad history of the Cherokee Indians from the 16th century to their removal from Georgia in 1837. (80 pages) YA

Perilous Journey of the Donner Party, The. Calabro, Marian. In 1846, 90 people traveling to California were trapped for the winter—a story of survival and cannibalism. (192 pages) YA

🎧 *Phineas Gage: A Gruesome but True Story about Brain Science.* Fleischman, John. After an iron rod went through his brain in 1848, a man lived for 11 years. (96 pages) YA

🎧 *Poet Slave of Cuba: A Biography of Juan Francisco Manzano, The.* Engle, Margarita, and Qualls, Sean. This biography tells of the suffering and the talent of a 19th-century Cuban poet. (192 pages) YA

Really Short History of Nearly Everything, A. Bryson, Bill. A very entertaining and complete explanation of key scientific concepts. Enjoyable for both scientific and nonscientific readers. (176 pages) YA

Red Scarf Girl. Jiang, Ji-Li. This Chinese writer tells about her difficult childhood in China during the Cultural Revolution. (285 pages) YA

Rosa Parks: My Story. Parks, Rosa, and Haskins, Jim. Rosa Parks tells of her life and her role in the civil rights movement in 1950s America. (188 pages)

🎧 *Three Cups of Tea.* Mortenson, Greg; Relin, David Oliver; and Thompson, Sara L. How one man dedicated his life to making the lives of children better by building schools in Pakistan and Afghanistan. (349 pages)

When I Was a Soldier: A Memoir. Zenatti, Valerie. The author writes about her two years in the Israeli army; the difficulties, dangers, and lessons. (240 pages)

🎧 *Zlata's Diary: A Child's Life in Wartime Sarajevo.* Filipovish, Zlata. Ten-year-old Zlata tells in her diary about the bombings and hardship of life in Sarajevo. (240 pages) YA

Vocabulary Building

Introduction

In this part of *Reading Power 3* you will work on vocabulary. You will learn ways to build a larger vocabulary and find out more about how words are used. This will help you become a better reader.

> **Remember**
>
> If you want to build your vocabulary, it's not enough to study words. You also need to read a lot. When you read, you will see the words many times in different contexts. This will help you learn the meanings of words and how they fit into sentences. It will also allow you to read faster, understand better, and remember the words better. For all these reasons, you should read as much as possible—during the course and afterward.

> **Note:** In this part of the book, you will often need to write the definitions of words—in the exercises, in your notebook, and on study cards. Check with your teacher about which language to use—English or your first language.

Making Good Use of the Dictionary

In this unit, you will learn how to make use of the information in learner dictionaries. This includes:

- pronunciation
- spelling
- parts of speech
- definitions
- the way words are used

Choosing a Good Dictionary

You will need a dictionary for some of the exercises in this unit and for other vocabulary work.

There are two kinds of dictionaries that are useful for vocabulary work: bilingual dictionaries and learner dictionaries. If possible, you should have one of each.

- *Bilingual dictionaries* (English and your language) are easier to use because the definitions are easier to understand than in an English dictionary. It may also be easier to find the English words you need when you are writing.
- *Learner dictionaries* in English have more examples and information about words and their usage than most bilingual dictionaries. For this same reason, they are also better than regular English language dictionaries.

Examples of learner's dictionaries are the Longman Dictionary of American English, the Longman Advanced Dictionary of American English, and the Longman Dictionary of Contemporary English for Advanced Learners (British and American).

Pronunciation

Everyone knows that pronunciation is important in speaking. However, many students may not know that it is also important in reading.

- Research has shown that you can read faster and better if you know what words sound like. That's because when you read, your brain makes a connection between the letters on the page and the sound of the word. When your brain can make this connection, it can more easily find other information about the word in your memory, including information about the meaning.

- Knowing the pronunciation of a word also makes it easier to remember. In fact, your memory has trouble holding onto a word if you can't say it. You may have noticed this about the names of people or places that you can't pronounce—they're easily forgotten.

Most dictionaries tell you how to pronounce words in English. They use special pronunciation symbols (letters) after each word. They usually contain a pronunciation table on the inside of the front or back cover that explains these symbols. If the table is not on the cover, look for it in the table of contents. Then put a tab (a post-it note or a taped piece of paper) on that page so you can find it easily when you use the dictionary.

In Appendix 1 on page 289, you will find a Pronunciation Key with example words for each symbol.

EXERCISE 1

A. *Work with another student. Look at the pronunciation key in Appendix 1 on page 289. Take turns saying the example words for each symbol. Then check your pronunciation with your teacher.*

B. *Read the pronunciation symbols and the words silently. Then take turns reading them aloud with a partner.*

1. / eɪ /   a. break   b. wait   c. eight
2. / ʌ /   a. trouble   b. fun   c. money
3. / ʃ /   a. station   b. special   c. machine
4. / s /   a. sword   b. science   c. listen

C. *Work with your partner. For each group of words in Part B, circle the letters in each word that make the sound shown by the symbol.*

EXERCISE 2

A. *Work with another student. Follow these directions for each group of words:*

- Take turns reading the words aloud.
- If you are not sure how to say a word, look it up in the dictionary.
- Check with your teacher if you still are not sure.
- Practice saying the words correctly.

1. a. pretty   b. enjoy   c. equal   d. eye   e. level
2. a. hear   b. heart   c. heavy   d. reach   e. bear
3. a. iron   b. kind   c. limit   d. machine   e. thin
4. a. fruit   b. guilty   c. sugar   d. suite   e. cruel
5. a. headache   b. much   c. choose   d. machinery   e. Christmas
6. a. mall   b. fact   c. match   d. shake   e. water
7. a. foreign   b. general   c. organize   d. thought   e. gift
8. a. trouble   b. doubt   c. though   d. amount   e. would

B. *In each group of words in Part A, circle the two words that include the sound given below. For example, circle* **enjoy** *and* **level** *for number 1.*

1. / ɛ / (as in pen) 5. / ʧ / (as in chair or itch)
2. / i / (as in free) 6. / æ / (as in cat)
3. / ɪ / (as in hit) 7. / g / (as in get)
4. / u / (as in true) 8. / aʊ / (as in out)

C. *Discuss these questions with another student:*

- What can you say about spelling and pronunciation in English?
- What can you say about spelling and pronunciation in your language?

Remember

When you look up a new word, check the pronunciation and say the word aloud.
A letter (or group of letters) may be pronounced in many ways.
 Examples: r**a**ther / æ /, sh**a**pe / eɪ /, f**a**ther / ɑ /
Different letters (or groups of letters) may have the same pronunciation.
 Examples: r**ou**gh, s**u**bject, m**o**ther / ʌ / (u as in fun)
Look for the ways that sounds relate in regular ways to spelling.
 Examples: h**o**p / ɑ / + e = h**o**pe / oʊ /   f**i**n / ɪ / + e = f**i**ne / aɪ /
        m**e**t / ɛ / + e = m**ee**t / i /   **a**m / æ / + i = **ai**m / eɪ /

Spelling

Another important kind of information about words is their spelling. If you know the spelling of a word, you know what it looks like on the page. Then when you see it, you recognize it more quickly.

When you learn new words, you should always learn the spelling.

EXERCISE 3

A. *Cover Exercise 2 with a notebook or piece of paper. Your teacher will read the words in the first column (column a). Listen and write the words.*

1. _____ 5. _____
2. _____ 6. _____
3. _____ 7. _____
4. _____ 8. _____

B. *Look back at the words in Exercise 2. Correct your spelling if necessary.*

A. **Work with another student. Give each other a spelling quiz on some words from Exercise 2.**
    Student A: Copy 10 words from columns b and c under List 1.
    Student B: Copy 10 words from columns d and e under List 2.

List 1   **List 2**

_____   _____

_____   _____

_____   _____

_____   _____

_____   _____

_____   _____

_____   _____

_____   _____

_____   _____

_____   _____

B. **Test your partner.**

1. Student A: Read your List 1 words to your partner. Read slowly two times.

2. Student B: Listen and write the words your partner says under List 1.

3. Change roles. Student B: Read List 2. Student A: Listen and write.

C. **Compare lists with your partner. Then look at Exercise 2 and check both lists. Correct your mistakes. Number of words spelled correctly:** _____

Parts of Speech

In a dictionary entry, the next information after the pronunciation is usually the part of speech.

Noun (n):	*a person, place, thing, quality, action, or idea*
Examples:	**Dorothy** lived on a small **farm** in **Kansas**.
	The **book** tells about the **destruction** caused by the **war**.
	Their **happiness** was not affected by the bad **weather**.
Verb (v):	*a word (or words) that show an action, experience, or state*
Examples:	Stuart **shouted** "good bye!" into the telephone and **hung up**.
	The teacher **didn't understand** why everyone **was laughing**.
	Tell Ted that he **should be** there at 10:00.
Pronoun (pron):	*a word that is used instead of a noun or noun phrase*
Examples:	**We** thought **you** might like to meet **him**.
	Your cat is destroying **my** furniture.
	She didn't know **who it** belonged to.
	I had dinner at the new restaurant **that** opened last month.
Adjective (adj):	*a word that describes a noun*
Examples:	A **little** girl with a **red** coat walked away from the crowd.
	The judge was **angry**, but he spoke in a **quiet** voice.
Adverb (adv):	*a word that tells you more about a verb, an adjective, or another adverb*
Examples:	My father wanted **very much** to go home.
	It snowed **heavily** all day. It was **almost** impossible to get around the city.
Preposition (prep):	*a word that is put in front of a noun to show where, when, or how*
Examples:	Your dinner comes **with** potatoes or rice.
	The cat climbed **up** the tree and sat **on** a branch.
	He ran home **at** top speed.
Conjunction (conj):	*a word that connects parts of sentences or phrases*
Examples:	My aunt has two cats, a sheep, **and** a horse, **but** no dogs.
	Put your hand up **if** you know the right answer.
	Though Pam knew the answer, she didn't raise her hand.

When you look up a word, notice the part of speech and write it down with other information about the word. You need to know this in order to learn to use the word correctly.

You may sometimes need to figure out the part of speech from the sentence where you found a word. This may help you understand the grammar and meaning of the sentence. It may also be necessary in order to look up the word in the dictionary, since some words can be more than one part of speech.

A. *Write the part of speech for each underlined word.*

1. The house was <u>valued</u> at over one million dollars.

   Part of speech: _____

2. The hotel is not responsible for <u>valuables</u> left in the rooms.

   Part of speech: _____

3. Politicians often talk about family <u>values</u>, but they don't really help families.

   Part of speech: _____

4. When traveling, it is best not to wear anything <u>valuable</u>.

   Part of speech: _____

---

val•u•a•ble /ˈvælyəbəl/ *adj.* **1** worth a lot of money: *a valuable ring.* **2** valuable help, advice, etc. is very useful → INVALUABLE: *I think we've all learned a valuable lesson today.*

val•u•a•bles /ˈvælyəbəlz/ *n.* [plural] things that you own that are worth a lot of money, such as jewelry, cameras, etc.: *Guests should leave their valuables in the hotel safe.*

val•ue¹ /ˈvælyu/ *n.* **1** [C,U] the amount of money that something is worth: *the value of the house* | *The dollar has been steadily increasing/decreasing in value.* | *Did the thieves take anything of value (=worth a lot of money)?* **2** [U] the importance or usefulness of something: *His research was of great value to doctors working with this disease.* | *These earrings have sentimental value (=are important to you because they were a gift, remind you of someone, etc.).* **3** values [plural] your beliefs about what is right and wrong, or about what is important in life: *traditional family values* **4 good/great etc. value** something that is worth the amount you pay for it [ORIGIN: 1300–1400 Old French, Vulgar Latin *valuta*, from Latin *valere* "to be worth, be strong"]

value² *v.* [T] **1** to think that something is important and worth having: *I value your friendship.* **2** to say how much something is worth: *a painting valued at $5 million*

B. *Use the dictionary entries and example sentences to check your answers to Part A. Then on a separate piece of paper, make a chart (see example below). Write the words from Part A in the chart.*

EXAMPLE

	Noun	Verb	Adjective	Adverb
1.		*valued*		
2.				

Check the answers to this Practice activity on page 285.

A. *Write the part of speech for each underlined word.*

1. The <u>economically</u> strong countries in Europe must help those that are weaker.

   Part of speech: _____

2. A new highway through this area would bring great <u>economic</u> benefits to the region.

   Part of speech: _____

3. Over the past 20 years, the local <u>economy</u> has lost many jobs to overseas companies.

   Part of speech: _____

4. It's more <u>economical</u> to rent a car than to buy one if you only need it occasionally.

   Part of speech: _____

5. During the war, families had to <u>economize</u> on many basic foods, such as sugar and coffee.

   Part of speech: _____

6. This year fewer students are majoring in <u>economics</u> than last year.

   Part of speech: _____

---

ec•o•nom•ic /ˌɛkəˈnɑmɪk/ *adj.* ECONOMICS relating to business, industry, and managing money: **Economic growth** has been slow. | *the country's economic system* | *Economic conditions have changed.*

ec•o•nom•i•cal /ˌɛkəˈnɑmɪkəl/ *adj.* using time, money, products, etc. without wasting any: *an economical way to produce energy* | *Smaller goods are more economical to transport than large, heavy goods.*

ec•o•nom•i•cally /ˌɛkəˈnɑmɪkli/ *adv.* **1** ECONOMICS in a way that is related to systems of money, trade, or business: *economically depressed areas of the country* | *Economically, our city has never been stronger.* **2** in a way that uses money, goods, time, etc. without wasting any → EFFICIENTLY: *We need to produce food as economically as possible.*

ec•o•nom•ics /ˌɛkəˈnɑmɪks/ *n.* [U] ECONOMICS the study of the way in which money, goods, and services are produced and used: *One law of economics says that competition drives down prices.* | *market economics*

e•con•o•mist /ɪˈkɑnəmɪst/ *n.* [C] ECONOMICS someone who studies economics

e•con•o•mize /ɪˈkɑnəˌmaɪz/ *v.* [I] to reduce the amount of money, time, goods, etc. that you use

e•con•o•my[1] /ɪˈkɑnəmi/ *n.* (plural **economies**) **1** [C] ECONOMICS the way that money, businesses, and products are organized in a particular country, area, etc.: *the growing economies of southeast Asia* | *The project will add 600 jobs to the* **local economy** (=in a particular town or city). | *the* **global/world economy** **2** [U] the careful use of money, time, products, etc. so that nothing is wasted: *For reasons of economy, the oil is cleaned and reused.* [ORIGIN: 1400-1500 French, Greek *oikonomia*, from *oikonomos* "manager of a house"]

B. *Use the dictionary entries and example sentences to check your answers to Part A. Then, on a separate piece of paper, make a chart (see example on page 38). Write the words from Part A in the chart.*

Choosing the Best Definition

Many words have more than one definition in the dictionary. In fact, these different definitions often are similar or have something in common.

For example, look at the definitions of *value* on the dictionary page for Practice 1 on page 38.

They all include one of these words: *connection, between,* or *family.* Or look at the definitions of *last* on the dictionary page in Practice 2. They almost all include one of these words: *recent, after, before, final,* or *continue*—all words involving time and sequence.

It is important to notice the common meaning. This will help you understand and remember the word better.

Guidelines for Choosing the Right Dictionary Definition

1. Read the sentence where you found the word and figure out the part of speech. Find the entry for that part of speech in the dictionary.

2. When there is more than one definition, they are numbered. Start with the first one. (This is the most common.)

3. Look for the definition that makes the most sense in the sentence where you found the word.

4. Read the example sentences to help you decide.

A. Write the part of speech and definition for each underlined word as it is used in the sentence.

1. The new washing machines don't <u>last</u> as long as the old ones.

   Part of speech: _____

   Definition: _____

   _____

2. The <u>last</u> time I went to the mountains, it rained every day.

   Part of speech: _____

   Definition: _____

   _____

3. James arrived <u>last</u> in the bike race because he had a flat tire.

   Part of speech: _____

   Definition: _____

   _____

4. Of all her friends, Jana was the <u>last</u> to hear the news.

   Part of speech: _____

   Definition: _____

   _____

last¹ /læst/ *determiner, adj.* **1** most recent → NEXT: *Did you go to the last football game? | I saw Tim **last night/week/Sunday**. | The **last time** I saw Ken, we got into an argument.* **2** at the end, after everyone or everything else: *The last part of the song is sad. | He's **the last person** I'd ask for help* (= I do not want to ask him). **3** remaining after all others have gone: *The last guests were just putting on their coats. | Do you want the last piece of cake?* **4 on its last legs** likely to fail or break: *The truck was on its last legs.* **5 have the last word** to make the last statement in an argument, which gives you an advantage

last² *adv.* **1** most recently before now: *When did you see her last?* **2** after everything or everyone else: *Harris is going to speak last.* **3 last but not least** said when making a final statement, to show that it is just as important as your other statements: *Last but not least, I'd like to thank my mother.*

last³ *n., pron.* [C] **1 the last** the person or thing that comes after all the others: *Joe was the last of nine children* (=he was born last). *| Les was the last to go to bed that night.* **2 at (long) last** if something happens at last, it happens after you have waited a long time: *At last, we were able to afford a house.* **3 the day/week/ year before last** the day, week, etc. before the one that has just finished **4 the last I/we …** (informal) used when telling someone the most recent news that you know: *The last we heard, Paul was in Brazil.* **5 the last of sth** the remaining part of something: *This is the last of the paint.*

last⁴ *v.* [I] **1** to continue to happen or exist: *Jeff's operation lasted three hours. | I wish this moment would last forever.* **2** to continue to be effective, useful, or in good condition: *Most batteries will **last for** up to eight hours.*

B. Compare answers with another student. What do all the definitions have in common?

_____

_____

Check the answers to this Practice exercise on page 285.

A. *Write the part of speech and the definition of each underlined word as it is used in the sentence.*

1. You don't need to come to the meeting. These problems don't <u>concern</u> you.

   Part of speech: _____

   Definition: _____

   _____

2. The parents' main <u>concern</u> was the health of their children.

   Part of speech: _____

   Definition: _____

   _____

3. That professor is only <u>concerned</u> with his research. He doesn't care about teaching.

   Part of speech: _____

   Definition: _____

   _____

4. There was a terrible storm in her home town and she's very <u>concerned</u> about her family.

   Part of speech: _____

   Definition: _____

   _____

5. The president of the company said there was no cause for <u>concern</u>.

   Part of speech: _____

   Definition: _____

   _____

---

con•cern¹ /kən'sɚn/ *n.* **1** [U] a feeling of worry about something important: *There is growing **concern about/over** ocean pollution.* | *There is **concern that** the war could continue for a long time.* | *The police officer said that there was **no cause for concern.*** **2** [C] something important that worries you or involves you: *The destruction of the rainforest is a **concern to** us all.* | *Our **main/primary/major concern** is safety.*

concern² *v.* [T] **1** to affect someone or involve him/her: *What we're planning doesn't concern you.* **2** to make someone feel worried or upset: *My daughter's problems at school concern me greatly.* **3** to be about something or someone: *Most of her books concern the problems of growing up.* **4 concern yourself (with sth)** to become involved in something that interests or worries you: *You don't need to concern yourself with this, Jan.*

con•cerned /kən'sɚnd/ *adj.* **1** [not before noun] involved in something or affected by it: *It was a shock for **all concerned** (=everyone involved).* | *Everyone **concerned with** the car industry will be interested.* **2** worried about something important: *We're **concerned about** the results of the test.* | *letters from concerned parents* **3** believing that something is important: *They seem to be only **concerned with** making money.* **4 as far as sth is concerned** used in order to show which subject or thing you are talking about: *As far as money is concerned, the club is doing fairly well.* **5 as far as sb is concerned** used in order to show what someone's opinion on a subject is: *As far as I'm concerned, the whole idea is crazy.*

con•cern•ing /kən'sɚnɪŋ/ *prep.* (formal) about or relating to something: *We have questions concerning the report.*

B. *Compare answers with another student. What do all the definitions have in common?*

_____

The Way Words Are Used

The example phrases and sentences in dictionaries can tell you how words are used and what words are often used together.

PRACTICE 3

Use the example sentences for record *to complete the sentences below. (More than one answer may be possible.)*

record *n.*
  Keep a **record** of how much you spend on this trip.
  This summer has been the driest on **record**.
  She holds the world **record** for the long jump.
  The movie broke all box office **records**.
  …an airline with a good/bad safety **record**
  Does he have a criminal **record** (=has he committed any crimes)?
  …a huge **record** collection

record *v.*
  All the events were **recorded**.
  The group has just **recorded** a new album.

1. Last year was the wettest year _____ record.

2. A Kenyan runner _____ the world record.

3. The police discovered that he had a _____ record in Canada.

4. When he died, the family sold his record _____ for a lot of money.

Check the answers to this Practice exercise on page 285.

EXERCISE 7

A. *Read the example phrases and sentences on the dictionary page in Exercise 5, page 39. Then complete each sentence. Use the part of speech given. (More than one answer is possible.)*

1. Noun

   a. Since the beginning of the year, economic _____ has slowed down.

   b. No other country has an economic _____ like the one in China.

2. Adjective

    a. Professor Gorton is studying the _____ economy of India.

    b. Taking a taxi is not a very economical _____ to get around.

    c. People generally have more health problems in economically _____ areas.

    d. Brazil now plays an important role in the _____ economy.

3. Preposition

    a. For reasons _____ economy, the university turns off the heat on weekends.

    b. They promised to do the job _____ economically _____ possible.

B. *Compare answers with another student.*

EXERCISE 8

A. *Read the example phrases and sentences on the dictionary page in Exercise 6, page 42. Then complete each sentence. Use the part of speech given. (More than one answer is possible.)*

1. Preposition

    a. The doctor said there was no cause _____ concern.

    b. Many people are concerned _____ the violence in video games.

    c. The high cost of health care is a concern _____ us all.

    d. It was a surprise _____ all concerned.

    e. Everyone concerned _____ education will be interested in this book.

    f. The professor was concerned _____ the low grades on the exam.

2. Adjective

    a. The government's _____ concern now is the economy.

    b. His mother's _____ concern was always to keep him out of trouble.

    c. A _____ concern of the government is to create more jobs.

3. Pronoun

He has never concerned _____ with his wife's family problems.

B. *Compare answers with another student.*

Learning New Vocabulary from Your Reading

In this unit you will find out how you can become a more effective vocabulary learner. This includes making choices about the words and phrases you want to learn and using an effective study method.

Choosing Words and Phrases to Learn

It would be very difficult, probably impossible, to learn *all* the new words and phrases you find in your reading. Instead, you should select some words to study. But *which words*?

- Learn the words and phrases that are used most often in general and academic English. These are listed in the Appendix that starts on page 290.
  If you know all the words and phrases on the list, you will know about 90 percent of the words and phrases in most texts.
- Learn the words and phrases that will be most useful for you:
  - words and phrases you have seen before and think you will meet again
  - words and phrases that are connected to your school subjects, interests, or job

EXAMPLES

- In a newspaper article about a famous singer, you find the word *remark* several times. You see that it is on the list on page 295. Look it up in your dictionary and learn it.
- In your economics textbook, you find the word *scarce*. It's not on the list, but it is repeated several times in that chapter. Look it up and learn it.
- You also find the phrase *in a pinch*. It is not on the list, and you only see it once. From the sentences around it, you can understand the general meaning (if necessary). You do not need to look up the phrase or learn it.

Guidelines for Choosing Words and Phrases to Learn*

1. Read to the end of the passage. Do not stop to look up new words or phrases.
2. Read the passage again and underline the new words and phrases.
3. Look for the new words on the list on page 290. (The list does not include phrases.) If you find a word on the list, circle it in the passage.
4. For words and phrases that are not on the list, decide if they are useful to you. Ask yourself: *Have I seen or heard this word before? Is it related to my schoolwork, interests, or job?* If so, circle the word or phrase in the passage.
5. Look up all the circled words in the dictionary. Then write them in your vocabulary notebook. (See page 149.)

   *These guidelines should not be used with extensive reading books unless you want to do extra vocabulary work on parts of a book you have already read.

A. *Read the passage to the end. Do not stop to look up new words.*

Unexpected Effects

Which finger do you use to press a doorbell? The answer may depend on your age. People who are over 30 will almost certainly do it with their index finger. However, those who are under 30 will probably use their thumbs. Young people have spent many hours exercising their thumbs by sending text messages and playing video games. Thanks to all that exercise, their thumbs have become stronger and more skillful. That is why they often use their thumbs in situations where older people use their index fingers.

Skillful thumbs are only one of the many unexpected effects of new technology. In fact, today's new products are influencing not only physical skills, but also mental skills. Most of the time people are not aware of what's happening. They change their behavior as necessary, little by little. The new skills they develop may include texting, for example, or how to make an online flight reservation.

As for the old skills, most of the time people do not even realize what they have lost. For instance, how many people can do mental arithmetic these days? It is rarely necessary with calculators in every office and on every phone and computer. Another lost skill is map reading. With GPS in many cars, there is little need to know how to read a map.

Some researchers are concerned about the consequences of losing the old mental skills. If GPS stopped functioning, for example, would anyone know how to find their way around? More importantly, since the collapse of all technology is unlikely, scientists wonder about our brains. What will happen to them if we no longer exercise them in the same way?

B. *Read the passage again. Underline the words and phrases that are new to you.*

C. *Look on the list on pages 290–297 for the words and phrases you underlined. In the passage, circle the words that you find on the list.*

D. *Think about the phrases and underlined words that were not on the list. Are they useful? Circle the ones you want to learn. Then show them to your teacher.*

E. *Look in the dictionary for all the circled words and phrases in the passage. Write the parts of speech and the definitions in the margins.*

A. *Read the passage to the end. Do not stop to look up new words.*

Making It Easy

In the 1990s, when the Internet was new, the most popular password was "12345." According to a recent study, 20 percent of Internet users still choose a very simple password. The top favorite now is "123456." Other popular passwords are "abc123," "iloveyou," and "password."

5   In terms of data protection, passwords like these are not very effective. According to computer security specialists, this is like leaving a house key under the mat at the front door. It is very easy to discover.

Most people should know by now that an easy password is not a good idea. This is not a new issue and there have been lots of stories in the media about Internet security.
10   From the very beginning, the Web has been under attack by hackers looking for ways to make trouble or money. They enter e-mail or other accounts, steal personal information, and use it to empty bank accounts or credit cards.

To protect their customers, some websites will not allow common passwords. Others require people to mix numbers, letters, and symbols in their passwords. This is the best
15   way to make a password safe. When the password is mixed, it is much harder for a hacker to discover.

However, many companies prefer not to have these requirements for their websites. They fear that their business could suffer if people think their site is hard to use. In fact, if a password is complicated enough to be secure, it may not be easy to keep in mind. That
20   may be the main reason why people continue to use easy-to-guess passwords. These days, there are so many passwords to remember—for bank machines, voice mail, email—that people tend to keep them simple.

The ideal password, according to computer experts, is one that is mixed, but memorable. This may involve dates, numbers, and letters that have special meaning.
25   Another possibility is to form a message, like the ones used in texting, such as "MglvsRk4evr" (Meg loves Rick forever).

B. *Read the passage again. Underline the words and phrases that are new to you.*

C. *Look on the list on pages 290–297 for the words and phrases you underlined. In the passage, circle the words that you find on the list.*

D. *Think about the phrases and underlined words that were not on the list. Are they useful? Circle the ones you want to learn. Then show them to your teacher.*

E. *Look in the dictionary for all the circled words and phrases in the passage. Write the parts of speech and the definitions in the margins.*

A. *Read the passage to the end. Do not stop to look up new words.*

Is Txting Bad 4 English?

People tend to have definite opinions about texting. There are those who love it, and those who hate it. Among the haters, some have expressed their opinion in very strong terms. One British journalist said that "texters are doing to our language what Genghis Khan did to his neighbors 800 years ago. They are destroying . . . our punctuation . . . our sentences . . . our vocabulary. And they must be stopped."*

This is not the first time people have said that technology was bad for language. In the 15th century, some scholars opposed the invention of the printing press. Common people shouldn't read books, these scholars argued, or the language might begin to reflect their common ways of thinking and speaking. More recently, the telegraph and then the telephone were also viewed as tools of linguistic destruction. And yet, the English language has survived.

There is reason to think that texting will not be any more harmful to the language than those past inventions. Research has shown that many of the claims made by text haters are not based on reality. These people especially dislike the way words in messages may be shortened, and numbers and symbols used instead of words. But only about 20 percent or fewer messages actually do contain these shorter forms. In most messages, traditional spellings and whole sentences are used. The reason for this is practical: the majority of senders are not teenagers, but schools, banks, or companies. They want to make sure they will be understood.

Among texters who do use the shortened forms, certain forms appear frequently, such as C=see, U=you, and 4=for. However, there is also a lot of variation. That is because texting can actually be quite creative and fun. It could be considered a kind of word play, like doing crosswords or puzzles.

---

*John Humphreys, "I h8 txt msgs: How texting is wrecking our language," *The Daily Mail,* 24 September 2007.

B. *Read the passage again. Underline the words and phrases that are new to you.*

C. *Look on the list on pages 290–297 for the words and phrases you underlined. In the passage, circle the words that you find on the list.*

D. *Think about the phrases and underlined words that were not on the list. Are they useful? Circle the ones you want to learn. Then show them to your teacher.*

E. *Look in the dictionary for all the circled words and phrases in the passage. Write the parts of speech and the definitions in the margins.*

A. *Read the passage to the end. Do not stop to look up new words.*

Virtual Games but Real Problems

Some analysts say 15 million. Others say 20 million. The exact number is uncertain, but there is no doubt that millions of people now play online video games like "World of Warcraft." As the number of players has risen, so has the number of people who suffer from game addiction. Psychologists report that it is becoming a serious problem in many countries, including China, Japan, the Netherlands, France, and the United States.

According to psychologists, video game addiction is not very different from other kinds of addiction (for example, to alcohol or gambling). Game addicts become so involved in their favorite game that they lose control of their lives. They do little else but play the game all day or night, which naturally has consequences in their lives. It leads to poor performance at school or at work, and it destroys friendships and families.

Most of these video gamers are men. Women are evidently not as attracted to the game universe of wild adventures, monsters, and wars. Most women also do not care for the game system of rules and levels. For men, on the other hand, this system offers a sense of control and satisfaction that may be missing from their real lives.

Moreover, many gamers are young—teenagers or a little older—though there are also some older men. What they have in common is their urge to escape from the real world. Some of them are very shy and have never been comfortable relating to real people. Others use the video world to escape from problems in their lives, such as academic failure, unemployment, or the breakup of a marriage or family.

Researchers have calculated that 2 to 4 percent of all players become addicts. These statistics have led to increasing concern. Psychologists at addiction clinics have developed guidelines for the prevention of addiction. These guidelines try first of all to identify people who might have a weakness for the games. Then they make recommendations for ways to limit game playing. For instance, they recommend keeping computers in more public areas of the home, rather than in the bedroom. They also suggest getting rid of very powerful computers and replacing them with small laptops that cannot handle most games.

B. *Read the passage again. Underline the words and phrases that are new to you.*

C. *Look on the list on pages 290–297 for the words and phrases you underlined. In the passage, circle the words that you find on the list.*

D. *Think about the phrases and underlined words that were not on the list. Are they useful? Circle the ones you want to learn. Then show them to your teacher.*

E. *Look in the dictionary for all the circled words and phrases in the passage. Write the parts of speech and the definitions in the margins.*

Studying Vocabulary

Check what you know about learning vocabulary. Research has shown that:

- Learning a word does not mean just memorizing a definition. There are lots of other things to learn about a word: the pronunciation, the spelling, different meanings, the way it is used, the words used with it.

- Your memory is not a computer. It cannot automatically take in and keep every word you encounter (meet). If you want to be able to understand or use a word six months from now, you must do something to help your memory.

- Repetition is essential in vocabulary study. You need to encounter a word at least 7–10 times before you will remember it. Reading is one way to have repeated encounters with words. A good study method will make it possible for you to have many more encounters.

- You are much more likely to remember a word if you work with it *actively*. The more ways you work with it (reading, listening, speaking, writing), the better you will remember it.

Did you know these facts about learning vocabulary? If you want to expand your vocabulary, you need to take them into account. When you study vocabulary, you need to include information about the way words are used. Then, you need to find a way to increase the number of times you encounter a word and the different ways you work with it.

Students and teachers have found two effective tools for vocabulary study: vocabulary notebooks and word study cards.

Vocabulary Notebooks

- You will need a small notebook that you use only for vocabulary. When you write words or phrases in your notebook, put them in some kind of order so you can find them again. You can order them by the alphabet, by topic, by the source (the place you found them), by the date, or by any other system. Do not just write words as you find them.

- Pronounce each new word/phrase aloud when you write it. Look at the pronunciation symbols in the dictionary. If you are still unsure, check with your teacher. Remember: it is important to know how to say words.

- Follow this format for writing words in your notebook:
  - On the left-hand page, write the new word or phrase. Beside the word, write the part of speech.
  - Below the word or phrase, write the sentence or sentences where you found it.
  - Write the dictionary definition on the right-hand page.

concern (noun)	the feeling of worry about
The parents' main <u>concern</u> was the health of their children.	something important
economical (adjective)	using time, money, products, etc.,
It's more <u>economical</u> to rent a car than to buy one if you only need it occasionally.	without wasting any

Guidelines for Using Your Vocabulary Notebook

When you review words in your vocabulary notebook, follow these steps:

1. Cover the words/phrases and try to remember the definitions.
2. Cover the definitions and try to remember the words or phrases.
3. Make a pencil mark beside words/phrases or definitions that you cannot remember well. Review them again.
4. Ask another student to test you:
   • Give the other student your notebook.
   • Tell him or her to ask you about words/phrases or definitions.
   • Write the answers. Did you remember them and write them correctly?

EXERCISE 5

A. *Look back at Exercises 1–4 in this unit. Choose 10–15 of the words and phrases you circled and looked up. Write them in your vocabulary notebook. Write the part of speech of each word or phrase, the sentence(s) where you found it, and the definition (as in the Example).*

B. *Compare notebooks with another student. Did you choose any of the same ones? Show your notebook to your teacher.*

C. *Review the words and phrases in your notebook. Follow steps 1–3 in the guidelines above.*

D. *Exchange notebooks with another student. Each student chooses 10 words and tests the other. Follow step 4 above. Then change roles.*

E. *Check your answers (including spelling). How many were correct?*

EXERCISE 6

A. Look back at the fiction passage in Part 1, Unit 2, Exercise 1 (page 8). Read the passage again and underline any words or phrases you do not know.

B. Look for the words you underlined on the list on pages 290–297. In the passage, circle the words that are on the list.

C. Think about the phrases and underlined words that were not on the list. Are they useful? Circle the ones you want to learn. Then show them to your teacher.

D. Look in the dictionary for all the circled words and phrases. Write them in your vocabulary notebook with the parts of speech, the sentences where you found them, and the definitions.

E. Review the new words and phrases.

EXERCISE 7

A. Look back at the nonfiction passage in Part 1, Unit 2, Exercise 2 (page 12). Read the passage again and underline any words or phrases you do not know.

B. Look for the words you underlined on the list on pages 290–297. In the passage, circle the words that are on the list.

C. Think about the underlined words and phrases that were not on the list. Are they useful? Circle the ones you want to learn. Then show them to your teacher.

D. Look in the dictionary for all the circled words and phrases. Write them in your vocabulary notebook with the parts of speech, the sentences where you found them, and the definitions.

E. Review the new words and phrases.

Study Cards

You will need small cards (3 x 5 inches or 7 x 12 cm).

Follow this system for writing words or phrases on the cards:

- On one side of the card, write the new word or phrase.
- Write the part of speech beside the single words.
- Below the word or phrase, write the sentence(s) where you found it.
- On the other side of the card, write the definition.

EXAMPLE

Side A

> concern (noun)
>
> The parents' main concern was the health of their children.

Side B

> a feeling of worry about something important

Keep your cards up to date.

- Take out a word or phrase when you have learned it very well. (You remember the definition or the word/phrase immediately.)
- Add new cards for words or phrases that you want to learn.
- Keep about 15–20 cards at a time.

A. *Review the words in your vocabulary notebook.*

B. *Choose 10–15 words or phrases from your notebook that you have trouble remembering well. Write them on study cards. Follow the example on page 53.*

C. *Show your study cards to your teacher.*

D. *Review your cards until you remember both the words/phrases and the definitions immediately.*

E. *Exchange 10 cards with another student and test each other. Write your answers on a separate piece of paper.*

F. *Check your answers (including spelling). How many were correct?*

Guidelines for Using Your Study Cards

Use the study cards in addition to your vocabulary notebook. They can be used in many different ways. Find a way that works well for you. Here are some ideas:

- Use the cards for the words or phrases you have trouble remembering. At the end of each week, choose new words or phrases from your vocabulary notebook to write on your cards. Take out the words or phrases you know well.
- Carry your cards with you all the time. Review them while you are waiting for class, while you are on a bus, before dinner, etc.
- When you make new cards, keep them all together in one pocket of a jacket or bag. When you know a word or phrase well, move that card to a different pocket. When all the cards are moved, review them again. If you know them all well again, make new cards.
- Instead of cards, use sticky notes. On the front, write the word or phrase, the part of speech, and the sentence. On the other side, write the definition. Stick the note on your desk, the refrigerator, or any place where you spend time. Test yourself whenever you look at the notes. Then write new notes with the definition on the front and the word/phrase on the back. Change the words/phrases when you know them well.

Remember

To learn words or phrases well, you need to review them often. You should review them:
- the same day you write them in your notebook
- a day later (in your notebook or on study cards)
- a week later
- at the end of the month
- at the end of the semester

Keywords

You may have heard stories about people with exceptional powers of memory who could look at a long series of numbers, for example, and memorize them instantly. Some of these people are born with special skills. But many of them have improved their memory by using something like the keyword technique.

This technique can be used for all vocabulary study, or just for words that are more difficult to learn.

The Keyword Technique*

- Choose a word in your vocabulary notebook or on your study cards that you want to learn (the target word).
- Think of a word in your language that sounds like the target word. (It can sound like the whole word or just the beginning.) This is your *keyword*.
- Think of an image (picture in your mind) that includes the meaning of the target word and the meaning of the keyword. You should actually see this picture in your mind. (This is very important.)

EXAMPLES

1. An Italian student wants to learn the meaning of the word *available*. He thinks of an Italian phrase that sounds similar, *a vela* (with sails). He imagines a beautiful big sailboat with sails up and ready to be taken out.
2. A Tanzanian student wants to learn the meaning of the word *twist*. She thinks of the Swahili word, *twiga* (giraffe). She imagines a giraffe's long neck and the way it can bend and twist in all directions.

The keyword technique works because it makes you think about the word in two important ways. You focus first on the sound of the word, and then on its meaning. These are connected to the sound and meaning of a word in your language. Your memory then has a much better hold on the target word.

*This idea was taken from I.S.P. Nation, *Teaching Vocabulary: Strategies and Techniques*, Heinle Cengage Learning, 2008.

A. *Choose five words that you have trouble learning. Write them under Target words.*

Target Words

1. _____   4. _____

2. _____   5. _____

3. _____

B. *For each target word in Part A, think of a keyword in your language. Write it under Keywords. Then think of an image that includes the meaning of the target word and the keyword. Write a short description of the image.*

Keywords   **Images**

_____   _____

_____   _____

_____   _____

_____   _____

_____   _____

C. *Discuss your keywords with another student. Did you choose any of the same target words? It so, do you have the same keywords and images?*

Reflecting on Your Learning

At the beginning of this unit, you learned that repetition and working with new words are important in learning vocabulary.

Now take a few minutes to reflect on your work in this unit.

1. Look at the words you wrote in the margins of the exercises and in your notebook. Which words or phrases did you write the most times? the least?
2. Look at all the words or phrases in your notebook. How well do you know each of them now?
3. Which words or phrases do you (still) have trouble remembering? Why?
   Have you encountered it/worked with it enough?
   Is it difficult to pronounce?
   Is the meaning complex or unclear to you?

Guessing Meaning from Context

You can learn a lot about a word or phrase from the context (the sentence or sentences around it). In Unit 1 you learned to use the sentence to decide on the part of speech of a word and to choose a dictionary definition.

In this unit, you will learn to use the context to guess the meaning of a new word or phrase. Sometimes you can get a clear idea of the meaning. Other times, you can only get a general idea. But even the general meaning is often helpful. It may be enough to allow you to keep reading and following the ideas in a story or passage.

Guessing the meaning is usually the best strategy for dealing with new words in your extensive reading. It can be useful in other kinds of reading, too, because it means you can stay focused on your reading.

This strategy may not always be appropriate, however. In some cases, it may not be possible to guess even a general meaning from the context. There are also times when you might need an exact meaning of a word (in a textbook, for example). Then you should look it up.

> **Note:** Check with your teacher about whether to use English or your first language to write the general meaning in these exercises.

Using the Context of the Sentence to Guess Meaning

The sentence in which you find a word or phrase can often tell you a lot about it.

Example: The *eruption* of a volcano in Indonesia killed over a hundred people.

You can tell from the sentence that *eruption* is something that happens to volcanoes. What happens to volcanoes? They explode and hot gas and rocks come out. This is probably what an *eruption* is. This meaning makes sense in the sentence, since it says the *eruption* killed people.

Example: The swimming pool was *shallow* at one end, but very deep at the other.

This sentence is about the two ends of a swimming pool. Notice the word *but*, which means that the second part of the sentence contrasts with the first part. We can guess that *shallow* probably means the opposite of *deep*. This makes sense when we think about the way swimming pools are often built.

Guidelines for Guessing Meaning from the Sentence

1. If it is a word, decide on the part of speech. If it is a phrase, think about how it fits in the sentence.

2. Look at the words next to it for clues (information) about the meaning.

3. Think about the meaning and the structure of the sentence.

4. Make a guess about the meaning. Give a synonym or a phrase to explain the general meaning.

5. Read the sentence again with your guessed meaning instead of the word or phrase. Does it make sense?

PRACTICE 1

Use the context to figure out the part of speech and general meaning of the underlined words. Follow the guidelines above. Give a synonym or a phrase to explain the general meaning.

1. William took the <u>lid</u> off the pot to see what his mother was cooking for supper.

   Part of speech: _____

   General meaning: _____

2. There was only one place to <u>plug in</u> the computer and DVD player—on the back wall of the classroom.

   Part of speech: _____

   General meaning: _____

3. Ellen's parents were very <u>strict</u> and did not allow her to go out in the evening.

   Part of speech: _____

   General meaning: _____

Check your answers to this Practice exercise on page 285.

A. **Use the context to figure out the part of speech and general meaning of the underlined words and phrases.**

1. When he won the race at the Olympics, he was at the <u>peak</u> of his career.

   Part of speech: _____

   General meaning: _____

2. Jill's skating accident made her foot <u>swell up</u> until she could no longer wear her shoe.

   Part of speech: _____

   General meaning: _____

3. We were all surprised by the <u>foul</u> language that came out of Ricky's mouth. You might expect it from a teenager, but not such a little boy.

   Part of speech: _____

   General meaning: _____

4. I'll wash the shirt in cold water so it won't <u>shrink</u>. It's already a little small for me.

   Part of speech: _____

   General meaning: _____

5. If you can't find the book now, don't worry about it. I'm sure it will <u>turn up</u> soon.

   Part of speech: _____

   General meaning: _____

6. Those women work very hard and in difficult conditions. They <u>deserve</u> to be paid more.

   Part of speech: _____

   General meaning: _____

B. **Compare answers with another student. Then look up the words and phrases in the dictionary. How well did you guess the meanings?**

A. *Use the context to figure out the part of speech and general meaning of the underlined words and phrases.*

1. The public will receive full information <u>in due course</u>. Until then, please check the website for updates.

   Part of speech: _____

   General meaning: _____

2. That morning she walked across the field on her way to school. Her shoes got all wet from the <u>dew</u>.

   Part of speech: _____

   General meaning: _____

3. Once again, my mother had put too much tomato and mayonnaise on the sandwich, and the bread was all <u>soggy</u>.

   Part of speech: _____

   General meaning: _____

4. When the war ended, the museum was still standing, but there was <u>scarcely</u> anything in it.

   Part of speech: _____

   General meaning: _____

5. The young people had tents and sleeping bags <u>strapped</u> to their backpacks. They planned to stay in the mountains for at least two weeks.

   Part of speech: _____

   General meaning: _____

6. Rosa <u>patched</u> up the hole on Bruno's jacket so well that his mother never noticed.

   Part of speech: _____

   General meaning: _____

B. *Compare answers with another student. Then look up the words and phrases in the dictionary. How well did you guess the meanings?*

A. *Use the context to figure out the part of speech and general meaning of the underlined words and phrases.*

1. Some politicians were against the new banking laws. They feared that the laws would <u>hinder</u> economic growth.

   Part of speech: _____

   General meaning: _____

2. Many of the vegetables you buy in the winter are grown in <u>greenhouses</u>.

   Part of speech: _____

   General meaning: _____

3. These technological changes <u>have given rise</u> to important new social developments.

   Part of speech: _____

   General meaning: _____

4. Frank didn't enjoy the summer vacation. His friends were all away, and he didn't know what to do with all those <u>idle</u> hours.

   Part of speech: _____

   General meaning: _____

5. When deciding on the points for an Olympic diver, the judges <u>take into account</u> the difficulty of the dive.

   Part of speech: _____

   General meaning: _____

6. A long line of people waited in the <u>chilly</u> midnight air. Some had brought blankets; others danced around to stay warm.

   Part of speech: _____

   General meaning: _____

B. *Compare answers with another student. Then look up the words and phrases in the dictionary. How well did you guess the meanings?*

A. *Use the context to figure out the part of speech and general meaning of the underlined words and phrases.*

1. The new type of heating system costs more to put in, but it saves money <u>in the long run</u>.

   Part of speech: _____

   General meaning: _____

2. The young Bulgarian violinist gave an <u>outstanding</u> performance of the Beethoven concerto.

   Part of speech: _____

   General meaning: _____

3. In the past few years, potato <u>yields</u> have fallen, mostly due to the very dry weather.

   Part of speech: _____

   General meaning: _____

4. In some countries, such as Italy, high school students often cheat on tests because they know they can probably <u>get away with it</u>.

   Part of speech: _____

   General meaning: _____

5. As the man shouted, Daisy stood <u>awkwardly</u> by the door, her arms full of books. He had asked for the books, but perhaps this was not a good moment.

   Part of speech: _____

   General meaning: _____

6. It happened right there as he was watching. A very large bird, probably an eagle, flew down and <u>snatched</u> the little kitten.

   Part of speech: _____

   General meaning: _____

B. *Compare answers with another student. Then look up the words and phrases in the dictionary. How well did you guess the meanings?*

Guessing Meaning from a Passage

In a reading passage, the sentences before or after the word or phrase can sometimes give you more clues about the meaning.

In this section you will find exercises to practice finding clues in the context of the passage.

Guidelines for Guessing Meaning from the Context of a Passage

1. Decide on the part of speech.

2. Look at the words close to it.

3. Think about the meaning of the sentence and the topic of the passage.

4. Look to see if the word is repeated in the passage.

5. Look for synonyms or opposites.

6. Look for an explanation or definition of the word (especially in a textbook or a technical passage).

7. Make a guess about the meaning.

8. Read the sentence again with your guessed meaning instead of the word or phrase. Does it make sense?

EXERCISE 5

The passages below are from the book, **The Outsiders,** *by S. E. Hinton. In this story, a teenager tells about his experiences in a youth gang.*

A. *Use the context of the passage to figure out the part of speech and the general meaning of the underlined words and phrases. Circle the clues you use to make your guesses. (The first clue is circled for you.)*

1. When I stepped out into the bright sunlight from the darkness of the movie house, I had only two things on my mind: Paul Newman and a ride home. . . .

I had a long walk home and no company, but I usually go alone anyway, for no reason except that I like to watch movies <u>undisturbed</u> so I can get into them and live them with the actors. When I see a movie with someone it's kind of uncomfortable, like having someone read your book over your shoulder. I'm different that way. I mean, my second-oldest brother, Soda, who is 16 going on 17, never <u>cracks</u> a book at all, and my oldest brother, Darrel, who we call Darry, works too long and hard to be interested in a story.

    a. *undisturbed*   Part of speech: _____

                          General meaning: _____

    b. *cracks*   Part of speech: _____

                          General meaning: _____

2. It was almost four months ago. I had walked down to the DX station to get a bottle of pop[1] and to see Steve and Soda because they'll always buy me a couple of bottles and let me help work on the cars. I don't like to go on weekends, because then there is usually a <u>bunch</u> of girls down there flirting with Soda. . . .

It was a warmish spring day with the sun shining bright, but it was getting chilly and dark by the time we started for home. We were walking because we had left Steve's car at the station. At the corner of our block there's a wide, open field where we play football and <u>hang out</u>. It's a place where there are often fist fights.

[1]**pop**   soda, such as Coca Cola

    a. *bunch*   Part of speech: _____

                     General meaning: _____

    b. *hang out*   Part of speech: _____

                     General meaning: _____

B.   **Compare answers with another student. Then check with your teacher.**

EXERCISE 6

The passages below are from **The Diary of Anne Frank,** *by Anne Frank. It tells the true story of how a young Jewish girl and her family hid from the German soldiers in Holland during World War II.*

A.   **Read the passages. Use the context to guess the part of speech and the general meaning of the underlined words and phrases. Circle the clues you use to make your guesses.**

1.   Daddy, Mummy, and Margot can't get used to the sound of the Westertoren clock yet, which tells us the time every quarter of an hour. I can. I loved it from the start, and especially in the night it's like a faithful friend.

I expect you will be interested to hear what it feels like to "disappear"; well, all I can say is that I don't know myself yet. I don't think I shall ever feel really at home in this house, but that does not mean that I <u>loathe</u> it here, it is more like being on vacation in a very peculiar <u>boardinghouse</u>. . . .[It] is an ideal hiding place. Although it leans to one side and is damp, you'd never find such a comfortable hiding place anywhere in Amsterdam, no, perhaps not even in the whole of Holland.

    a. *loathe*   Part of speech: _____

                     General meaning: _____

    b. *boardinghouse*   Part of speech: _____

                     General meaning: _____

2. The four of us went to the private office yesterday evening and turned on the radio. I was so terribly frightened that someone might hear it that I simply <u>begged</u> Daddy to come upstairs with me. Mummy understood how I felt and came too. We are very nervous in other ways, too, that the neighbors might hear us or see something going on. We made curtains straight away on the first day.

There are some large business <u>premises</u> on the right of us, and on the left a furniture workshop; there is no one there after working hours but even so, sounds could travel through the walls. We have forbidden Margo to cough at night, although she has a bad cold, and make her swallow large spoonfuls of codeine.[1]

[1]**codeine**   a medicine given for coughing and pain

    a. *begged*   Part of speech: _____

                      General meaning: _____

    b. *premises*   Part of speech: _____

                      General meaning: _____

B.   ***Compare answers with another student. Then check with your teacher.***

PRACTICE 2

Use the context of the passage to figure out the part of speech and the general meaning of the missing word. Circle the clues you use to make your guesses.

For some countries, such as Russia, a xxxxxx is required. Travelers who arrive without one will not be allowed to enter. Those arriving by plane can usually get a xxxxxx at the airport. It is also possible to get one at the border for those arriving by car. However, in both cases, there may be long lines and the Russian officials sometimes refuse entry for little reason. These problems can be avoided by getting a xxxxxx from the Russian embassy before leaving home.

    Part of speech: _____

    Possible word or meaning: _____

Check the answers to this Practice exercise on page 285.

A. *Use the context of the passage to figure out the part of speech and the general meaning of the missing words and phrases. Circle the clues you use to make your guesses.*

1. Trains connect the larger cities in Tunisia, but there are not many smaller train lines. To travel between the smaller cities and towns, most Tunisians take buses or xxxxxxs. These xxxxxxs are often cheaper than the buses. They leave as soon as they have at least five people who want to go to the same place. That might be a distant city or a town nearby. The destination of the xxxxxx is written on a sign on the roof. Other travelers who wish to go there can wave to the driver to stop. Officially there is a maximum number of passengers allowed, but in reality the xxxxxxs sometimes carry many more.

Part of speech: _____

Possible word or meaning: _____

2. Various kinds of xxxxxxs are available in Oslo. Some are good for a day, while others are for three days or a week. They all allow unlimited travel on the local buses and subway. These xxxxxxs are useful for tourists who want to visit different parts of the city. There is also another kind of weekly xxxxxx that allows unlimited travel on buses and trains and boats anywhere in the country. This is quite expensive, but it is worth getting if you are planning to move around the country a lot. Otherwise, it is better to pay separately for each trip.

Part of speech: _____

Possible word or meaning: _____

3. Foreign drivers in the United States should pay attention to the rules of the road. If they do not follow the rules carefully, they may get into trouble. For instance, the police are very strict about the speed limit. Drivers going only five miles (8 kilometers) per hour over the limit may just get a warning. But drivers going ten miles per hour or more over the limit will get a xxxxxx. The cost of a xxxxxx can vary, but it may be as much as $250. Furthermore, information about all xxxxxxs is put into the police computer system. This can cause problems for drivers later if, for example, they want to rent a car. The car rental companies can find out the names of drivers who have gotten xxxxxxs in the past and may refuse to rent to them.

Part of speech: _____

Possible word or meaning: _____

B. *Compare answers with another student. Then check with your teacher.*

A. *Use the context of the passage to figure out the part of speech and the general meaning of the missing words or phrases. Circle the clues you use to make your guesses.*

1.   Nobody wants a xxxxxx near their home. First of all, these places usually do not smell very pleasant. Second, they often attract lots of insects, such as flies and mosquitoes, as well as animals such as rats and mice. A nearby xxxxxx may also mean that you will have noisy trucks on your street all day. Finally, the most serious problem with xxxxxxs is that they may pollute (dirty) the drinking water. In the garbage, there may be some things that contain dangerous chemicals. When it rains, the chemicals are washed out of the garbage and into underground water. This water then becomes unsafe to drink.

   Part of speech: _____

   Possible word or meaning: _____

2.   Xxxxxxs are one cause of water pollution that is not well known. There are more and more xxxxxxs around the world. This is due to the fact that the wild fish in the oceans are disappearing because they have been overfished. At the same time, especially in developed countries such as the United States and Europe, the demand for fish is increasing. In the oceans, fish do not cause pollution, but in xxxxxxs, the situation is different. Many fish are kept in a small amount of water, which means that the water must be changed often. Each time it is changed, the dirty water is goes directly into a river or ocean. This is very bad for the plants, animals, and fish living naturally in that river or ocean.

   Part of speech: _____

   Possible word or meaning: _____

3.   In many countries these days, governments are facing a serious problem: what to do with the garbage. Every year there is more of it. But putting garbage in the ground pollutes the water. Burning it pollutes the air. The only way to solve this problem is to reduce the amount of garbage. For this reason, in many places, people are encouraged to xxxxxx as much as possible. Not all kinds of garbage can be xxxxxxxed. The easiest materials are glass, paper, and plastic. They can be used to make new glass, paper, and plastic. It is also possible to xxxxxx food and organic material from kitchens and yards. That can be made into garden soil (dirt).

   Part of speech: _____

   Possible word or meaning: _____

B. *Compare answers with another student. Then check with your teacher.*

Word Parts

Many words in English are made up of several parts. These parts all contribute to the meaning and the grammar of a word. If you make a change in a word by adding or taking away a part, you change the meaning or the grammar.

You will learn vocabulary better if you can recognize word parts and understand how they can change a word. There are two reasons for this:

1. You will have more complete understanding of the words.
2. You will remember the words better because you will be able to connect them to something you already know (the parts or other words with the same parts).

In this unit, you will practice dividing words into parts, and you will learn about some parts that are found in many words.

Parts of Words

The root is the most important part of a word. It gives the word its basic meaning.
   Example: appear

A prefix is a part added before the root.
   Example: *dis* + appear = disappear

A suffix is a part added after the root.
   Example: appear + *ance* = appearance

Some words contain both a prefix and a suffix.
   Example: *dis* + appear + *ance* = disappearance

Roots

There are two kinds of roots in English:

- Roots that can stand alone as words. These are usually not difficult to recognize. They may also be used with a prefix and/or a suffix.

   Examples:

Root	Prefix	/	Root	/	Suffix
appear	dis	+	appear	+	ance
success	un	+	success	+	ful
build	re	+	build	+	ing

- Roots that cannot stand alone in English. These may be harder to recognize and understand because they often come from other languages, such as Latin or Greek.

Examples:

Root	Source	Prefix	/	Root	/	Suffix
annu	Latin *annus*: year	bi	+	annu	+	al
nation	Latin *natus*: born	inter	+	nation	+	al
geo	Greek *ge*: earth	geo	+	ge	+	ology

Note: The spelling of a root may change in the English word.

Example: *nunc* (from Latin *nuntius* meaning messenger)—*pronounce*

EXERCISE 1

A. **Work with a partner. In each of the words below, find a root from the box and circle it. Then think of another word for each root and write it.**

Roots

cycle (Greek *kyklos*: circle)	invent (Latin *invenire*: to find)	nation (Latin *natio*: born)
dict (Latin *dicere*: to say)	ject (Latin *jacere*: to throw)	nunc (Latin *nuntius*: messenger)
duct (Latin *ducere*: to lead)	loc (Latin *locus*: place)	path (Greek *pathos*: suffering)
form (Latin *forma*: shape)	lit (Latin *litteratus*: writing)	phone (Greek *phone*: sound, voice)
geo (Greek *geo*: earth)	meter (Greek *metron*: measure)	port (Latin *portare*: to carry)

	Root	New Word		Root	New Word
1.	(loc)al	*location*	7.	information	_____
2.	kilometer	_____	8.	pronunciation	_____
3.	predict	_____	9.	literate	_____
4.	invention	_____	10.	introduce	_____
5.	bicycle	_____	11.	project	_____
6.	sympathy	_____	12.	informal	_____

Root	New Word		Root	New Word
13. inventory	_____		17. geography	_____
14. conduct	_____		18. export	_____
15. announce	_____		19. multinational	_____
16. dictation	_____		20. recycling	_____

B. Compare answers with another student. Do you know the meanings of the words?

C. Check your work with your teacher. Write any new words in your vocabulary notebook.

Prefixes

Most prefixes change the meaning in some way.

Example: *un* + certain = not certain

A few prefixes change the part of speech.

Example: *a* + live (verb) = alive (adjective)

> **Note:** Sometimes a hyphen is put between the prefix and the root.
> **Examples:** non-native, pre-existing

EXERCISE 2

A. Find the prefix in each word and write it on the line.

1. incomplete   _____   7. unable   _____
2. misplace   _____   8. nonsense   _____
3. disagree   _____   9. invisible   _____
4. unreal   _____   10. mispronounce _____
5. impossible   _____   11. imperfect   _____
6. discover   _____   12. nonstop   _____

B. Discuss the meanings of the words from Part A with another student. Look up any new words in the dictionary.

C. *Now think about the prefixes. How do they change the meaning of the words?*

_____

D. *Write any new words in your vocabulary notebook.*

EXERCISE 3

A. *Find the prefix in each word and write it on the line.*

1. bicycle _____
2. triple _____
3. century _____
4. uniform _____
5. centigrade _____

6. triangle _____
7. universe _____
8. triathlon _____
9. bimonthly _____
10. union _____

B. *Discuss the meanings of the words from Part A with another student. Look up any new words.*

C. *Write the four prefixes from Part A. Then make a guess about the meaning of prefixes.*

    Prefix   **Meaning**

1. _____ _____
2. _____ _____
3. _____ _____
4. _____ _____

D. *Check your guesses with your teacher. Correct them if necessary. Write any new words in your vocabulary notebook.*

A. *Find the prefix in each word and write it on the line.*

1. preheat _____		9. outgrow _____
2. outnumber _____		10. preview _____
3. underrate _____		11. refill _____
4. review _____		12. outrun _____
5. overeat _____		13. relocate _____
6. underpay _____		14. underline _____
7. overcook _____		15. reconsider _____
8. predict _____		16. overprice _____

B. *Discuss the meanings of the words from Part A with another student. Look up any new words.*

C. *Write the five prefixes from Part A. Then make a guess about the prefixes' meanings.*

Prefix	Meaning
1. _____	_____
2. _____	_____
3. _____	_____
4. _____	_____
5. _____	_____

D. *Check your guesses with your teacher. Correct them if necessary. Write any new words in your vocabulary notebook.*

A. *In each line, all the words <u>except one</u> start with the same prefix. Find the word that is different and cross it out. Then write the prefix (from the other words) and its meaning.*

1. reflect   report   ~~regular~~   recognize   return

   Prefix: _re-_   Meaning: *again, back, as before*

2. unlike   unknown   unofficial   until   unsure

   Prefix: _____   Meaning: _____

3. pressure   prepare   preposition   prevent   prejudice

   Prefix: _____   Meaning: _____

4. combination   comparison   committee   companion   comeback

   Prefix: _____   Meaning: _____

5. misjudge   mismanage   miserable   mislead   misunderstand

   Prefix: _____   Meaning: _____

6. disability   distance   disappointment   discount   disagreement

   Prefix: _____   Meaning: _____

7. industry   indirect   inefficient   independent   indeterminate

   Prefix: _____   Meaning: _____

8. bilingual   bilateral   biennial   binoculars   bitter

   Prefix: _____   Meaning: _____

B. *Compare answers with another student. Look up any new words. Write them in your vocabulary notebook.*

Suffixes

Most suffixes change the part of speech of a word or the verb tense.

   Example: safe (adjective)   + *ly* = safely (adverb)

           cook (present tense verb) + *ed* = cooked (past tense verb)

Some suffixes also influence the meaning of the word.

   Example: young (adjective)   + *est* = youngest (superlative form of adjective)

Note: Sometimes the spelling of the root changes when you add a suffix.

Examples: simple + *ly* = simply (the letter *e* is dropped)
busy + *ness* = business (y → i)

EXERCISE 6

A. *Find the suffix in each word and circle it. Write the part of speech of the word. Then write the root (without the prefix) and the part of speech of the root.*

Word	Part of Speech	Root (without prefix)	Part of Speech of Root
1. unfaithful	adjective	faith	noun
2. strangely			
3. powerless			
4. restful			
5. broadly			
6. unbelievable			
7. widely			
8. watchful			
9. childless			
10. invaluable			
11. careful			
12. noticeable			

B. *Write the four suffixes from Part A. Then write the parts of speech of the words with the suffix and the words without the suffix.*

Suffixes	Part of Speech: Words with Suffix	Part of Speech: Words without Suffix
1.		
2.		
3.		
4.		

C. *Compare answers with another student. Look up any new words and write them in your vocabulary notebook. Then check your answers with your teacher.*

A. *Find the suffix in each word and circle it. Write the part of speech of the word. Then write the root (without the prefix) and the part of speech of the root.*

Word	Part of Speech	Root (without prefix)	Part of Speech of Root
1. annoying			
2. influential			
3. demanding			
4. expressive			
5. independent			
6. existing			
7. insensitive			
8. judgmental			
9. confident			
10. informal			
11. massive			
12. environmental			

B. *Write the four suffixes from Part A. Then write the parts of speech of the words with the suffix and the words without the suffix.*

Suffixes	Part of Speech: Words with Suffix	Part of Speech: Words without Suffix
1.		
2.		
3.		
4.		

C. *Compare answers with another student. Look up any new words and write them in your vocabulary notebook. Then check your answers with your teacher.*

A. *Find the suffix in each word and circle it. Write the part of speech of the word. Then write the root (without the prefix) and the part of speech of the root.*

Word	Part of Speech	Root (without prefix)	Part of Speech of Root
1. generalize	_____	_____	_____
2. addition	_____	_____	_____
3. impossibility	_____	_____	_____
4. invention	_____	_____	_____
5. weaken	_____	_____	_____
6. specialize	_____	_____	_____
7. freshness	_____	_____	_____
8. reproduction	_____	_____	_____
9. simplicity	_____	_____	_____
10. modernize	_____	_____	_____
11. preparation	_____	_____	_____
12. lengthen	_____	_____	_____
13. popularity	_____	_____	_____
14. forgetfulness	_____	_____	_____

B. *Write the five suffixes from Part A. Then write the parts of speech of the words with the suffix and the words without the suffix.*

Suffixes	Part of Speech: Words with Suffix	Part of Speech: Words without Suffix
1. _____	_____	_____
2. _____	_____	_____
3. _____	_____	_____
4. _____	_____	_____
5. _____	_____	_____

C. *Compare answers with another student. Look up any new words and write them in your vocabulary notebook. Then check your answers with your teacher.*

Word Families

A word family is a group of different forms of a word that all include the same root. The word forms in a word family are closely related in meaning, but they are different parts of speech.

Example:

Noun	Verb	Adjective	Negative Adjective	Adverb
direction	*direct*	*direct*	*indirect*	*directly*

Notes:

- Some words do not have a negative adjective form. In this case, the negative is expressed with *not*.

Example: not hungry

- Sometimes the same word form can be more than one part of speech.

Examples:

Noun	Verb	Adjective
care	care	
cold		cold
	direct	direct
end	end	

- There may be more than one form for a part of speech. The different forms usually have somewhat different meanings.

Example: *careful* (adjective), *careless* (negative adjective), *caring* (adjective)

careful = trying hard not to make mistakes, damage something, or cause problems

careless = not paying enough attention to what you are doing so that you make mistakes, damage things, or cause problems

caring = someone who is caring is kind to other people and tries to help them

A. **Work with another student. Write the missing forms for each word. Do not use the dictionary. If you do not know a form, make a guess. An X means that form is rare or doesn't exist. (More than one form may be possible.)**

	Noun	Verb	Adjective	Negative Adjective	Adverb
1.	reason	reason	reasonable	unreasonable	reasonably
2.			fresh	X	
3.		X	possible		
4.				unrelated	
5.		prepare			X
6.		serve		X	X
7.	sense				
8.	profit				
9.					really
10.	limit				X
11.		operate			
12.			special	X	

B. **Use a dictionary to check your answers to Part A. Correct them if necessary. Write any new words in your vocabulary notebook.**

A. **Work with another student. Write the missing forms for each word. Do not use the dictionary. If you do not know a form, make a guess. When there is an X, no form exists. (More than one form may be possible.)**

	Noun	Verb	Adjective	Negative Adjective	Adverb
1.		organize			X
2.				unrecognizable	
3.	production				
4.		unite			X
5.					substantially
6.		suggest		X	X
7.	settlement				X
8.			equal		
9.			valuable		X
10.		develop			
11.				unaccountable	
12.		consider			

B. **Use a dictionary to check your answers to Part A. Correct them if necessary. Write any new words in your vocabulary notebook.**

A. Work with another student. Write the missing forms for each word. Do not use the dictionary. If you do not know a form, make a guess. When there is an X, no form exists. (More than one form may be possible.)

	Noun	Verb	Adjective	Negative Adjective	Adverb
1.		demand			X
2.				independent	
3.			formal		
4.	manager				
5.				disabled	
6.		agree			
7.			simple	X	
8.			noticeable		
9.					expressively
10.		report			
11.			popular		
12.	length			X	X

B. Use a dictionary to check your answers to Part A. Correct them if necessary. Write any new words in your vocabulary notebook.

A. *Work with another student. Write the missing forms for each word. Do not use the dictionary. If you do not know a form, make a guess. When there is an X, no form exists. (More than one form may be possible.)*

	Noun	Verb	Adjective	Negative Adjective	Adverb
1.				X	generally
2.			believable		
3.				unofficial	
4.	perfection				
5.				powerless	
6.		exist			X
7.	weakness			X	
8.			influential	X	
9.				X	additionally
10.		ensure			
11.	rest				
12.				unpredictable	

B. *Use a dictionary to check your answers to Part A. Correct them if necessary. Write any new words in your vocabulary notebook.*

Collocations

What Is a Collocation?

A collocation is a group of words that are frequently used together. There are many collocations in English because people tend to use the same groups of words again and again. This is easier than trying to think of new ways to say things each time. It is also easier for listeners and readers to understand. If they recognize the collocation, they do not have to think about each word separately.

Most collocations are simply frequent combinations of words (phrases). It is usually possible to understand the meaning of these collocations from the meanings of the words.

Common Types of Collocations

Verb + noun:
We decided to <u>join the club</u>.
We need to <u>make a plan</u> for next month.

Verb + adverb:
The teacher <u>read aloud</u> from the book.
Jared <u>looks well</u> today.

Phrasal verb (verb + preposition):
Americans <u>throw away</u> a lot of plastic bags.
Please <u>turn down</u> the television. It's too loud.

Adverbial phrase:
They traveled <u>even farther</u> on the second day.
Betsy is my cousin and a good friend <u>as well</u>.
<u>Just a moment</u>, please. He'll be right there.

Noun + (preposition) + noun:
We checked the <u>weather forecast</u> before leaving.
Yesterday I bought a new <u>pair of shoes</u>.

Adjective + noun:
Only one student was a <u>native speaker</u> of English.
<u>Fast food</u> restaurants are popular with students.

Prepositional phrase:
It rained several times <u>during the night</u>.
<u>Over the years</u>, the company has grown.

Idioms

Some collocations are idioms. That is, the words together have a special meaning that is different from the meaning of each separate word. These include idiomatic expressions, as well as many phrasal verbs.

Idiomatic expressions:
She was feeling a little <u>under the weather</u>.
<u>By the way</u>, don't forget to check your e-mail.
He learned the whole poem <u>by heart</u>.
The prices have gone up, <u>of course</u>.

Phrasal verbs:
The doctor told him to <u>give up</u> smoking.
Don't worry, it's not lost. It will <u>turn up</u> later

Collocations in Other Languages

Collocations often differ from one language to another. You may have noticed that some English collocations are similar to ones in your language. However, there are probably many others—especially idioms—that are expressed in completely different ways in your language.

Do you say these phrases in your language ?. . .

• black and white	. . . with a similar phrase? The same word order?
• heavy rain	. . . with a similar adjective or a different one?
• give up	. . . with a preposition after the verb? The same one?
• take place	. . . with a verb + noun?
• under the weather	. . . with a similar idiom? A different idiom?

Learning Collocations

Choosing Collocations to Learn

It is important to become familiar with common collocations. They will make your speech and writing seem more natural. Recognizing them will also help you become a more efficient reader.

However, there are thousands of collocations in English. You could not possibly learn them all. As with single words, you need to choose the collocations that will be most useful to you and learn those.

You should focus on:

- The most common collocations. A good learner dictionary includes the most common phrases. If a collocation is not in a learner dictionary, it is probably not very common.
- Collocations that are related to your studies, work, or interests. If you find a collocation several times you probably should learn it.

Finding Collocations in the Dictionary

Collocations are usually listed under the noun or the verb, if there is one. Phrasal verbs are listed under the verb, usually in a separate entry (as in the example on the next page).

under the weather

weath•er[1] /'wɛðə-/ *n.* **1** [singular, U] the temperature and other conditions such as sun, rain, and wind: *What's the weather like today?* | *Our flight was delayed because of **bad weather**.* | *very **cold/warm/ hot/dry weather*** **2 under the weather** (informal) slightly sick: *I'm feeling a little under the weather.* [ORIGIN: Old English *weder*]

as well

well[1] /wɛl/ *adv.* (comparative **better**, superlative **best**) **1** in a good, successful, or satisfactory way: *Did you sleep well?* | *She doesn't hear very well.* | *Is the business **doing well**?* | *I hope your party **goes well**.* **2** thoroughly or completely: *I don't know her very well.* | *Mix the flour and eggs well.* **3 as well (as sb/sth)** in addition to someone or something else: *I'm learning French as well as Italian.* **4 may/might/could well** used in order to say that something is likely to happen or is likely to be true: *What you say may well be true.*

turn up

turn up *phr. v.*
1 turn sth ↔ **up** to make a machine such as a radio, OVEN, etc. produce more sound, heat, etc.: *Turn up the radio a little.*
2 to be found, especially by chance, after being searched for: *The keys turned up in the silverware drawer.*
3 turn sth ↔ **up** to find something by searching for it thoroughly: *An inspection of the brakes turned up no defects.*
4 to arrive: *Danny turned up late as usual.*
5 if an opportunity or situation turns up, it happens, especially when you are not expecting it: *Don't worry, a job will turn up soon.*

pair of shoes

pair[1] /pɛr/ *n.* (plural **pairs** or **pair**) [C] **1** something made of two similar parts that are joined together: *a **pair of** scissors* | *two pairs of jeans* | *a pair of glasses* **2** two things of the same kind that are used together: *a **pair of** earrings* | *She has 12 pairs of shoes!* **3** two people who are standing or doing something together: *a **pair of** dancers*

Studying Collocations

- In your vocabulary notebook, include the context (book, article, etc.) in which the new phrase or idiom was used, including the sentence where you found the phrase.
- When you meet a new phrase or idiom, think about how you say it in your language. You will remember better when the English idiom or phrase is similar. But just thinking about this will help you learn the idiom or phrase.
- Look for a connection between the meanings of the single words and the whole phrase/ idiom. If you cannot find one, invent something that will help you remember it. Drawing a little picture can also help.

Example: under the weather

One student's idea: The weather comes from the sky, so I am under it. I live in a place with a cold climate, and when there's a lot of (bad) weather, people often get sick.

A. *In each sentence, underline a phrasal verb from the box. (The verb may be in a different form: go on → is going on.)*

> point out   run into   turn up

1. The teacher <u>pointed out</u> to the students that the exam was the following week.
2. Don't worry; your gloves will <u>turn up</u> sooner or later.
3. Paul sometimes <u>ran into</u> his colleague, Tim, at the supermarket after work.

B. *Complete each sentence with a form of a phrasal verb from Part A. Change the form if necessary.*

1. If you _____ Mark, tell him I need to talk to him.

2. The director _____ that since there were fewer students, they did not need as many teachers.

3. Our cat finally _____ after a week. We were very worried about her.

C. *Work with another student. Discuss the meanings of the phrasal verbs in the box. Look up any you are not sure about.*

D. *Make up a story with your partner using the phrasal verbs in the box. Then tell your story to another pair of students and listen to their story.*

Example:

"Last weekend, I <u>ran into</u> my friend Sian at the bookstore. She told me she had lost her passport. She had looked everywhere in the apartment, but couldn't find it. I told her not to worry, it would <u>turn up</u> sooner or later. She said that luckily she had changed her vacation plans. She wasn't going to Europe anymore, but to Canada, so she didn't need her passport. I <u>pointed out</u> to her that now you need a passport to go from the United States to Canada."

E. *Write the phrasal verbs you want to learn in your vocabulary notebook. Remember to write the sentences where you found them.*

Note: There may be more than one definition of each phrasal verb in the dictionary. Make sure you find the one that fits the way it is used in these sentences.

Check the answers to this Practice exercise on page 285.

A. *In each sentence, underline a phrasal verb from the box. (The verb may be in a different form: go on → is going on.)*

bring about	carry on	go on	slow down
bring up	figure out	sign up	take up

1. He'd better slow down, or the police will give him a speeding ticket.
2. My friend Susan and I both signed up for an evening class in Spanish.
3. After his grandmother died, his grandfather had to bring up the three boys.
4. The teacher couldn't figure out how to make the computer work.
5. Financial problems take up a lot of his time.
6. After her teacher left, the young artist carried on with the project.
7. What is going on in that company? Why is it losing money?
8. We cannot expect to bring about environmental change in a short time.

B. *Complete each sentence with a form of a phrasal verb from Part A. (More than one form of the verb may be possible.)*

1. My sister's clothes _____ most of the space in the closet.

2. It's hard for a single parent to _____ a child alone.

3. The teacher knew perfectly well what _____ behind her back.

4. The new president was hoping to _____ some real change in Washington.

5. Production _____ in the factory because of electrical problems.

6. All students who need help in math should _____ for tutoring after class.

7. It is not easy to _____ the real cost of this project.

8. The professors at the university _____ teaching as usual until the fighting started.

C. Work with another student. Discuss the meanings of the phrasal verbs in the box. Look up any you are not sure about.

D. Make up a story with your partner using at least four of the phrasal verbs in the box. Then tell your story to another pair of students and listen to theirs.

E. Write the phrasal verbs you want to learn in your vocabulary notebook.

A. In each sentence, underline a collocation from the box.

> cheap source   dramatic sight   new opportunities   technological improvement
> close contact   full story   severe weather   terrible shock

1. Because of the severe weather, there will be no classes at the university today.
2. We did not hear the full story about his death until many years later.
3. When the police arrived at the scene, they were met with a dramatic sight.
4. It was a terrible shock for him when he lost his job.
5. For many years, eastern Europe was a cheap source of labor (workers) for western Europe.
6. Modern technology has opened up new opportunities in many parts of the world.
7. The police were in close contact with the FBI about the murder case.
8. The cell phone is a technological improvement that has made a real difference in Africa.

B. Complete each sentence with a collocation from Part A. (More than one form of the verb may be possible.)

1. She suffered a _____ when she saw her mother after the accident.

2. Skype was one _____ she could not live without after she moved to Japan.

3. The new skyscraper, the tallest in the city, was a _____ .

4. _____ is predicted for the next three days.

5. In poor countries people eat beans because they are a

   _____ of vitamins, minerals, and protein.

6. If you want to know the _____, you'll have to ask my boss.

7. My cousin and I stayed in _____ for many years, but then we lost touch.

8. There are lots of _____ for work in the fields of renewable energy.

C. Work with another student. Discuss the meanings of the collocations in the box. Look up any you are not sure about.

D. Make up a story with your partner using at least four of the collocations in the box. Then tell your story to another pair of students and listen to theirs.

E. Write the collocations you want to learn in your vocabulary notebook.

A. *In each sentence, underline a collocation from the box.*

advantage over	interest in	limit to	problem with
doubts about	lack of	position as	right to

1. According to the United Nations, all children have the right to an education.
2. The teacher had some doubts about the test. Was it a good measure of the students' abilities?
3. One problem with the book was its length—500 pages.
4. Our new refrigerator has one big advantage over the old one. It consumes much less energy.
5. In his position as the president of the college, he had to be careful about his words.
6. His real problem was not lack of skill, but lack of confidence.
7. There is a limit to the number of students who can sign up for certain courses.
8. The media has shown a great deal of interest in the situation.

B. *Complete each sentence with a collocation from Part A.*

1. The director has taken an _____ the boy's situation and wants to meet him.

2. There is no _____ the number of times you can use the subway pass in a week.

3. Because of the _____ funding, the music and art courses will not continue.

4. The home team had a big _____ the other team.

5. The main _____ his paper was the poor structure.

6. Microsoft still holds its _____ the leader in the field.

7. The bank manager had serious _____ the loan.

8. The woman was very angry. She said she had paid for her ticket, so she had the

   _____ a seat.

C. **Work with another student. Discuss the meanings of the collocations in the box. Look up any you are not sure about.**

D. **Make up a story with your partner using at least four of the phrasal verbs in the box. Then tell your story to another pair of students and listen to theirs.**

E. **Write the collocations you want to learn in your vocabulary notebook.**

A. *In each sentence, underline a collocation from the box. (There may be additional words, such as adjectives, included in the collocations in the sentences. Example: join a new club)*

have access to	make a difference in	raise money for	take care of
join a club	make progress in/on	run the business	take charge of

1. College students need to learn to take charge of their learning.
2. The government is making little progress in the war on crime.
3. The majority of people in the United States have access to Internet.
4. The parents decided to raise money for the school trip.
5. The travel agent took care of all the reservations for the trip.
6. She really believed that she could make a difference in the company.
7. For thirty years, he ran the business successfully.
8. Most students join some kind of club while they are in college.

B. *Complete each sentence with a phrase from Part A.*

1. Getting enough sleep before an exam can _____ the results.

2. My neighbor will _____ my house plants when we go away.

3. Marc loved playing chess, so in Paris he _____ for chess players.

4. Thorvald is _____ on his thesis and should be finished by June.

5. Berlusconi ran the Italian government the same way that he _____.

6. The college needs to _____ the new sports center.

7. When she arrived, she immediately _____ the situation.

8. People in some poor countries do not _____ basic health care.

C. *Work with another student. Discuss the meanings of the collocations. Look up the meanings of any you are not sure about.*

D. *Five of the collocations are followed by prepositions in the sentences in Parts A and B. Write the phrases with the prepositions and the nouns that follow.*

1. *have access to Internet/basic health care*
2. _____
3. _____
4. _____
5. _____

E. *Make up a story with your partner using at least four of the phrasal verbs in the box. Then tell your story to another pair of students and listen to theirs.*

F. *Write the collocations you want to learn in your vocabulary notebook.*

Collocations in Academic Writing

Certain collocations are often used by writers of textbooks and other academic material. They help the writers explain and discuss ideas and information.

Common Collocations in Academic Writing

Talking about work/research:
The tests <u>show that</u> there are problems.
She <u>made a good point</u> in her paper.
<u>According to</u> Ansari, the pattern is clear.
The results <u>tend to</u> follow a pattern.
In the study, we <u>focused on</u> young learners.

Explaining or describing:
It is not the <u>main factor</u>, but it is important.
There is a <u>wide range</u> of courses to choose from.
The test can be used for <u>a variety of</u> purposes.
There are <u>a number of</u> reasons why it failed.

Referring to time:
<u>In recent years</u>, research has been limited.
His solution is not practical <u>in the long run</u>.

Giving an example:
<u>For instance</u>, Ford has developed a new strategy.
Companies <u>such as</u> Nike are known worldwide.

Adding a new idea to a series of ideas:
<u>In addition</u>, we will discuss possible solutions.
The age of the student is a factor, <u>as well</u>.

Introducing a contrasting idea:
<u>At the same time</u>, costs are rising.
<u>On the other hand</u>, the market is still weak.

Explaining a cause or effect:
<u>As a result</u>, many people left the country.
<u>In order to</u> lower costs, the heat was turned down.

A. In each sentence, underline the academic collocations from the box. There are two or more collocations in most sentences. (The forms may be slightly different.)

a great deal of	based on	effect on	so far
a number of	carry out	raise issues	such as
a variety of	current theory	reach a goal	suggest that
argues that	deal with	set up	support a theory

1. Professor Wu argues that the new laws will have no effect on the situation.
2. The book raises important issues about current theories of global economics.
3. The results suggest that further research needs to be carried out.
4. To deal with this problem, we set up the equipment in a different lab.
5. Her research was based on interviews with people from a variety of backgrounds.
6. In order to reach our goal, a great deal of work still needs to be done.
7. So far, test results support our theory that technology has a positive effect on learning.
8. There are a number of factors to consider, such as size, weight, and color.

B. Work with another student. Discuss the meanings of the collocations in the box. Look up any you are not sure about.

C. Write the collocations you want to learn in your vocabulary notebook.

EXERCISE 6

A. In each sentence, underline the academic collocations from the box. (There are two or more collocations in most sentences.)

a number of	data show	in the long run	possible causes
according to	dramatically changed	lack of	results suggest
carry out	focus on	little difference	serve a purpose
current theory	in recent years	main reason	solve the problem

1. According to research, the skin serves an important purpose in keeping the body healthy.
2. In recent years, technological improvements have dramatically changed the way people work.
3. According to current theory, global warming will have a significant effect on ocean life.
4. There are good reasons for focusing on this particular issue.

5. The results suggest that there is little difference between age groups.
6. To solve the problem in the long run, we need to focus on the possible causes.
7. The data show a number of possible causes, which we will deal with one at a time.
8. A number of factors are involved, but the main reason is lack of funds.

B. *Work with another student. Discuss the meanings of the collocations in the box. Look up any you are not sure about.*

C. *Write the collocations you want to learn in your vocabulary notebook.*

EXERCISE 7

A. *Read these paragraphs from textbooks. Underline the academic collocations listed in the boxes in Exercises 5 and 6 or in the Examples box on page xxx.*

1. Teamwork

Research suggests that the best way to carry out certain kinds of projects is to have a number of people working together on a team. The main reason why a team is better than a single person is that a group of people has a wider range of knowledge and skills. In addition, with more hands and minds focused on the project, it can usually be completed more quickly. Moreover, studies show that working as a team also has an effect on creativity. People who work in a group tend to take more risks than people working alone. Each person in the group feels freer to experiment with a variety of solutions because the group as a whole is responsible, and not the individuals in it. As a result, the group can solve problems better

2. The Study of Sleep

It is possible that sleep plays an important role in health, but scientists are not yet sure what it is. Some psychologists argue that it allows the brain to rest and store information. However, it is difficult for scientists to study sleep effectively because they have no way to find out exactly what is going through a person's head while he or she is asleep. What people remember afterward may not be accurate or complete. However, in recent years, experiments have been carried out with new technology that has made it possible to learn a great deal more about sleep. Scientists placed special equipment on the heads of sleeping people to measure the electrical activity of the brain. Based on the results of these studies, the scientists now think that sleep may serve a number of purposes for the brain and the body.

B. *Work with another student. Look in the paragraphs for collocations that are not in the boxes. Circle them and show them to your teacher.*

C. *Write the collocations you want to learn in your vocabulary notebook.*

UNIT 6

Structure and Reference

Understanding a sentence or passage means more than just understanding words. You also need to understand the structure of sentences and the ways that writers refer to things or ideas and show relationships among them. In this unit you will practice identifying:

- key parts of sentences
- signal words or phrases
- pronouns
- synonyms or related words

Key Parts of Sentences

The key parts of a sentence are the subject and the verb.

The **subject** tells who or what the sentence is about.

The **verb** tells what the subject does—or—gives information about the subject.

Notes:

- The subject can be
  - a pronoun.   ***Example:*** *I, you, he, she, it, we, they, this, that, these, those, there, who, which*
  - a whole phrase.   ***Example:*** *The tallest mountain in the world* is Mount Everest.
    Learning vocabulary requires time and effort.

- The verb can
  - be in any tense.   ***Example:*** *is selling, sold, had sold, will sell, is going to sell*
  - include a modal.   ***Example:*** *may sell, can sell, could sell, must sell, should sell, has to sell*
  - be negative.   ***Example:*** *does not like, didn't like, won't like*
  - include adverbs.   ***Example:*** *has just arrived, will never believe*

- Sentences can have multiple subjects and/or verbs.
  - multiple subjects.   ***Example:*** The youngest child and the oldest man were sitting side by side.
  - multiple verbs.   ***Example:*** They looked at each other and laughed.
  - multiple subjects and verbs.   ***Example:*** Though the runner could hardly lift his legs, he did not stop.

Underline the subject and verb in each sentence. Write S under the subject and V under the verb.

Experiments have shown that some animals have a very good sense of direction. The Monarch butterfly is a good example of this. A beautiful orange and black color, the Monarch is quite a large butterfly. However, it is still only an insect with a very small brain. In spite of this fact, each year thousands of Monarchs travel from Mexico to the northern United States and Canada and back again.

Check the answers to this Practice exercise on page 285.

EXERCISE 1

A. *Underline the subject(s) and verb(s) in each sentence in the passages. Write S under the subjects and V under the verbs.*

1. Bus Passes in Oslo

Various kinds of bus passes are available in Oslo. Some are good for a day, while others are good for three days or a week. They all allow unlimited travel on the local buses and subway. These passes are useful for tourists who want to visit different parts of the city. There is also another kind of weekly pass that allows unlimited travel on buses and trains and boats anywhere in the country. This pass is quite expensive, but it is worth getting if you are planning to move around the country a lot. Otherwise, it is better to pay separately for each trip.

2. Foreign Drivers in the United States

Foreign drivers in the United States should pay attention to the rules of the road. If they do not follow the rules carefully, they may get into trouble. For instance, the police are usually very strict about the speed limit. Drivers going only five miles per hour over the limit may just get a warning. However, drivers going ten miles per hour or more over the limit will get a ticket. The cost of tickets can vary, though it may be as much as $250. Furthermore, information about all tickets is put into the police computer system. This can cause problems for drivers if, for example, they want to rent a car. The car rental companies can find out about the tickets and refuse to rent to those drivers.

B. *Compare answers with another student. Are they the same?*

Signal Words and Phrases

Writers often use signal words or phrases to help readers understand how an idea relates to other ideas in the sentence or in the passage.

> **Notes:**
> - You have seen some of these signal phrases already in Unit 5 in the section on Collocations in Academic Writing.
> - Many of them are also used to signal patterns of organizations (See Part 3, Unit 4).

Function in the Passage	Signal Words and Phrases
Adding new idea to a series of ideas *Example:* The police are looking for an older man, <u>as well as</u> a young woman.	*also, another, other, additional, as well as, furthermore, moreover*
Referring to time or to a step in a process *Example:* The new bus line will be running <u>by next week</u>.	*last month, next week, in a year, before the war, in 2001, in recent years, after that, then, first, last*
Introducing a contrasting idea *Example:* There was no evidence of murder. <u>However</u>, there was something strange about the death.	*but, however, though, although, instead, in contrast, yet, otherwise, while*
Explaining a cause or effect *Example:* Many young people are out of work <u>as a result</u> of the economic situation.	*since, because, for, as, consequently, so, as a result, due to, therefore, thus*
Giving an example *Example:* Many kinds of birds fly long distances. <u>One good example</u> is the arctic tern.	*for example, for instance, a good example of, in particular*
Offering a more detailed explanation *Example:* He was not the only student to fail the exam. <u>In fact</u>, over half the class failed.	*in fact, indeed, that is*

EXAMPLE

In this paragraph the signal words or phrases are underlined.

Foreign drivers in the United States should pay attention to the rules of the road. If they do not follow the rules carefully, they may get into trouble. <u>For instance</u>, the police are usually very strict about the speed limit. Drivers going only five miles per hour over the limit may just get a warning. <u>However</u>, drivers going ten miles per hour or more over the limit will get a ticket. The cost of tickets can vary, <u>though</u> it may be as much as $250. <u>Furthermore</u>, information about all tickets is put into the police computer system. This can cause problems for drivers if, <u>for example</u>, they want to rent a car. The car rental companies can find out about the tickets and refuse to rent to those drivers.

A. *Underline the signal words or phrases in the passage.*

Unexpected Effects

Which finger do you use to press a doorbell? The answer may depend on your age. People who are over thirty will almost certainly do it with their index finger. However, those who are under thirty will probably use their thumbs. Young people have spent many hours exercising their thumbs when sending text messages or playing video games.
5 Thanks to all that exercise, their thumbs have become stronger and more skillful. That is why they often use their thumbs instead of their index fingers.

Skillful thumbs are only one of the many unexpected effects of new technology. In fact, today's new products are influencing not only physical skills, but also mental skills. Most of the time people are not aware of what's happening. They change their behavior
10 as necessary, little by little. The new skills they develop may include texting, for example, or how to make an online flight reservation.

As for the old skills, most of the time people do not even realize what they have lost. For instance, how many people can do mental arithmetic these days? It is rarely necessary with calculators in every office and on every phone or computer. And with GPS in many
15 cars, there is little need to be able to follow directions or read a map.

Some researchers are concerned about the consequences of losing the old mental skills. If GPS stopped functioning, for example, would anyone know how to find their way around? More importantly, since the collapse of all technology is unlikely, scientists wonder about our brains. What will happen to them if we no longer exercise them in the
20 same way?

B. *Compare your work with another student. Do you agree?*

A. *Underline the signal words and phrases in the passage.*

The Early Cinema

The cinema had its beginnings at the end of the 19th century in the United States. It grew out of several earlier forms of entertainment, including theater, and out of the technology developed for so-called "peep shows."

Peep Shows

5 In the 1890s peep shows were popular in many American cities. In a peep show, a film was viewed through a small opening in a machine that was created for that purpose.

Among those who worked on peep shows was Thomas Edison, who invented a peep show machine in 1894. He then opened several special shops for his machines, where customers paid 25 cents to move from one machine to another and view short films.

New Technology

In these same years, however, other inventors began to look ahead. They realized that there was a basic limit to the peep show machines: Only one person at a time could look at a film. They wanted to improve the technology so they could show films to more people, so they worked on developing film projectors.

Edison did not become involved in this development because he believed he could make money with his peep show machines. In fact, he missed a major opportunity.

Entertainment for Everyone

By 1895, the first film projectors were in use in theaters, halls, and fairs. From the point of view of the producer, film production had several important advantages over theater or music hall productions. First of all, the material was recorded. Once the film was produced, there was no need for the actors, singers, lighting people, or make-up people. Furthermore, each film could be shown to much larger numbers of people. In other words, a successful film could make a lot more profit.

Audiences were also immediately enthusiastic about these early films. Unlike the peep shows, the cinema experience could be shared with others. And unlike the theater, where audiences were limited, there were almost no limits to the number of viewers for a film. This was the real beginning of the mass entertainment of the 20th century.

B.   Compare your work with another student. Do you agree?

Pronouns

Writers use pronouns to continue to talk about the same thing without repeating all the same words. There are several different kinds of pronouns.

Personal Pronouns and Possessive Adjectives

These are the most common pronouns.

Subject pronouns:	I	you	he	she	it	we	they
Object pronouns:	me	you	him	her	it	us	them
Possessive adjectives:	my	your	his	her	its	our	their

A personal pronoun takes the place of a noun or noun phrase. That noun or noun phrase is the referent.

The pronoun can be the subject of the sentence.
   Example: Maria knew that <u>she</u> wanted to continue studying French.
         The referent for *she* = *Maria*

The pronoun can also be the object of a verb or preposition.
   Example: Peter decided to major in psychology, a subject that had always interested <u>him</u>.
         The referent for *him* = *Peter*

A possessive adjective shows that something belongs to someone (or something). That someone or something is the referent.
   Example: Sula made an important decision about the course of <u>her</u> life.
         The referent for *her* = *Sula*

In this paragraph, the personal pronouns and possessive adjectives are underlined and marked with S (subject pronouns), O (object pronouns), or P (possessive adjectives).

In Tunisia, trains connect the larger cities, but there are not many smaller train lines. To travel between the smaller cities and towns, most Tunisians take buses or taxi vans. These taxi vans are often cheaper than the buses. They leave as soon as they have five

S   S

people who want to go to the same place. That might be a distant city or a town nearby. The driver puts a sign with their destination on the roof of the van. Other travelers

P

who want to go there can wave to him. He will stop and let them on. Officially there is

O   S   O

a maximum number of passengers allowed, but in reality the taxi vans sometimes carry many more.

EXERCISE 4

A. *Underline the personal pronouns and possessive adjectives. Write S under the subject pronouns, O under the object pronouns, and P under the possessive adjectives.*

Pedicabs

A pedicab is a small cab that is pulled by a bicycle. It has been popular in Asian countries for many years. About ten years ago, it was introduced in Denver, Colorado. Before long, there were pedicabs in many cities in the United States. These cabs do not take the place of taxis because people use them mainly just for short rides. The passengers

5   of pedicabs are often people who do not want to walk because they are well-dressed for an evening event. Tourists also take them as a fun and unusual way to get around a city.

The drivers of pedicabs are usually friendly students with strong legs. They pay the owner of the cabs a certain amount to use one for a day or evening. Any money they earn from passengers above that amount is their own. Typically, a pedicab driver earns about

10   as much as he or she would earn by working in a restaurant. However, students who have chosen pedicabs say they prefer this kind of work. It may be more tiring, but they enjoy being outdoors. They also like the fact that no one is telling them what to do.

B. *Compare answers with another student. Are they the same?*

Demonstrative Pronouns and Adjectives

Writers use demonstrative pronouns and adjectives to refer to something they have already mentioned and to connect it with a new idea. These words are very common in academic writing.

	Demonstrative Pronouns	Demonstrative Adjectives
Singular:	*this*, *that*	*this* idea, *that* effect
Plural:	*these*, *those*	*these* people, *those* years

When demonstrative pronouns and adjectives are used as pronouns, they take the place of a phrase or an idea. This phrase or idea is the referent.

Example: The taxi vans leave as soon as they have five people who want to go to the same place. That might be a distant city or a town nearby.

The referent for *That = the same place*

They are also used as adjectives, together with nouns. They can take the place of a longer phrase or idea.

Example: Before long, there were pedicabs in many cities in the United States. These cabs do not take the place of taxis because people use them mainly just for short rides.

The referent for *These cabs = pedicabs*

EXAMPLE

In this paragraph, the referent for each underlined demonstrative pronoun or adjective is circled and there is a line from the referent to the pronoun.

Monarch Butterflies

Experiments have shown that some animals have a very good sense of direction. The Monarch butterfly is a good example of this. A beautiful orange and black color, the Monarch is quite a large butterfly. However, it is still only an insect with a very small brain. In spite of that, each year thousands of Monarchs fly from Mexico to the northern United
5   States and Canada and back again. It is a remarkable trip, especially because it takes several generations. The butterflies that spend the winter in Mexico start north in early spring. Within two months, those butterflies lay eggs and die. The next generation is born and continues traveling north. This may happen one or two more times before the butterflies reach their summer home. The butterflies born in early fall are different from the others.
10 These butterflies live for seven months or more and fly all the way back down to Mexico.

EXERCISE 5

A. **Circle the referent for each underlined demonstrative pronoun or adjective. Then draw a line to the pronoun.**

Is Txting Bad 4 English?

People tend to feel strongly about texting. Some people love it, while others hate it. Among the haters, some have expressed their opinion in very strong terms. One British journalist said that "texters are doing to our language what Genghis Khan did to his

(continued)

neighbors 800 years ago. They are destroying . . . our punctuation . . . our sentences . . .
our vocabulary. And they must be stopped."*

This is not the first time that people have said that technology was bad for language. In the 15th century, some scholars opposed the invention of the printing press. Common people should not read books, these scholars argued, or the language might begin to reflect their common ways of thinking and speaking. More recently, the telegraph and then the telephone were also viewed as tools of linguistic destruction. And yet, the English language has survived.

In fact, there is reason to think that texting will be no more harmful to the language than any of those past inventions. Research has shown that many of the claims made by text haters are not based on reality. They especially dislike the way words in messages may be shortened, and numbers and symbols used instead of words. However, only about 20 percent or fewer messages actually do contain these shorter forms. In most messages, traditional spellings and whole sentences are used. The reason for this is practical: the majority of senders are not teenagers, but schools, banks, and companies. They want to make sure they will be understood.

Among texters who do use the shortened forms, certain forms appear frequently, such as c=see, u=you, and 4=for. However, there is also a lot of variation. That is because texting can actually be quite creative and fun. It could be considered a kind of word play, like doing crosswords or puzzles.

---

*John Humphreys, "I h8 txt msgs: How texting is wrecking our language," *The Daily Mail,* 24 September 2007.

B. ***Compare answers with another student. Are they the same?***

Relative Pronouns

Relative pronouns connect several ideas in one sentence. The pronoun takes the place of a noun or an idea already mentioned in the sentence.

Relative Pronouns: who   which   that   where

- *Who* and *that* refer to people.

    Examples:
    The number of children <u>who</u> suffer from asthma is increasing.
    The number of children <u>that</u> suffer from asthma is increasing.
    (who/that = number of children)
    Marzia spoke to the bank president, <u>who</u> told her that the bank was not going to fail.
    (who = bank president)
- *Which* and *that* refer to things.

    Examples:
    My husband cannot eat foods <u>that</u> are very spicy.
    My husband cannot eat foods <u>which</u> are very spicy.
    (that/which = foods)

- *Which* also can refer to ideas.

  Example:
  He was the only man in the room, <u>which</u> made him feel uncomfortable.
  (which = the fact that he was the only man in the room)
- *Where* refers to places.

  Example:
  We would like to go someplace <u>where</u> we can truly relax.
  (where = someplace)

EXERCISE 6

A. *Underline the relative pronouns (who, which, that, where) in these sentences. Then circle the referent and draw a line to the pronoun. (Remember: **that** can also be a demonstrative pronoun.)*

The Tuaregs: From Nomads to Farmers

For the Tuareg people of north-central Africa, life has changed dramatically in recent years. Historically, the Tuaregs led the life of nomads, people with no permanent home. They traveled across the Sahara Desert in caravans of camels, carrying goods between Arab Africa in the north and black Africa in the south.

5   Neither Arab nor black African, the Tuaregs were a light-skinned Berber people, who had a culture and a language of their own. To Europeans, they were the "blue men" of the desert because they dressed all in blue. They were known for their great skill in finding their way across the open desert, with only the stars to guide them.

They were also known for their independent spirit. In fact, they loved the nomad
10   way of life, which allowed them to come and go as they chose. National borders had no meaning for them in the desert. During the 19th century, Africa was divided up and ruled by various European countries, but this did not affect the Tuaregs, who continued to move freely. In the 20th century, however, many of the new African nations closed their borders, which forced the Tuaregs to limit their travels and trade.

15   At the same time, another big change had come to the area. People began to use motor vehicles for travel across the desert, which meant the Tuareg camel caravans lost their important role. Then came the great drought (dry weather) of the 1970s and 1980s. Many animals died, including the Tuaregs' camels. Their old way of life was now definitively over.

20   In recent years, some of the Tuaregs have managed to make a new life for themselves as farmers. They have settled near the old water holes, such as Timia, in central Niger. In the past, it was just a place in the middle of the desert where travelers stopped to rest. Now it has a population of about 10,000. Most of the people who live there were nomads in the past, but now they make a living from their fruit and vegetable gardens. They grow
25   oranges, grapefruits, pomegranates, dates, and corn, which they send by truck to Agadez, the nearest city.

B. *Go through the passage again and make a box around the signal words and phrases.*

C. *Compare your work with that of another student. Is it the same?*

Synonyms and Related Words

Writers tend to repeat important words in their writing to remind the reader what it is about. However, they do not want to use the same word too many times, so they often use other words with similar meanings: synonyms or related words.

A synonym is a word or phrase that has the same or a similar meaning as another word or phrase.

Examples
often = frequently   help = assist
hard = difficult   important = significant

A related word also refers to something similar, like a synonym, but it is more specific or more general.

Examples

General	→	→	→	Specific
reading material	book	autobiography		*The Diary of Anne Frank*
clothes	formal wear	suit		tuxedo
meal	breakfast	American breakfast		pancakes

EXAMPLE

In this paragraph the words and phrases that are synonyms or related to the underlined words are circled.

Experiments have shown that some (animals) have a very good sense of direction. The Monarch butterfly is a good example of this. A beautiful orange and black color, the Monarch is quite a large (butterfly). However, it is still only an (insect) with a very small brain.

EXERCISE 7

A. *Read the sentences. Underline the words that are synonyms or related to the underlined words.*

1. Scientists have found evidence of communities living in Kunda, northern Estonia, around 6500 BCE. These groups of people had not yet started farming, but lived by hunting and fishing.

2. In the last two hundred years, Estonia has been occupied and ruled by forces from Germany, Sweden, Russia, and other countries. This small eastern European nation has had a difficult and often violent past.

3. During the 20th century, one <u>war</u> after another brought suffering to Estonians. They were involved in fighting against the Russians and the Germans.

4. Talinn is the <u>capital</u> of Estonia. It is also the historic heart of Estonian history and culture. The walls and gates of the old city center date back to the 13th century.

5. Estonians are very fond of <u>singing</u>. There are often choral concerts in the churches and concert halls and also many informal opportunities to hear vocal music.

6. Every year, a <u>national song contest</u> is held in Estonia. Singers from all over the country meet and sing in the competition. This event is shown on television and is very popular with young Estonians.

7. The <u>old city hall</u> stands in the main square in the center of Talinn. This beautiful medieval building is no longer the seat of the city government. It is now used for special events.

8. The <u>University of Tartu</u> is in the smaller city of Tartu, to the southeast of Tallinn. Estonia's oldest and largest educational institution, it attracts students from many other countries. For this reason, many courses are held in English.

9. Many people who live in Talinn also have <u>vacation homes</u> on the nearby island of Saaremaa in the Baltic Sea. These may be just simple cottages, but they are often surrounded by large gardens full of flowers, fruit trees, and vegetables.

10. Estonians love a good <u>cup of coffee</u>. In the center of Talinn, there are many small coffee shops where they can enjoy their favorite drink and also chat with friends.

B. **Compare your work with another student. Do you agree?**

EXERCISE 8

A. **Find synonyms or related words in the passage. Follow these instructions:**
   If a word is underlined, underline the synonyms and related words.
   If a word is circled, circle the synonyms and related words.
   If a word is boxed, box the synonyms and related words.
   (One synonym has been underlined for you.)

1. The Rise of Factories

The first <u>factories</u> opened in the United States after 1815, and soon there were factories in all the major cities. <u>Industrialization</u> had direct consequences on the American labor force. Before the factories, most manufacturing was done at home, where people had control over the way they worked, in particular their movements and their time. With factories, however, workers lost all control over their jobs. The new methods of production required a stricter sense of time. Work began at the sound of a bell and workers had to keep machines operating all day. They could not be late or absent, as that could interfere with production. Furthermore, in the industrial system, there was no room for personal invention or creativity. Workers were not encouraged to think for themselves or to take pride in the products, but simply to follow instructions—and above all, keep production moving. In this way, industrialization not only made a difference in the way work was organized; it completely changed the nature of work.

2. Workers' Reactions to Industrialization

The first workers to arrive in the factories had trouble getting used to the new methods of production. They did not have an easy time, first of all, adapting to the strict schedule. Some of them began to hate the sound of the bell that signaled the beginning of their working day. It came to represent their loss of freedom. Furthermore, the conditions in the factories were terrible by modern standards. The workers had to work quickly to keep up with the machines, which meant repeating the same movements rapidly all day. Factory days were also very long—10 or even 12 hours a day, six days a week. And finally, the machines were noisy, dirty, and dangerous, often injuring or killing the people working with them. It is not surprising that a certain number of workers could not cope with the situation and left the factories. Others looked for ways to protect themselves and formed the first unions.

B. *Compare your work with another student. Do you agree?*

Comprehension Skills

Introduction

Reading is a complex process. First of all when you read, you need to recognize the letters and words on the page. Your eyes send this information to your brain, which then tries to make sense of it by connecting it with information or ideas already stored in your memory . . .

> . . . about the sentence,
> . . . about the passage,
> . . . about the topic and writer,
> . . . about language and the world.

If you are a good reader, most of this happens automatically—very, very quickly. You do not have to spend time thinking about the letters, the words, and the sentences. This means you can concentrate on the ideas in the text.

To become a good reader, you need to learn the skills that good readers use to make the reading process more efficient. In Part 2, you learned about and practiced some word- and sentence-level skills. In Part 3, you will focus on and practice the skills that readers use to discover and follow ideas in a text.

Scanning and Previewing

In this unit, you will learn about and practice ways to get information quickly from a text.

Scanning

You scan when you are looking for a specific piece of information in a text. Scanning is a very useful skill that you use often in daily life. For example, you might scan a course listing, a website homepage, or the index of a book.

Practice in scanning will also help your reading. You will learn to recognize words faster and develop more flexibility in the way you move your eyes when you read.

How to Scan

In this kind of reading, your eyes need to move quickly. They also need to move up and down and around the page—not just from left to right along the lines of print.

It is not actually necessary to read many words when you scan. You should read just enough of the text to find what you are looking for. How much you read will depend on the text you are scanning and the information you are looking for.

There are two groups of exercises in this section:

- Scanning for information in different kinds of text
- Scanning for key words in a passage

Scanning for Information

In these exercises, you will scan to find the answers to "Wh-" questions (*who, what, why, where, when,* and *how*). You may not know exactly what words to look for, but you do know what kind of information you need. For example:

"When . . . ?"	Look for a time, day, or date
"How many . . . ?"	Look for a number
"Where . . . ?"	Look for the name of a place

Some questions also include words that can help you. For example:

"Which person . . . ?"	Look for a name
"What book . . . ?"	Look for the title of a book

> **Notes:**
> - You do not need to understand all the words in these exercises. Use the words you understand to look for the answers to the questions.
> - Exercises with a ⊗ have a time limit. You need to work quickly. Your teacher will time you.

A. *Read the questions. Then scan the list of websites on the next page and underline the answers. You will have two minutes.*

1. Where can you find out about hotels in South Africa?
2. How can you win a Hyundai?
3. Where can you read about the history of the World Cup?
4. On which site can you watch World Cup matches live?
5. For which country does David James play?
6. Where can you buy tickets to soccer games in Brazil?

B. *Write three more questions about the list of websites. Then ask another student to scan for the answers.*

_____

_____

_____

C. *Discuss these questions with your partner.*

1. Do you ever watch soccer games or other sports events? If so, do you watch them on TV or online?
2. What are the differences between watching a sports event on TV and on the computer?
3. Do you play or do any sports? If so, which sport(s)?

WORLD CUP SOCCER

FIFA.com - Fédération Internationale de Football Association (FIFA)
18 Jun 2010 Upload your *World Cup* photos and you could win a Hyundai! Every FIFA *World Cup* match day, FIFA.com users can vote for. . . .
www.fifa.com/

FIFA *World Cup* - Wikipedia, the free enclopedia
The FIFA *World Cup,* also called the Football *World Cup* or the Soccer *World Cup,* is an international association football competition contested by the men's. . . .
*en.wikipedia.org/wiki/FIFA_* **World_Cup**

Schedule - 2010 FIFA World Cup South Africa ...—2014 World Cup in Brazil
*en.wikipedia.org/wiki/2010_FIFA_* **World_Cup**

News for WORLD CUP
   Friday's *World Cup* 2010 round-up - 1 hour ago
   Former France captain Zinedine Zidane has criticized coach Raymond Domenech after the 2-0 defeat by Mexico which left Les Bleus on the brink of *World Cup*. . . .
   Goalie David James should start for England
   BBC Sport
   World Cup 2010: Player Of The Day: Argentina's Gonzalo Higuain
   Goal.com

Watch *World Cup* 2010 Live Online ...
There will be more Group A action on Wednesday in the 2010 *World Cup* when France plays against Mexico. This is sure to be a thrilling encounter so. . . .
www.watchfootballnow.com/ - United Kingdom

World Cup 2010 South Africa
18 Jun 2010 . . . *World Cup* 2010 news from South Africa with opinion, hotels, accommodation, safety information, and team schedule and group news.
www. **worldcup** *2010southafrica.com/*

FIFA *World Cup* 2010 - Football / Soccer - ESPN Soccernet
Get complete, live coverage of the 2010 *World Cup* from South Africa including expert analysis, schedules, statistics, highlights, and more.
soccernet.espn.go.com/ **world-cup** */*

World Cup

World Cup football website on the history of the *world cup*, providing all the information, scores, results, news on the football competition and we have a. . . .
www. **worldcup** *years.com/*

FIFA *World Cup* 2010 | Scores | Results | News - Yahoo! Eurosport UK
The latest FIFA *World Cup* 2010 news, results and scores on Yahoo! Eurosport, UK. Find fixtures, group tables, team and player profiles, match coverage, . . .
uk.eurosport.yahoo.com/.../ **world-cup** */ - United Kingdom*

2010 *World Cup* Tickets — Soccer Tickets Online
We have tickets to every game for the *World Cup* in South Africa in 2010. We also have tickets for all England, USA, Brazil, and Argentina. . . .
www.soccerticketsonline.com/ **world-cup** *-tickets/*

allAfrica.com: *World Cup* 2010
Briefing: Africa Competes in 2010 FIFA *World Cup* . . . Features about the *World Cup* from around Africa by the journalists of the Twenty Ten project. . . . *allafrica.com/* **worldcup** */*

A. **Read the questions. Then scan the Table of Atomic Weights on the next page and underline the answers. You will have two minutes.**

1. What are the four kinds of information given in this table?
2. What is the symbol for iron?
3. What is the atomic number for tin?
4. Which elements have an atomic number of 100 or above?
5. Which has a lighter atomic weight, zinc or lead?
6. What are the highest and lowest atomic numbers?
7. What has an atomic weight of 83.80?
8. What does the symbol Au stand for?

B. **Write three more questions about the table. Then ask another student to scan for the answers.**

_____

_____

_____

C. **Discuss these questions with your partner.**

1. Do you like reading or watching documentaries about science?
2. Have you ever taken a chemistry course? Was it interesting?
3. Are any of the names of these elements new to you? If so, which ones?

Table of Atomic Weights*

Element	Symbol	Atomic number	Atomic weight	Element	Symbol	Atomic Number	Atomic weight
Actinium	*Ac*	*89*	*(277)*	*Mercury*	*Hg*	*80*	200.59
Aluminum	Al	13	26.9815	Molybdenum	Mo	42	95.94
Americium	Am	95	(243)	Neodymium	Nd	60	144.24
Antimony	Sb	51	121.75	Neon	Ne	10	20.179
Argon	Ar	18	39.948	Neptunium	Np	93	237.0482
Arsenic	As	33	74.9216	Nickel	Ni	28	58.71
Astatine	At	85	(210)	Niobium	Nb	41	92.9064
Barium	Ba	56	137.34	Nitrogen	N	7	14.0067
Berkelium	Bk	97	(249)	Nobelium	No	102	(254)
Beryllium	Be	4	9.01218	Osmium	Os	76	190.2
Bismuth	Bi	83	208.9806	Oxygen	O	8	15.9994
Boron	B	5	10.81	Palladium	Pd	46	106.4
Bromine	Br	35	79.904	Phosphorus	P	15	30.9738
Cadmium	Cd	48	112.40	Platinum	Pt	78	195.09
Calcium	Ca	20	40.08	Plutonium	Pu	94	(242)
Californium	Cf	98	(251)	Polonium	Po	84	(210)
Carbon	C	6	12.011	Potassium	K	19	39.102
Cerium	Ce	58	140.12	Praseodymium	Pr	59	140.9077
Cesium	Cs	55	132.9055	Promethium	Pm	61	(145)
Chlorine	Cl	17	35.453	Protactinium	Pa	91	231.0359
Chromium	Cr	24	51.996	Radium	Ra	88	226.0254
Cobalt	Co	27	58.9332	Radon	Rn	86	(222)
Copper	Cu	29	63.546	Rhenium	Re	75	186.2
Curium	Cm	96	(247)	Rhodium	Rh	45	102.9055
Dysprosium	Dy	66	162.50	Rubidium	Rb	37	85.4678
Einsteinium	Es	99	(254)	Ruthenium	Ru	44	101.07
Erbium	Er	68	167.26	Samarium	Sm	62	150.4
Europium	Eu	63	151.96	Scandium	Sc	21	44.9559
Fermium	Fm	100	(253)	Selenium	Se	34	78.96
Fluorine	F	9	8.9984	Silicon	Si	14	28.086
Francium	Fr	87	(223)	Silver	Ag	47	107.868
Gadolinium	Gd	64	157.25	Sodium	Na	11	22.9898
Gallium	Ga	31	69.72	Strontium	Sr	38	87.62
Germanium	Ge	32	72.59	Sulfur	S	16	32.06
Gold	Au	79	196.9665	Tantalum	Ta	73	180.9479
Hafnium	Hf	72	178.49	Technetium	Tc	43	98.9062
Helium	He	2	4.00260	Tellurium	Te	52	127.60
Homium	Ho	67	164.9303	Terbium	Tb	65	158.9254
Hydrogen	H	1	1.0080	Thallium	Ti	81	204.37
Indium	In	49	114.82	Thorium	Th	90	232.0381
Iodine	I	53	126.9045	Thulium	Tm	69	168.9342
Iridium	Ir	77	192.22	Tin	Sn	50	118.69
Iron	Fe	26	55.847	Titanium	Ti	22	47.90
Krypton	Dr	36	83.80	Tungsten	W	74	183.85
Lanthanum	La	57	128.9055	Uranium	U	92	238.029
Lawrencium	Lr	103	(257)	Vanadium	V	23	50.9414
Lead	Pb	82	207.2	Xenon	Xe	54	131.30
Lithium	Li	3	6.941	Ytterbium	Yb	70	173.04
Lutetium	Lu	71	174.97	Yttrium	Y	39	88.9059
Magnesium	Mg	12	24.305	Zinc	Zn	30	65.37
Manganese	Mn	25	54.9380	Zirconium	Zr	40	91.22
Mendelevium	Md	101	(256)				

*Based on atomic weight of Carbon-12 = 12.0000. Numbers in parentheses are mass numbers of most stable isotopes.

A. *Read the questions. Then scan the list of paperback best sellers on the next page and underline the answers. You will have three minutes.*

1. In which book is a person sentenced to death?
2. Which book focuses on a sport?
3. What is the title of the book by Sherman Alexie?
4. Which two books are about people and events in Africa?
5. In which book is there an autistic character?
6. Where does *Mister Pip* take place?
7. Which book tells about historical events in China?
8. Who is the author of the book about John Lennon?

B. *Write three more questions about the bestseller list. Then ask another student to scan for the answers.*

_____

_____

_____

C. *Discuss these questions with your partner.*

1. Which books seem most interesting to you? Why?
2. Do you ever look for the most popular books or movies on newspaper lists or websites?
3. What are some other ways you find books you want to read?

RECOMMENDED READING on contemporary issues and themes (fiction and nonfiction)

Alexie, Sherman. *The Absolutely True Diary of a Part-Time Indian.* 2007. Little, Brown. Fiction. A young American Indian draws cartoons to deal with the family disasters and racism on an Indian reservation. When he goes to an all-white high school, he gains respect and acceptance through his determination.

Anderson, M. T. *Feed.* 2002. Candlewick. Fiction. In a possible future society, each person is fed an endless stream of virtual information, entertainment, and advertising. Suddenly Violet is no longer connected, and she and others are forced to reexamine the power of the cyber-feed in their lives.

Beah, Ishmael. *A Long Way Gone: Memoirs of a Boy Soldier.* 2008. Farrar, Straus and Giroux. Nonfiction. The dramatic autobiography of Ishmael Beah, a 12-year-old child who becomes a child soldier and gets caught in the horrors of civil war in his African homeland.

Chang, Iris. *The Rape of Nanking: The Forgotten Holocaust of World War II.* 1998. Penguin. Nonfiction. The horrific torture and murder of hundreds of thousands of Chinese citizens by the invading Japanese army took place over the course of just seven weeks.

D'Orso, Michael. *Eagle Blue: A Team, a Tribe, and a High School Basketball Season in Arctic Alaska.* 2006. Bloomsbury. Nonfiction. While focusing on the high school basketball team, this book tells of the tiny village of Fort Yukon, Alaska, the native population, their cultural heritage, and how they relate to mainstream American culture.

Eggers, Dave. *What Is the What: The Autobiography of Valentino Achak Deng: A Novel.* 2007. Knopf/Vintage. Fiction (based on real events and memories). Six-year-old Valentino watched Arab militia destroy his village in southern Sudan, and then joined the "Lost Boys" in the desert, surviving hunger, violence, and disease to tell his story to Dave Eggers, who tells it to us.

Gaines, Ernest. *A Lesson Before Dying.* 1997. Knopf/Vintage. Fiction. A disillusioned teacher, Grant Wiggins is sent to talk with Jefferson, a young black man in jail and sentenced to death, to help him gain a sense of dignity and self-esteem before his execution.

Haddon, Mark. *The Curious Incident of the Dog in the Night-Time.* 2004. Knopf/Vintage. Fiction. In his own special way (he has Asperger Syndrome, a form of autism), Christopher tries to solve two mysteries: who killed his dog Wellington and what happened to his mother?

Jones, Lloyd. *Mister Pip.* 2008. Dell Publishing/Dial Press. Fiction. Civil war breaks out on a Pacific Island, and in the village, Mr. Watts, a lonely Englishman, reads Dickens's Great Expectations aloud to the village children, transforming their lives.

McCormick, Patricia. *Sold.* 2006. Hyperion. Fiction. Thirteen-year-old Lakshmi is sold into prostitution by her stepfather and her life becomes a nightmare in the slums of Calcutta. This novel reflects the real-life situation of millions of girls around the world.

Partridge, Elizabeth. *John Lennon: All I Want Is the Truth.* 2005. Penguin/Viking. Nonfiction. An objective view of the work and life of one of the most influential and complicated persons in the history of popular music.

Picoult, Jodi. *Nineteen Minutes.* 2008. Simon & Schuster/Washington Square Press. Fiction. Why does a 17-year-old get up one day, load his backpack with guns, walk into his high school, and kill nine students and a teacher? This novel explores the psychology of the boy, his family, and his friends.

Rogers, Elizabeth, and Kostigen, Thomas. *The Green Book: The Everyday Guide to Saving the Planet One Simple Step at a Time.* 2007. Crown Publishing/Three Rivers Press. Suggestions from many, including celebrities like Ellen DeGeneres, Jennifer Aniston, Tim McGraw, and Dale Earnhardt, Jr., for ways to be more green: small changes that will have a positive impact on the health of our planet.

A. *Read the questions. Then scan the article on the next page and underline the answers. You will have three minutes.*

1. What are the names of two dentists in the article?
2. What foundation is mentioned?
3. Which workers suffer the most?
4. How long do some people grind their teeth at night?
5. What should patients not drink before going to bed?
6. How much do bite guards cost?

B. *Write three more questions about the article. Then ask another student to scan for the answers.*

_____

_____

_____

C. *Discuss these questions with your partner.*

1. How does stress affect you?
2. Do you have any habits you would like to stop, such as grinding your teeth or biting your nails?
3. Have you ever tried any relaxation techniques, such as meditation or yoga? Do you think they are/would be helpful?

Economic Hard Times Are Good Times for Dentists

Growing numbers of men and women are suffering from eating problems, serious headaches, and mouth pain because they grind their teeth[1] at night. Dentists in the UK say this increase comes from people worrying about their jobs. Levels of unemployment have gone up dramatically in recent months.

In the past year, more patients have seen dentists for treatment because of the effects of their grinding. These include headaches, pain in their whole mouth, or damage to the teeth, including pieces falling off and cracked molars (back teeth). Many patients take painkillers to help with their symptoms. Even with the painkillers, some are not able to keep up with their work or to maintain their normal lifestyle.

According to Sharif Kahn, a cosmetic dentist, "Ambitious people and perfectionists who work in business are the worst affected by grinding."

Workers in the financial sector suffer more than those in other sectors. Dentist Yann Maidment says he has seen a 10–20% increase in such patients over the past 18 months, especially those working in banks and financial services businesses.

"There's a lot of anxiety about job loss," said Maidment. Business people who travel frequently for work also grind their teeth more than others, he said. He is giving bite guards to more and more patients. These are thin pieces of plastic that protect the teeth, similar to the mouth guards used by sports players. Bite guards cost from $400–$700 and they are worn at night to cover the teeth. Most of those people who grind their teeth do it for up to two hours per night.

An adviser at the British Dental Health Foundation says there has been an increase in calls about the problem. "Stress is probably the major reason—people not being able to cope with things going on in their work or love life, or having money worries."

There is no specific cure for teeth grinding, but patients are encouraged to use relaxation techniques and told not to drink tea, coffee, or alcohol before they go to bed.

[Adapted from *Surge in Teeth Grinding Linked to Recession,* by Dennis Campbell/ Janet Hardy-Gould, Guardian Weekly, April 09, 2010]

[1] **grind teeth**   to rub your upper and lower teeth together

Scanning for Key Words

In these exercises you will continue to practice moving your eyes quickly as you look for the key words. Later you will use this skill to help you find the answers to questions about the ideas in passages.

Remember, you are not working on comprehension. You are just practicing moving your eyes quickly. Do not worry about the meaning of the words or about unfamiliar words.

EXERCISE 5

A. *Turn back to the article about dentists in Exercise 4, page 115. Scan it again for the key words below. Scan for one word at a time and circle that word every time you find it. Then write the number of times you found each key word.*

Key words	Number of times
a. dentist(s)	_____
b. teeth	_____
c. patient(s)	_____

B. *Now turn to the passage about texting in Part 2, Unit 2, page 48. Scan it for the key words below and then write the number of times you find each word.*

Key words	Number of times
a. text (ing/er)	_____
b. language	_____
c. message	_____

C. *Compare answers with another student.*

Previewing

Previewing is what you should do *before* you read. (It is closely related to skimming, as you will learn in Unit 6.) When you preview, you take a very quick look at a passage so you can get a sense of what it is about—the *gist*—and how to read it. This will help you read it more effectively.

Previewing can help you with all of your reading. It is particularly helpful for course assignments and for reading comprehension tests or exams. Though it takes a little time to preview, just a few seconds of previewing can make a difference in your reading later.

Focusing on the Title

Start previewing by looking at the title and using it to think of previewing questions about the ideas and information in the passage.

EXAMPLE

Headline of newspaper article:

> **Workers Block Factories**

Possible previewing questions:

- Where did workers block factories?
- Why did they block the factories?
- When did they block the factories?
- Who owns the factories?
- How long did the workers block the factories?
- What were the effects of blocking the factories?

A. *Work with another student. Read these newspaper headlines. Then write three previewing questions for each title.*

1.
Storm Recovery Slowed

   a. _____

   b. _____

   c. _____

2.
Operation Stops Star

   a. _____

   b. _____

   c. _____

3.
Not the Real Fish

   a. _____

   b. _____

   c. _____

4.
Cash Helps the Medicine Go Down

   a. _____

   b. _____

   c. _____

5.
Kenya Bombing Kills Five

   a. _____

   b. _____

   c. _____

B. *Compare questions with another student.*

A. *Preview each article. Read the first sentence and look through the rest quickly. Then write a headline from Exercise 6 for each article.*

1. _____

The winner of last year's U.S. Open tennis tournament, Juan del Potro, has had surgery on his right wrist, according to the Argentine news agency Telam. The Argentine del Potro is right-handed. He is expected to be out of action for at least the next four months. This will mean missing the French Open, Wimbledon, and probably the U.S. Open. The 21-year-old became a major player last year, winning against many top players. The operation was performed at the Mayo Clinic in Minnesota by Dr. Richard Berger, a leading hand surgeon, who has helped many professional athletes.

2. _____

Two bombs exploded in the middle of a crowd in Nairobi on Sunday, killing 5 people and wounding more than 100. Many of the wounded are in critical condition. Kenyans fear this may signal a return to the political violence that killed more than 1,000 people in 2008. That violence was set off by divisive election results. The bombs on Sunday may also have been politically motivated. The country will soon be voting on a referendum* for a new constitution and the crowds on Sunday were attending a political rally.

*referendum when the people vote to make a decision about something (not to elect someone)

3. _____

Lack of power is slowing rescue workers and residents as they try to clear homes and businesses in Nashville, Tennessee after several days of violent storms and flooding. Heavy rain caused the Cumberland River to overflow its banks and much of downtown was underwater until yesterday. The flooding caused extensive damage to many buildings in the area, including the Opryland Hotel and Resort—famous for its country music. The flooding has caused 20 deaths in Tennessee and 10 more in neighboring Kentucky, though officials said that more victims may be discovered.

4. _____

One-third to one-half of all patients do not take their medication as prescribed. These patients often become sicker, requiring hospitalization and more costly treatment, raising medical costs by more than $100 billion annually, according to a recent study. Now many doctors, hospitals, and insurance companies in the United States are promoting a new solution to the problem: pay patients to follow their treatments. Patients who take their medication regularly (as confirmed by their doctor), receive a small payment every month. The study showed that this makes a significant difference in patient behavior. Not only does it mean a savings in medical costs; it also saves the patients from illness and suffering.

5. _____

Many English people are not getting what they think in their favorite dish—"fish and chips." The fish is supposed to be cod or haddock. But according to a new survey at least 25% is made from some other kind of fish. As a result of overfishing, supplies of cod and haddock have decreased in recent years and prices have risen dramatically. This explains why producers of fish and chips often make it with cheaper kinds of fish, such as pollack, saithe, or whiting. This should be written on the package if it is frozen, or in the shop—but few people notice the writing.

B. *Read the articles again carefully. Then look back at the questions you wrote in Exercise 6. Which ones were answered in the articles? Did the questions help you understand the article?*

Guidelines for Previewing Longer Passages

How you preview depends on the kind of passage and your reason for reading it. In general, follow these steps:

1. Focus on the title and ask yourself questions about it.

2. Think about the kind of writing—is it an email, a web or newspaper article, part of a story?

3. Look at headings or illustrations, if there are any. How do they relate to the title?

4. Read the first few lines—Do they tell you more about the title?

5. Notice the language—Is it formal or informal, technical or personal?

6. Notice the content—Are there lots of names, numbers, difficult words?

EXERCISE 8

A. *Work with another student. Read the title of the passage. Then write three previewing questions on a separate piece of paper.*

The Early Cinema

B. *Follow the previewing steps. Then look quickly for the answers to your previewing questions.*

The cinema had its beginnings at the end of the 19th century in the United States. It grew out of several earlier forms of entertainment, including theater, and out of the technology developed for so-called "peep shows."

Peep Shows

In the 1890s peep shows were popular in many American cities. In a peep show, a film was viewed through a small opening in a machine that was created for that purpose.

Among those who worked on peep shows was Thomas Edison, who invented a peep show machine in 1894. He then opened several special shops for his machines, where customers paid 25 cents to move from one machine to another and view short films.

New Technology

In these same years, however, other inventors began to look ahead. They realized that there was a basic limit to the peep show machines: Only one person at a time could look at a film. They wanted to improve the technology for showing films to more people, so they worked on developing film projectors.

Edison did not become involved in this development because he believed he could make money with his peep show machines. In fact, he missed a major opportunity.

Entertainment for Everyone

By 1895, the first film projectors were in use in theaters, halls, and fairs. From the point of view of the producer, film production had several important advantages over theater or music hall productions. First of all, the material was recorded. Once the film was produced, there was no need for the actors, singers, lighting people, or makeup people. Furthermore, each film could be shown to much larger numbers of people. In other words, a successful film could make a lot more profit.

Audiences were also immediately enthusiastic about these early films. Unlike the peep shows, the cinema experience could be shared with others. And unlike the theater, where audiences were limited, there were almost no limits to the number of viewers for a film. This was the real beginning of the mass entertainment of the 20th century.

C. *Discuss these questions with your partner. Do not look back at the article.*

1. Did you find the answers to your previewing questions?   2. What is the passage about?   3. Where do you think it came from?   4. Will it be difficult to read?

D. *Read the passage carefully. Then talk with your partner. Can you explain the headings?*

A. *Work with another student. Read the title of the article. Then write three previewing questions on a separate piece of paper.*

Carver Children Safe after Night Out

B. *Follow the previewing steps. Then look quickly for the answers to your previewing questions.*

SOUTH CARVER – February, 13, 2010 Cold, wet and afraid, the three children who were lost all last night were found this icy morning. The discovery by a team of searchers brought an end to a rescue operation involving hundreds of local and state officials.

The children had spent the night in a swamp (wet land), on some higher ground, holding tight to each other and to their dog. Sam and Cathy Ryan, 7 and 5, and their cousin Bill McCarthy, 11, were found by two Carver police officers at 8:15 a.m.

George Hammond, one of the officers, was out all night searching in the swamp. He said he fell twice into water that was over his head. The rescuers brought the children back through a mile of swamp, with Cathy in Hammond's arms. An ambulance brought them to Plymouth Hospital, where the children and Officer Hammond were treated for minor injuries.

Hospital officials said the children would remain overnight for observation, but added that they seemed to be in good condition. They asked for hamburgers and French fries soon after their arrival.

The police had been using special high-tech equipment in their 18-hour hunt. But in the end, it was common sense that led to the children. Officer Hammond said that he and another officer tried to figure out which direction the children could have taken. They then pushed their way through some of the worst parts of the swamp, shouting the children's names until they got an answer.

The children said that they had been very afraid at times, but had never given up hope. Bill McCarthy knew from his boy scout training that they should stay in one place after they got lost. At one point, they heard a helicopter overhead, but they had no way of making themselves seen or heard.

C. *Discuss these questions with your partner. Do not look back at the article.*

1. Did you find the answers to your questions?
2. What is the passage about?
3. Where do you think it came from?
4. Will it be difficult to read?

D. *Read the article carefully. Then, with your partner, retell the events.*

A. *Work with another student. Read the title of the textbook passage and write three previewing questions on a separate piece of paper.*

The Law of Demand

B. *Follow the previewing steps. Then look quickly for the answers to your previewing questions.*

Anyone who has ever spent money will easily understand the **law of demand**. The law of demand says that when a good's price is lower, consumers will buy more of it. When the price is higher, consumers will buy less of it. All of us act out this law of demand in our everyday purchasing decisions. Whether your income is $10 or $10 million, the price of something will strongly influence your decision to buy it.

Ask yourself this question: Would I buy a slice of pizza for lunch if it cost $2? Many of us would, and some of us might even buy more than one slice. But would you buy the same slice of pizza if it cost $5? Fewer of us would buy it at that price. Even real pizza lovers might reduce their consumption. How many of us would buy a slice for $10? Probably very few. As the price of pizza gets higher and higher, fewer of us would be willing to buy it. That is the law of demand in action.

The law of demand is the result of not one pattern of behavior, but of two separate patterns that overlap. These two behavior patterns are the **substitution effect** and the **income effect.** The substitution effect and the income effect describe two different ways that a consumer can change his or her spending patterns. Together, they explain why an increase in price decreases the quantity purchased.

The Substitution Effect

When the price of pizza rises, pizza becomes more expensive compared with other foods, such as tacos and salads. So, as the price of pizza rises, consumers become more and more likely to buy one of those alternatives as a substitute for pizza. This causes a drop in the amount of pizza demanded. For example, instead of eating pizza on Mondays and Fridays, a student could eat pizza on Mondays and a bagel on Fridays. This change in spending is known as the substitution effect. It takes place when a consumer reacts to a rise in the price of one good by consuming less of that good and more of a substitute good.

The Income Effect

Rising prices have another effect that we have all felt. They make us feel poorer. When the price of movie tickets, shoes, or pizza increases, your limited budget just won't buy as much as it used to. You can no longer afford to buy the same combination of goods, and you must cut back your purchases of some goods. If you buy fewer slices of pizza, for example, without increasing your purchases of other foods, that is the income effect.

The income effect also operates when the price is lowered. If the price of pizza falls, all of a sudden you feel wealthier. If as a result you buy more pizza, that is also the income effect.

[Adapted from *Economics: Principles in Action*, by Arthur O'Sullivan and Steven M. Sheffrin, Prentice Hall/Pearson, 2003, pp. 80–81]

C. *Discuss these questions with your partner. Do not look back at the passage.*

1. Did you find the answers to your previewing questions?
2. What is the passage about?
3. Where do you think it came from?
4. Will it be difficult to read?

D. *Read the passage carefully. Then talk with your partner. Can you explain the title and the headings?*

> **Remember**
>
> Always preview when you read something new.

Focus on Vocabulary

Target Vocabulary

Check your knowledge of these words and phrases. (Do not look in the dictionary.)

Mark each one: ✔ *You are sure of the meaning.*
                 ? *You have seen it before, but are not sure of the meaning.*
                 X *You have not seen the word before.*

_____ carry out	_____ charge with	_____ extend	_____ finances
_____ operation	_____ massive	_____ statement	_____ estimate
_____ currently	_____ acquire	_____ strike	_____ revenue
_____ branch	_____ wealth	_____ significant	_____ exceed

EXERCISE 1

A. *Preview and then read the passage. Do not stop to look up new words.*

Police Arrest Hundreds in Italy

ROME—Police carried out one of the biggest operations ever against the 'Ndrangheta (pronounced n-DRANG-gay-tah), currently one of the most powerful Italian crime organizations. More than 300 people were arrested in Calabria in the south of Italy, and also in Lombardy in the north.

Among those arrested was Domenico Oppedisano, 80, the man believed to be the organization's boss of bosses, and Pino Neri, the leader of the Milan branch, as well as several local government officials. Those arrested are charged with criminal association, murder, arms and drug trafficking, and other serious crimes. In the raids, police seized millions of dollars worth of weapons, cash, and property, as well as massive amounts of drugs.

Traditionally based in Calabria, the 'Ndrangheta recently has been acquiring property and political influence in the north of Italy, particularly in Lombardy. Authorities now consider it to be Italy's most dangerous crime group, due to increasing wealth from its trafficking of drugs from South America.

Like other Italian crime organizations, such as Cosa Nostra in Sicily, or the Camorra, based in Naples, the 'Ndrangheta has extended its reach far beyond Italy's borders. In 2007, six people linked to the group were killed in Duisburg, in northern Germany, in a shoot-out between competing families. The Italian police report finding connections between the leadership in Calabria and crime organizations based in Australia and Canada, but arrests have not yet been carried out for technical reasons.

According to a statement from the Ministry of the Interior, the 'Ndrangheta is believed to be involved in commercial activities, politics, and the local administration in both Calabria and Lombardy. Interior Minister Roberto

Maroni said in a telephone interview that the predawn operation had involved more than 3,000 police officers across the country. In his view, it struck a significant blow to the 'Ndrangheta's leadership structure and its finances.

Experts in Italian crime and organizations estimate that the revenue of Italy's main crime groups, including the 'Ndrangheta, rose by about 4 percent in 2009 to 135 billion euros. That is almost 9 percent of Italy's gross domestic product and exceeds the revenue of the country's largest company.

B. *Read the passage again. Circle all of the words and phrases from the target vocabulary list. Underline all of the words and phrases you don't know.*

C. *For each underlined word or phrase, look at the context (the words and sentences around it). Make a guess about the meaning. Write your guess in the margin.*

D. *Check your comprehension. Write T (True) or F (False) after each sentence.*

1. The 'Ndrangheta is a criminal organization based in Calabria. _____

2. This organization operates only in the south of Italy. _____

3. It rarely uses violent methods. _____

4. It is involved in local politics. _____

5. The 'Ndrangheta controls very large amounts of money. _____

E. *Check the dictionary for the words and phrases you are not sure about. Compare the definitions with your guesses in Part C. Change your guesses if necessary.*

F. *Compare your work with another student.*

EXERCISE 2

A. *Read the two sentences. Choose the best definition for the underlined word or phrase. The first one has been done for you.*

1. Those arrested are <u>charged with</u> criminal association, murder, arms and drug trafficking, and other serious crimes.
   The young man was <u>charged with</u> drunken and disorderly conduct (behavior).
   a. cleared for
   b. accused of
   c. attacked for

2. According to a <u>statement</u> from the Ministry of the Interior, the 'Ndrangheta is believed to be involved in commercial activities. . . .
   The Chief of Police made a <u>statement</u> this morning about the case.
   a. a guess that is made about a situation or a problem
   b. a television appearance on a talk show or news program
   c. something that is said or written to give an opinion or facts

3. Police <u>carried out</u> one of the biggest operations ever against the 'Ndrangheta, currently one of the most powerful Italian crime organizations.
The students <u>carried out</u> a campaign against the new regulations.

   a. planned and completed
   b. worked for and voted for
   c. ordered and received

4. Police carried out one of the biggest <u>operations</u> ever against the 'Ndrangheta, currently one of the most powerful Italian crime organizations.
The fire department and the police worked together on the rescue <u>operation</u>.

   a. planned actions with a goal
   b. business activities for profit
   c. medical procedures

5. Authorities now consider it to be Italy's most dangerous crime group, due to increasing <u>wealth</u> from its trafficking of drugs from South America.
Simon Neill never had to work for his <u>wealth</u>; it came down to him from his mother's family.

   a. large house in the country
   b. the general condition of your body
   c. a large amount of money and possessions

6. That is almost 9 percent of Italy's gross domestic product and <u>exceeds</u> the revenue of its largest company.
The security costs of the president's visit could <u>exceed</u> $2 million.

   a. to plan for
   b. to be more than
   c. to be equal to

7. In the raids, police seized millions of dollars worth of weapons, cash, and property, as well as <u>massive</u> amounts of drugs.
Globalization has caused <u>massive</u> changes in both developed and developing countries.

   a. unusually large, powerful, or damaging
   b. not likely to make a difference
   c. frequent, happening often

8. Among the arrested was Domenico Oppedisano, 80, the man believed to be the organization's boss and Pino Neri, the leader of the Milan <u>branch</u>. . . .
After he graduated, he got a job at the local <u>branch</u> of Citizen's Bank.

   a. something that is growing
   b. a building or structure holding something
   c. part of a company or organization

B. *Compare answers with another student.*

A. *Cross out the word or phrase in each group that is NOT a possible synonym for the target word. The first one has been done for you.*

1. **strike**	hit	~~break~~	attack	harm
2. **massive**	interesting	large	enormous	huge
3. **significant**	noticeable	serious	several	important
4. **acquire**	have	buy	get	gain
5. **finances**	banking	job	accounts	money
6. **currently**	now	at the moment	at present	at least
7. **extend**	spread	make	continue	reach
8. **revenue**	property	earnings	gain	income

B. *Compare answers with another student.*

EXERCISE 4

A. *Complete the passage with words from the box. Change the word to fit the sentence if necessary.*

branch	charge with	massive	statement
carry out	currently	operation	strike

Yesterday the police arrested two men in Arizona who were

_____ illegal activities and disorderly behavior. The Chief
       1

of Police said the police had been planning the _____ for
                                                          2

months.

The arrest followed an attack on a teacher who was

_____ in the face and pushed to the ground. The two men
       3

are U.S. citizens and have no criminal record, but they are known in the state for their

extreme views.

They are _____ members of an organization that

_4_

aims to make all languages except English illegal in the U.S. The Arizona

_____ of this organization became well known to teachers

_5_

and parents last winter. The two men led a _____ effort to

_6_

influence state school programming using questionable methods, including offers of

money.

In a _____ read by their lawyer, the men say they were

_7_

only _____ orders given by other people in the organization.

_8_

B. *Compare answers with another student.*

EXERCISE 5

A. *Choose a word from the box that can be used with all the words/phrases in each group. The first one has been done for you.*

> acquire   carry out   exceed   extend
> branch   charge with   estimate   significant

1. _extend_____ + the reach / the theory / the period
2. _____ + wealth / property / knowledge
3. _____ + blow / difference / effect
4. _____ + an operation / a survey / orders
5. _____ + of a bank / of a company / of an organization
6. _____ + a crime / murder / criminal association
7. _____ + the cost / the damage / the wealth
8. _____ + the limit / the revenue / the amount

B. *Compare answers with another student.*

A. *Work with another student. Write different forms for each word. If you don't know a form, make a guess. Do not use the dictionary. (More than one answer is possible for some forms.)*

Noun	Verb	Adjective	Negative Adjective	Adverb
1.	acquire		X	X
2.	estimate		X	X
3.	exceed		X	
4.	extend		X	
5. finance			X	
6. operation				
7.		significant		
8. statement				
9.	strike		X	

B. *Compare your work with another pair.*

Vocabulary Review

- In your vocabulary notebook, write the words from this Focus on Vocabulary section that you want to learn. Include the parts of speech, the sentences, and the definitions (See Part 2, Unit 1).
- Review your notebook (See Part 2, Unit 2).
- Make study cards of 10–15 words that you have trouble remembering. Study them alone and then with another student.

UNIT 2 Making Inferences

An inference is a kind of guess. To infer, you use what you already know about something to try to guess more about it. In everyday life, you often make inferences.

EXAMPLES

- While you are riding the bus, you hear a young woman talking about exams. She looks too old to be a high school student, but too young to be a teacher. You infer that she is probably a college student.
- In New York's Italian neighborhood a crowd is watching a soccer match outside on a big screen. You know that there is a World Cup match between Italy and Brazil. Suddenly everyone gives a great shout. You infer that the Italian team has made a goal.

Good readers often make inferences while they are reading. For example, they infer the general meaning of new words when they do not want to stop and look them up in the dictionary. (Part 2, Unit 3, focuses on this important skill of guessing meaning from context.)

They also make inferences about the content of what they are reading:
- In fiction, they notice clues (pieces of information) in the descriptions or the dialogues. They use these clues to make inferences about the people, the situations, or the plot.
- In nonfiction, they make inferences from information in the text to fill in gaps in their knowledge about the topic or in their understanding of the ideas.

> **Notes:**
> - Some of the questions for the exercises in this unit have more than one possible answer. Any answer is acceptable if you can explain it with clues or information from the text.
> - For some difficult words, definitions have been given. These are not common words, so you should not spend time learning them.
> - Try to guess the general meaning of new words and continue reading.

Making Inferences from Conversations

When you hear part of a conversation and try to imagine more about the people and their situation, you are making inferences.

A. *Read the conversation. Then discuss the questions with another student.*

A: Excuse me. Do you live around here? Is this Chilton Street?

B: No, this is Garden Street.

A: Garden? Hmm . . . I don't see it here on my map.

B: Let me have a look. . . . Here. We're right here, at the corner of Garden and Somerset.

A: Oh. So where's Chilton?

B: You go to the end of Garden, take a right, and then, let's see, I think your second left. There's an intersection. . . . But you know, I'm going that way myself. I'll show you. I mean, if you want.

A: That would be great. I'm supposed to meet someone to get a key, and I'm late already.

B: Hey, that looks heavy. Let me take it.

A: Oh, it's all right. It's got wheels.

B: No, really. I'll take it.

1. Where are these people?
2. What are they doing?
3. What can you infer about A?
4. What can you infer about B?
5. What do you think will happen next?

B. *Compare answers with another pair.*

Check the answers to this Practice activity on page 285.

A. *Read the conversation. Then discuss the questions with another student.*

A: Why is he taking so long?

B: He has to get changed, you know. He's got all that makeup to take off.

A: We've been here nearly 40 minutes. It's cold out here. Are you sure we're at the right door?

B: Yes, I'm sure. Come on. Let's not give up now. I've just got to see him close up.

A: He's not so great looking.

B: That's not true. I've seen him on TV a couple of times. He's got this amazing smile.

A: But he's ancient! Anyway, I'm just about frozen. If he doesn't come out in another two minutes, I'm going home.

B: Look here he comes! Give me the pen!

1. Where are these people?
2. What are they doing?
3. Who are they talking about?
4. What can you infer about A?
5. What can you infer about B?
6. What do you think will happen next?

B. *Compare answers with another pair.*

EXERCISE 2

A. *Read the conversation. Then discuss the questions below with another student.*

A: Is this the kind of thing you're looking for?

B: It's so hard. You see, she's got very definite ideas about what she likes.

A: How about a nice little item like this?

B: Hmm. You'd think I'd know by now, but every year I have the same problem! Those do look nice, but they look a bit old-fashioned.

A: Then what about these? They're classic.

B: No, no. She's not the classic type. Something more up-to-date . . . like those over there.

A: These? Are you sure? Colors like these usually appeal to . . . to younger women.

B: She's fond of color. Always has been. Says I'm so dull in my suits. I'll take those.

A: Shall I gift wrap them for you?

B: No, that's not necessary. I'll just put the box in my pocket.

1. Where are these people?
2. What are they doing?
3. Who are they talking about?
4. What can you infer about A?
5. What can you infer about B?
6. What do you think will happen next?

B. *Compare answers with another pair.*

Making Inferences in Short Stories

In each of the following exercises, there is a passage from a story. You will try to infer more about the people and situations from the clues in the passage.

A. ***Read the passage from*** **The Darkness of the Night,** *a short story by Robert M. Coates. Then discuss the questions below with another student.*

. . . in the silence they couldn't help hearing the talk that was going on at the next table.

"Well, the old lady just looked at the kid and kept on stirring," a man in a dark-blue suit was saying. " 'I don't know where he is,' says she, 'All I know is he's never around when you want him.' "

5   When the man had finished speaking, a girl in a gray tailored coat and a short black skirt gave a whoop[1] and pushed herself back in her chair so hard that she almost lost balance. She grabbed at the red-faced man's arm to steady herself. "Oh, God!" she cried. "What a simply crazy story! Eddie where do you get them?" The red-faced man was laughing too. "Now, listen," he said. "Let me tell one."

10   Flora gave a little sigh. "Ah, Fred," she said. "People can have such good times, can't they?"

"Only us," Fred said.

"Only us."

"We could have good times, too."

She shook her head slowly at him, not speaking.

15   "Look," the red-faced man was saying, "This one's an Irish one, and you ought to know the accent to really put it over. But it seems there was a snowstorm in Ireland . . ."

Flora giggled suddenly. "You know, Fred," she said. "I busted[2] a light bulb yesterday!"

Fred stared at her, puzzled. "A light bulb?"

"Yes, you know, a light bulb. It was out in the kitchen over the sink, and it had burned

20   out, so yesterday I thought I would change it. And then, when I was screwing it out, it dropped, bang, into the sink. It smashed into a thousand pieces. Really, Fred, I bet if you'd count them. . . ."

She stopped for a second, looking at him. They were yelling again at the next table and Fred couldn't keep from grinning[3]; he couldn't help thinking there was a joke in what

25   Flora was saying, too.

"Right near where the stew[4] was," she went on. She had leaned forward a little, and there was something in her voice that made Fred stop grinning. For an instant his heart and his breathing stopped too. "The stew I was putting some vegetables in," she said. "For his supper. And I couldn't help thinking. . . ."

30   She had opened her purse and was fishing around in it. She pulled out a newspaper clipping. "Fred, did you notice this? Because I was reading it in the *News* just before I started fixing that bulb."

---

[1]**whoop** loud shout
[2]**bust** broke

[3]**grinning** smiling widely
[4]**stew** a dish with meat and vegetables

The clipping was a small one, and it was date-lined some place in Ohio. Fred could hardly read it, but it told how a woman had confessed[5] to feeding her husband almost the whole of two beer bottles, broken up, before the glass had killed him.

Fred's hand shook a little as he laid the clipping down. Then he picked it up again, squeezed it carefully into a ball, and dropped it under the table. They had talked of such things before.

[Adapted from the story published in *The New Yorker*, Sept. 5, 1942]

---

[5]**confess** admit or tell you have done something wrong

1. Where are Flora and Fred?
2. What is the relationship between them?
3. Who are the people at the next table?
4. Whose supper was Flora preparing?
5. What do you think will happen next in the story?

B. **Compare answers with another pair.**

EXERCISE 4

A. **Read the passage from "The Standard of Living," a short story by Dorothy Parker. Then discuss the questions below with another student.**

"All right," she said. "So you've got this million dollars. So what would be the first thing you'd do?"

"Well, the first thing I'd do," Midge said, "I'd get a mink[1] coat." But she said it mechanically, as if she were giving the memorized answer to an expected question.

"Yes," Annabel said. "I think you ought to. The terribly dark kind of mink." But she, too, spoke as if by rote[2]. It was too hot; fur, no matter how dark and sleek and supple[3], was horrid[4] to the thoughts.

They stepped along in silence for a while. Then Midge's eye was caught by a shop window. Cool, lovely gleamings[5] were there set off by chaste and elegant darkness.

"No," Midge said, "I take it back. I wouldn't get a mink coat the first thing. Know what I'd do? I'd get a string of pearls. Real pearls."

Annabel's eyes turned to follow Midge's.

"Yes," she said, slowly. "I think that's a kind of a good idea. And it would make sense, too. Because you can wear pearls with anything."

Together they went over to the shop window and stood pressed against it. It contained but one object—a double row of great, even pearls clasped by a deep emerald around a little pink velvet throat.

"What do you suppose they cost?" Annabel said.

"Gee, I don't know," Midge said. "Plenty, I guess."

"Like a thousand dollars?" Annabel said.

---

[1]**mink** a kind of animal
[2]**by rote** automatically
[3]**sleek and supple** smooth and soft

[4]**horrid** terrible
[5]**gleamings** shiny things

"Oh, I guess like more," Midge said. "On account of the emerald."

"Well, like ten thousand dollars?" Annabel said.

"Gee, I wouldn't even know," Midge said.

The devil nudged Annabel[6] in the ribs. "Dare[7] you to go in and price them," she said.

25 "Like fun!"[8]

"Dare you!" Annabel said.

"Why, a store like this wouldn't even be open this afternoon," Midge said.

"Yes, it is so, too," Annabel said. "People just came out. And there's a doorman on. Dare you."

30 "Well," Midge said. "But you've got to come too."

They tendered[9] thanks, icily, to the doorman for ushering[10] them into the shop. It was cool and quiet, a broad, gracious room with paneled walls and soft carpet. But the girls wore expressions of bitter disdain[11], as if they stood in a sty[12].

A slim, immaculate clerk came to them and bowed. His neat face showed no 35 astonishment at their appearance.

"Good afternoon," he said. He implied that he would never forget it if they would grant him the favor of accepting his soft-spoken greeting.

"Good afternoon," Annabel and Midge said together, and in like freezing accents.

"Is there something—" the clerk said.

40 "Oh, we're just looking," Annabel said. It was as if she threw the words down from a dais[13]. The clerk bowed.

"My friend and myself merely happened to be passing," Midge said, and stopped, seeming to listen to the phrase. "My friend here and myself," she went on, "merely happened to be wondering how much are those pearls you've got in your window."

45 "Ah, yes," the clerk said. "The double rope. That is two hundred and fifty thousand dollars, Madam."

"I see," Midge said.

The clerk bowed. "An exceptionally beautiful necklace," he said. "Would you care to look at it?"

50 "No, thank you," Annabel said.

"My friend and myself merely happened to be passing," Midge said.

They turned to go; to go, from their manner, where the tumbrel[14] awaited them. The clerk sprang ahead and opened the door. He bowed as they swept by him.

[Excerpt from the story first published in *The New Yorker*, Sept. 20, 1941]

---

[6]**nudged Annabel** gave her an idea
[7]**dare** try to make someone do something
[8]**Like fun.** (old-fashioned) You're joking.
[9]**tendered** offered
[10]**ushering** showing them the way
[11]**bitter disdain** feeling that something is not good enough

[12]**sty** place to keep pigs
[13]**a dais** platform used for giving speeches
[14]**tumbrel** cart used to carry prisoners during the French Revolution

1. Where are Annabel and Midge?
2. What is the relationship between them?
3. How did Annabel and Midge feel in the store?
4. What did the clerk think of them?
5. When do you think this story takes place?
6. What do you think will happen next in the story?

B. *Compare answers with another pair.*

Making Inferences in Nonfiction

In each of these exercises, you will practice making inferences to answer various kinds of questions about nonfiction passages.

EXERCISE 5

A. ***The paragraphs below are about different jobs. Read each paragraph and guess the job.***

1.   The minute you climb in, you start feeling excited. There's nothing so exciting for me, not even a jet plane. You get in and start up and off you go. And then you've got to pay attention every minute. There's always someone doing something crazy who's likely to end up under your wheels. I sometimes think it's a miracle if I can get all the way there with no accidents. You've always got to be thinking ahead. That's hard when you have to keep going for so many hours alone. A lot of people in this job have stomach problems from the tension. They lose their hearing, too, because of the noise. Sometimes you end up unloading stuff, too, and that can ruin your back. You've got to be tough on this job, you know.

Job: _____

2.   My day starts at four o'clock in the morning. That's when my feet hit the floor. I'm at work at five-thirty, and I finish at two in the afternoon. In between I do a lot of walking. I wear out a lot of shoes each year—maybe four or five pairs. And my poor feet, at the end of the day they're really hurting. The other problem is the dogs. Sometimes you can make friends with them and they'll follow you around. But other times, they can be mean. I've been bitten a couple of times. I can't say as I care much for dogs any more. But it's not all bad, my job. One thing I like is the way you meet a lot of people. You learn all about their private lives, too. It never gets boring.

Job: _____

3.   The most important thing is to understand people. You've got to know what they're thinking. If you can figure that out, you can get them to do anything. They come in with an idea about what they want. You get them talking about themselves, about what they like. If it's a man, you talk about baseball, or something like that. If it's a woman, you ask her about fashions. That way they get comfortable with you. You ask them a lot of questions and get them saying yes. Then they just get into the habit of saying yes. In the end, you can put them into anything you want, if you're really good. They need a little car for the city; you send them home with a truck. Of course, I wouldn't really do that. It wouldn't be right. You've got to sell on this job, but you also have to be fair. It's not fair to take advantage of people too much. There are some people in this business who'd do anything. But I don't believe in that.

Job: _____

B. ***Compare answers with another student.***

A. *These paragraphs are examples of different genres (kinds of writing). Read each paragraph and choose the appropriate genre from the box. (There are two extra.)*

> a. product information on a package e. e-mail message from a bank
> b. encyclopedia article f. newspaper article
> c. online advertisement g. college textbook
> d. letter from a nonprofit organization

1. New York. A metal suitcase caused a bomb scare near Times Square on Friday. The suitcase was discovered at the side of the road on Eighth Avenue between 46th and 47th Streets at 11:52 a.m. Part of Eighth Avenue was closed off to vehicles and pedestrians while the bomb squad examined the suitcase. According to city officials, it was not a threat. It contained tools, not explosives. Within an hour, the street had been reopened. It is likely that the suitcase fell off the back of a truck. The police are holding it for the owner at the central station.

Genre: _____

2. Every year, more than 10 million children in developing countries die before reaching their fifth birthday. Of these deaths, seven million are caused by one or more of five common conditions: pneumonia, diarrhea, malaria, measles, and malnutrition. These conditions can be prevented in simple and inexpensive ways: with vaccinations,[1] bed nets, food, clean drinking water, and basic medicine. So why do so many children still die every day? The aim of our organization is to reduce these numbers, to save as many children as possible from unnecessary suffering and death.

[1]**vaccinations** medicines that prevent disease

Genre: _____

3. This message is personal and confidential. If you are not the intended recipient, please notify the sender and do not use or share this message. This message does not include offers to buy or sell financial products or services. Any offers to buy or sell financial products or services that appear to be linked with this company are fraudulent.[2] You should not respond to such offers and you should notify the company immediately.

[2]**fraudulent** an illegal way to gain money

Genre: _____

4. For a delicious and satisfying cold snack, lunch, or meal, soak[3] 1/4 cup Heidi's Old Country Muesli in 1/2 cup yogurt for 5 to 10 minutes. (The Swiss soak it overnight.) Or try soaking it in fruit juice or milk. Makes 1 serving. For a wonderfully delicious hot cereal, add 1/2 cup Muesli to 1/2 cup water or milk and bring to a boil. Cook on low heat for 3 to 5 minutes. Microwave directions: Place in covered bowl and cook on high for 3 to 5 minutes. Makes 2 servings.

[3]**soak** to keep in a liquid

Genre: _____

5. Early Life. Anna Eleanor Roosevelt was born in New York City on Oct. 11, 1884. Her parents, Elliott and Anna Hall Roosevelt, were members of socially important families, and she was a niece of President Theodore Roosevelt. She had an intensely unhappy childhood. Her mother, widely known for her beauty, made fun of Eleanor for her plainness. Her father, whom she adored, was an alcoholic and often absent. Her parents died when she was still quite young, and she was raised strictly by her Grandmother Hall.

Genre: _____

B. Compare answers with another student.

EXERCISE 7

A. Read these short articles about scientific news. Discuss the questions with another student.

1. Fewer Snakes

A new study predicts that snakes will disappear in many areas as a result of climate change. This is the first major study of snake populations. In the study, scientists on three continents looked at 17 populations in a variety of habitats.[1] They reported finding significantly fewer snakes in 11 of them, while 5 remained the same, and only 1 showed a very small increase. The scientists believe in fact that snake populations are declining globally, and that this will have wider consequences. Snakes are vital predators[2] in many habitats, including rice fields.

[1]**habitat** the natural environment of a plant or animal
[2]**predator** an animal that kills and eats other animals

    a. How might the decline in snakes affect other animals?
    b. How might it affect people?
    c. Are the "wider consequences" positive or negative?

2. "Planned" Attacks

Until recently, scientists believed that only humans were able to plan for the future. A chimpanzee at the Furuvik zoo in Sweden has challenged this belief. Santino, an adult male chimpanzee, has been at the Furuvik zoo since the 1980s. As he grew to adulthood, he became quite aggressive[3] and he killed the only other male chimpanzee at the zoo. Then, in the late 1990s he become more aggressive toward human visitors and began throwing rocks at them. (A tall fence protected the visitors.) Zoo staff discovered that he would prepare and hide small piles of rocks early in the morning. Then when people arrived, he would start throwing the rocks. When zoo staff removed all rocks from his area, he began making things to throw. He would find weak places in the cement boulders[4] in his area and break them off so he could throw them.

[3]**aggressive** angry and violent   [4]**boulder** very large rock

    a. Why was Santino making piles of rocks?
    b. Why was he throwing rocks at the visitors to the zoo?
    c. How did Santino's behavior challenge scientists' "beliefs"?

B. Compare answers with another student.

A. *Read this article. Then discuss the questions below with another student.*

Undoing the Balance of Nature

What happens when people change the balance of nature by introducing new species? The events on Macquarie Island should be a lesson about how even the best intentions can lead to unfortunate results.

Macquarie Island, part of Australia, lies halfway between Australia and Antarctica. It
5   was first discovered by the English in 1810 and its problems began almost immediately. It became a popular stopping place for English and American whaling ships. Sailors from these ships killed thousands of seals and penguins for their meat, fur, and oil.

While the ships were at the island, rats and mice moved onto the land and stayed. At some point, some ships' cats also remained on the island. They may have been left to keep
10 down the mice and rats. With no large predators on the island, and with plenty of rats and mice, the cat population grew rapidly. Soon they had almost eliminated the rats and mice and needed other food, so they began eating other animals, including young birds. Two kinds of flightless birds that were unique to the island became extinct.

Meanwhile, by the late 19th century, there were few seals or penguins left on the
15 island, so sailors left some rabbits. These would provide food for ships that stopped there. In spite of the cats, the rabbit population increased over the next century. By the 1970s, scientists estimated that there were about 130,000 rabbits on the island. All these rabbits had damaged the natural environment. They ate all the vegetation,[1] leaving the island bare rock and earth, and they dug holes everywhere.

20 At this point, scientists decided to introduce a disease called myxomatosis. This reduced the rabbit population to under 20,000 in ten years. The island vegetation began to grow again. But with fewer rabbits around, the cats went after more birds. Several other species of ground birds were at risk of becoming extinct. In 1985, scientists came to the decision that it was necessary to shoot all the cats. The last one was killed in 2000.
25 Now that there were no cats, the rabbit population increased rapidly. In 2006, the rabbits were blamed for a big landslide that destroyed a whole penguin colony.[2]

The Parks and Wildlife Service now has plans to eliminate all the estimated 130,000 rabbits, along with the 36,000 rats and 103,000 mice. Scientists who have studied the island warn that this could result in more unexpected effects.

---

[1] **vegetation** plants
[2] **colony** group of birds

1. What animals lived on Macquarie Island before it was discovered by the English?
2. Why did whaling ships stop at Macquarie Island?
3. How did myxomatosis affect the bird population on the island?
4. Why were the rabbits blamed for the landslide?
5. What unexpected effects do you think the scientists fear?

B. *Compare answers with another student.*

Focus on Vocabulary

Target Vocabulary

Check your knowledge of these words and phrases. (Do not look in the dictionary.)

Mark each one: ✔ *You are sure of the meaning.*
                ? *You have seen it before, but are not sure of the meaning.*
                X *You have not seen the word before.*

_____ issue	_____ adopt	_____ vast	_____ rating
_____ unemployment	_____ effective	_____ apparently	_____ build
_____ presence	_____ reveal	_____ be aware of	_____ recommend
_____ joint	_____ myth	_____ emerge	_____ concern

EXERCISE 1

A. *Preview and then read the passage. Do not stop to look up new words.*

A Closer Look at New York Subway Rats

The city of New York has had to face a number of tough issues with long histories—including traffic, unemployment, and homelessness. Now we learn, in a study just published, that they are searching for a way to solve a problem that is as old as the subway system: rats.

Scientists and subway officials examined the entire system for the presence of rats, which have regularly been sighted in subway tunnels and stations since the subway opened more than a century ago. According to some estimates, the rat population in the city of New York is over a million.

A joint project of the city and the Metropolitan Transportation Authority (MTA), the study looked at the system over a two-year period. The MTA has fought rats for decades, though the methods adopted so far, including the use of traps and poison, have not been effective.

The findings, revealed yesterday, contrast with popular myths. The rats do not live deep in the subway tunnels in vast rat cities. Said to be very intelligent animals, they apparently are aware of the danger of touching the electrified tracks. In any case, they have no reason to go out into the tunnels; what they want is food, and they can find all they want in the stations. They live in cracks or openings in the station walls, and emerge regularly to look for food.

The authors of the study did not offer any permanent solutions to the rat problem, but they did give some practical advice, beginning with better maintenance and cleanliness in the subway stations. Station and track cleaners sometimes do not do their jobs as they should. More often, the fault is of the subway riders who leave food and trash in the stations.

Of the 18 stations examined in lower Manhattan, almost half received a rating of fair or poor. The main problem was litter[1] on the ground and overfull trash cans, particularly on weekends and holidays, when the trash quickly builds up.

The study also recommended keeping the storage rooms in the stations cleaner. Storage rooms filled with trash bags are like restaurants for rats. The study further recommended placing poison near the bags, removing full bags more often, and keeping the doors closed at all times. New high-tech systems for catching rats were also mentioned in the study, though with today's budget concerns it is unlikely that the city can afford to install them.

---

[1]**litter** leave paper or trash on the ground

B. *Read the passage again. Circle all of the words and phrases from the target vocabulary list. Underline all of the words and phrases you don't know in the passage.*

C. *For each underlined word or phrase, look at the context (the words and sentences around it). Make a guess about the meaning. Write your guess in the margin in pencil.*

D. *Check your comprehension. Write T (True) or F (False) after each sentence.*

1. The study concerned health problems due to the presence of rats. _____

2. Many rats live in the subway tunnels. _____

3. According to the study, the rat population has grown recently. _____

4. Putting poison on the tracks does not reduce the number of rats. _____

5. According to the study, cleaner stations would mean fewer rats. _____

E. *Check the dictionary for the words and phrases you are not sure about. Compare the definitions with your guesses in Part C. Change your guesses if necessary.*

F. *Compare your work with another student.*

EXERCISE 2

A. *Match each target word to its definition. There is one extra definition.*

1. adopt
2. emerge
3. effective
4. joint
5. presence
6. vast
7. myth
8. unemployment

a. involving two or more people or groups
b. extremely large
c. the number of people in a country who do not have a job
d. to start to use a particular way of thinking or doing something
e. not supporting one purpose or cause above another
f. producing the result that was wanted or intended
g. to appear or come out from somewhere
h. the fact that someone or something is in a place
i. an idea or story that many people believe, but which is not true

B. *Compare answers with another student.*

EXERCISE 3

A. *Find the word or phrase in each group that is NOT a possible synonym for the target word and cross it out.*

1. **issue**	problem	history	subject	matter
2. **apparently**	fortunately	evidently	obviously	clearly
3. **be aware of**	realize	understand	notice	choose
4. **build up**	increase	get bigger	bring together	develop
5. **rating**	class	idea	level	place
6. **concern**	belief	worry	care	problem
7. **recommend**	advise	learn	suggest	urge
8. **reveal**	show	disclose	make known	review

B. *Compare answers with another student.*

A. *Complete the passage with words from the box. Change the word to fit the sentence if necessary.*

> apparently   issue   rating   reveal
> build up   myth   recommend   unemployment

The new government has a number of major _____ it must deal with.
1

If it can resolve these problems effectively, there is no doubt that voters will reward the

president in the next election.

The most serious problem now is _____. Some economists believe that
2

this problem will take care of itself. This is a dangerous _____. The reality
3

is that jobs will not be created unless the government gives the economy a boost. At

the moment, millions of people in this country are without a job. Feeling against the

president and his government is _____.
4

The government needs to take effective measures soon. Already, it has lost a lot

of its popularity. If it does not act rapidly, its approval _____ will go down
5

even further.

According to the president, a new job creation plan will be _____ next
6

week. Though the content of the plan is not known, it will _____ include
7

significant amounts of money that will be invested in various sectors of the economy.

This is a good start. We _____ that the government also invest in education
8

and training programs to help workers find jobs in new fields.

B. *Compare answers with another student.*

A. *Choose a word or phrase from the box that can be used with all the words or phrases in each group.*

> adopt   effective   issue   reveal
> build up   emerge   joint   vast

1. _____ + findings / a secret / the name of the winner

2. _____ + operation / action / account

3. _____ + method / strategy / measure

4. _____ + majority / area / hall

5. _____ + an attitude / a philosophy / a method

6. anger / trash / pressure + _____

7. the rats / the truth / the sun + _____

8. tough / major / key + _____

B. *Compare answers with another student.*

EXERCISE 6

A. *Work with another student. Write different forms for each word. If you do not know a form, make a guess. Do not use the dictionary. (More than one answer is possible for some forms.)*

Noun	Verb	Adjective	Negative adjective	Adverb
1.	adopt		X	X
2.	X	aware		X
3. concern				X
4.		effective		
5.	emerge		X	X
6. employment				X
7.		joint	X	
8. myth	X		X	X
9. presence			X	
10. rating				X
11.	reveal			
12.	recommend		X	X
13.	X	vast	X	

B. *Compare your work with another pair.*

Vocabulary Review

- In your vocabulary notebook, write all the words from this Focus on Vocabulary section that you want to learn. Include the parts of speech, the sentences, and the definitions (See Part 2, Unit 1).
- Review your notebook (See Part 2, Unit 2).
- Make study cards of 10–15 words that you have trouble remembering. Study them alone and then with another student.

Understanding Paragraphs

A topic is a word or phrase that tells what something is about. English is a topic-centered language. Most nonfiction writing focuses on a topic. All the ideas and sentences are related to that topic.

In the first exercises, you will practice identifying the topics of lists of words. Then you will work with the topics of paragraphs.

Topics

The topic of each list in these exercises is a general word or phrase. The topic includes all the words in the list. These words are more specific. They are parts, details, or examples of the topic.

The topic can be:

- The name of a thing with many parts

   Example: Topic: _house_
   Parts: roof, walls, windows, stairs, doors

- The name for a general idea that includes more specific things

   Example: Topic: _camping_
   Details: tent, sleeping bag, campfire, water bottle, mosquitoes

- The name of a group of things or people

   Example: Topic: _airline companies_
   Examples: Lufthansa, United, Qantas, Delta

The topic should not be too general or too specific. It should just fit the words on the list.

In the last example above: *Airline companies* is a good topic for the list of words.
Companies is too general.
American airline companies is too specific. Only two of the companies are American.

PRACTICE 1

A. *Work with another student. Read each list of words and write the topic.*

1. Topic: _____

   Archimedes   Newton   Galileo   Copernicus   Einstein

2. Topic: _____

   photo editor   browser   email   word processor   media player

B. **Compare answers with another pair.**

Check the answers to this Practice activity on page 285.

EXERCISE 1

A. **Work with another student. Read each list of words and write the topic. Then write another word that fits the topic. Do not use a dictionary. (The first one has been done for you.)**

1. Topic: _foods made from milk_

   butter   milk   cream   cheese   yogurt   _ice cream_

2. Topic: _____

   trunk   branch   root   fruit   bark   _____

3. Topic: _____

   dictionary   biography   crime   history   self-help   _____

4. Topic: _____

   windshield   tires   seats   body   fenders   _____

5. Topic: _____

   circle   hexagon   rectangle   triangle   pentagon   _____

6. Topic: _____

   Quebec   Toronto   Vancouver   Halifax   Calgary   _____

7. Topic: _____

   microwave   stove   coffeemaker   toaster   grill   _____

8. Topic: _____

   walk   skip   march   stroll   race   _____

9. Topic: _____

   tables   waiter   chairs   kitchen   dishes   _____

10. Topic: _____

    pineapple   coconut   papaya   guava   mango   _____

11. Topic: _____

    mercury   tin   copper   aluminum   silver   _____

12. Topic: _____

    mountains   plains   cliffs   valleys   marshes   _____

B. *Compare answers with another pair. Use a dictionary to look up any words you want to know. Then write them in your vocabulary notebook. (See Part 2, Unit 2.)*

EXERCISE 2

A. *Work with another student. Read each list and cross out the word that does not belong. Then write the topic for the other words. Do not use a dictionary.*

1. Topic: *farm animals that are kept for meat*

    cows   sheep   pigs   ~~mice~~   goats   chickens

2. Topic: _____

    wasp   pigeon   bee   fly   butterfly   ant

3. Topic: _____

    steam   bake   roast   boil   stir   fry

4. Topic: _____

    wrist   rib   shoulder   elbow   knee   hip

5. Topic: _____

    apartment   palace   mansion   teepee   cottage   hut

6. Topic: _____

    Islam   Nationalism   Hinduism   Sikhism   Judaism   Protestantism

7. Topic: _____

    potatoes   lettuce   spinach   zucchini   cabbage   broccoli

8. Topic: _____

   towel   sand   sunglasses   waves   bicycle   swimsuit

9. Topic: _____

   cashier   teacher   nurse   mechanic   interpreter   ballet dancer

10. Topic: _____

    divide   review   cube   add   subtract   multiply

11. Topic: _____

    glass   mug   teacup   bottle   jar   goblet

12. Topic: _____

    spine   heart   stomach   liver   kidneys   lungs

B. *Compare answers with another pair. Use a dictionary to look up any words you want to know. Then write them in your vocabulary notebook.*

Topics of Paragraphs

The topic of a paragraph tells what the paragraph is about. In a well-written paragraph all the sentences are about that topic (directly or indirectly). It is very important to figure out the topic quickly. It is the key to understanding the paragraph.

EXERCISE 3

A. *Read the paragraph. The topic has been left out. What do you think it is?*

Topic: _____

Paragraph A:
Some of us have done this hundreds of times, but if it is your first time, don't worry. It really is very simple. First, you sort everything into piles. It is best to separate things carefully at this point, or you could be sorry later. When one pile is ready, you can let technology do the work for you. Be sure to follow the directions. Mistakes can be costly. After the first part is done, the next step depends on your equipment. You may be able to put technology to work again. Or you may have to use old-fashioned methods and take everything outside. In any case, in a while you will need to make piles again and put everything where it belongs. Then you are done—for now. Soon the time will come to do it again.

B. *Compare your guesses with other students. Turn to page 286 and read Paragraph B. Then look back at Paragraph A. Does it make more sense?*

Recognizing the Topic of a Paragraph

Knowing the topic is important. Even when you know all the words and grammar, you cannot understand a passage if you do not know the topic. The topic gives you a context for the ideas and information in the passage. It allows you to connect them to things you already know. Then the passage makes sense to you.

Good readers always look for the topic when they start reading. Writers usually try to help readers figure out the topic by stating it near the beginning and repeating it a number of times.

In a paragraph, you will also find specific facts and ideas that describe or explain the topic. These are the supporting facts and ideas. They may be parts, details, or examples of the topic (as with the topics of lists).

EXAMPLE

> *Read the paragraph. The topic has been circled. The supporting facts and details about the topic have been underlined. The diagram below shows how the supporting facts and details relate to the topic.*

⬭Monticello, in Charlottesville, Virginia, was the home of Thomas Jefferson,⬭ the third president of the United States. This house is a <u>fine example of early eighteenth-century American architecture.</u> <u>Jefferson designed it himself in a style he had admired in Italy</u>. Many American buildings of that time, in fact, imitated European styles. But while most were just imitations, his <u>Monticello is lovely</u> in itself. Furthermore, the design <u>combines a graceful style with a typical American concern for comfort</u>.

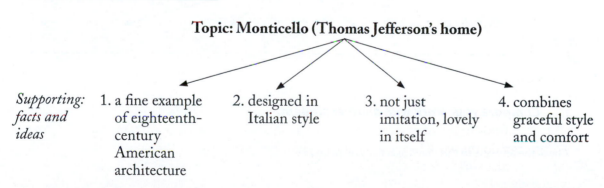

Topic: Monticello (Thomas Jefferson's home)

Supporting: facts and ideas
1. a fine example of eighteenth-century American architecture
2. designed in Italian style
3. not just imitation, lovely in itself
4. combines graceful style and comfort

When you work with topics in these exercises, keep in mind:

- The topic should not be too general or too specific.
- It should include all the facts and ideas in the paragraph.
- It should not refer to facts and ideas that are not in the paragraph.
- Writers often mention the topic in the first sentence.

A. *Read the paragraph and circle the best topic. Write too general or too specific after the other topics.*

Building Materials

People build their houses out of many different kinds of materials. They usually use the materials that are most easily available to them. In North America, for example, many people build their houses of wood. There are large areas of forests, so wood is easy to get and inexpensive. In countries around the Mediterranean Sea, there are few forests, so people use other materials, especially stone and brick. In tropical areas of Africa and Asia, people do not need thick walls, so they build houses with other kinds of material, like bamboo and other plants. Finally, in extremely cold climates such as northern Canada and Alaska, the only material that is easily available is ice. Until recently, people made their houses from blocks of ice (though now they use other materials).

          a. houses around the world _____

Topic: b. materials used for houses _____

          c. ice houses in Canada _____

B. *Discuss these questions with another student:*

1. Where can you find the topic in the paragraph? _____

2. What words are repeated most often in the paragraph? _____

C. *Complete the diagram with the topic and the supporting facts and ideas. (You do not need to write complete sentences—just a word or phrase.)*

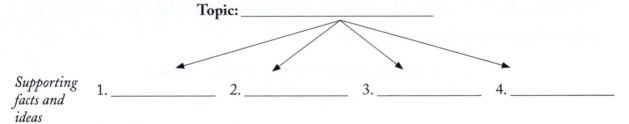

Topic: _____

Supporting facts and ideas

1. _____ 2. _____ 3. _____ 4. _____

D. *Compare your work with another student.*

Check the answers to this Practice activity on page 286.

Note: The title at the top of each exercise is a general category, not a topic.

A. *Read the paragraph and circle the best topic. Write* **too general** *or* **too specific** *after the other topics.*

Elephants

1. The elephant's trunk is a long nose with a strong sense of smell. It is also an upper lip[1] used for drinking and eating. To drink, elephants suck the water up into their trunk and blow it into their mouths. They eat by pulling up grass or leaves with their trunks and putting the food into their mouths. Because of the muscles at the end, the elephant's trunk is also like a hand that can pick up and carry things. With its flexibility, elephants can use their trunks for all kinds of things, including scratching themselves and throwing things. Furthermore, the trunk plays a part in elephants' interactions with each other. Elephants can use it to make a wide variety of sounds in order to communicate happiness, anger, or danger. They also use their trunks to touch each other and to show affection.[2]

[1] **lip** outer part of the mouth
[2] **affection** a feeling of love and caring

Topic:
    a. the elephant's trunk _____
    b. elephant communication _____
    c. the bodies of elephants _____

2. Elephants are the largest animals on land; whales are the largest animals in the sea. Apart from the fact that they are both large, these two animals share many characteristics. Some biologists, in fact, believe that they may be related. There is a lot of evidence to support this idea. The shape of an elephant's head, for example, is similar to a whale's. Both animals are also excellent swimmers. Whales live their whole lives in the sea, of course, while elephants have been known to swim up to 300 miles to get food on an island. Another similarity is the fact that both animals use sound to show anger and for other kinds of communication. Finally, their social organization is alike in some ways. Female elephants and whales stay close to other females in the group and help them when they give birth.

Topic:
    a. the largest animals in the world _____
    b. the characteristics of elephants _____
    c. the similarities of elephants and whales _____

3. Scientists and people who work with elephants have observed various kinds of behavior that show how intelligent these animals are. One mark of intelligence is the ability to use tools. Elephants sometimes use sticks to scratch[3] themselves in places they cannot reach with their trunks. Another mark of intelligence is the ability to plan ahead. Indian farmers who keep elephants as work animals have observed this ability. There is no fence that will keep their elephants out of an area where they want to go, such as a banana plantation. The only way the farmers can save their bananas is to tie bells around the

(continued)

[3] **scratch** to rub the skin with or against something

necks of the elephants. Then the farmers will hear the elephants if they try to eat the bananas. However, some elephants have figured out a way to silence the bells. They roll in mud until the bells are filled with mud and no longer make any sound.

a. tool use by elephants _____

Topic: b. animal intelligence _____

c. the intelligence of elephants _____

B. *On a separate piece of paper, draw a diagram for each paragraph to show the topic and the supporting facts and ideas (as in the Practice Exercise on page 152).*

C. *Compare your work with another student.*

Writing the Topic of a Paragraph

The topic should tell what the paragraph is about. It should just fit the information and ideas in the sentences. It should not be too general or too specific.

PRACTICE 3

A. *Read the paragraph and write the topic.*

Topic: _____

Bees

For one reason or another, people have been interested in bees for a long time. In ancient times, they were interested mostly in the bee's honey. Archaeologists have found evidence that the ancient Egyptians, Greeks, and Romans all gathered and ate honey. In more recent times, people have observed bees at work and made comparisons with humans. Expressions about bees have become common in some languages. In English, for example, you can describe someone who is working hard with the expression "as busy as a bee." Today, scientists are interested in another aspect of bees—the way they communicate. These insects with very small brains are able to tell each other important information, for example, about where to find food.

B. *Complete the diagram with the topic and the supporting facts and ideas.*

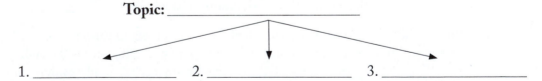

Topic: _____

1. _____   2. _____   3. _____

C. *Compare your work with another student.*

Check the answers to this Practice activity on page 286.

Note: Your diagram will look different depending on the number of supporting facts and ideas in a paragraph. Some paragraphs have just a few, while others may have many.

A. *Read each paragraph and write the topic.*

Giant Pandas

1. Giant pandas used to live in large areas of China, but they are now close to extinction.[1] In the past, they were spread throughout the forests of southern and eastern China. Each panda needed a large area of forest—and large amounts of bamboo—but there was enough forest and bamboo for tens of thousands of giant pandas. However, in the 20th century, people moved into the forests and cut down the bamboo. By the 1990s, scientists estimated that there were only about 1,000 wild pandas left. Fortunately, the Chinese government decided to try to save them. It created several panda reserves,[2] where the pandas and their forests were protected. Thanks to these reserves, panda populations are slowly growing and there are now from 1,500 to 2,000 in the wild. Pandas are still on the international list of endangered species, but scientists now hope it may be possible to save them.

[1]**extinction** the disappearance of a whole species
[2]**reserve** an area of land that is kept separate

Topic: _____

2. For the first year of their lives, giant panda cubs depend completely on their mothers. At birth, the babies are very small—about 5 ounces (140 g). They are also completely helpless. For several weeks, their eyes are closed. For at least the first three months, their legs are not strong enough for walking. When they are this small, they can easily be killed by other animals if they are not protected by the mother. At around six months, the young pandas start eating little bits of bamboo, but milk from their mothers is their main food until they are over nine months old. This milk is very rich, and the little pandas grow quickly. By the time they are a year old, they weigh at least 55 pounds (25 kg).

Topic: _____

3. Scientists report that panda mothers care for their babies in some of the same ways that human mothers do. For one thing, panda mothers keep their babies very clean. They do not give the little pandas baths, of course. Instead, they use their tongues to lick the babies clean. Any smell might attract predators that could attack and try to kill the baby. Like human mothers who hold their babies in their arms, mother pandas often hold their babies in their front paws. And just like humans, panda mothers rock their babies back and forth when they cry. Finally, as with humans, young pandas stay with their mothers for their early years. But their childhood ends much sooner than with human children. After about two years, mother pandas usually become pregnant with another baby and chase away the young pandas. Now they must become independent and live on their own.

Topic: _____

B. *On a separate piece of paper, draw a diagram for each paragraph to show the topic and the supporting facts and ideas.*

C. *Compare your work with another student.*

Main Ideas in Paragraphs

The main idea—the writer's idea about the topic—gives you a more complete understanding of the topic. When you are reading, you should first decide on the topic. Then ask yourself, "What does the writer want to say about this topic?"

For any topic, writers may develop different main ideas.

EXAMPLE

Topic: The effects of watching television.

Possible main ideas:

   a. Children who watch a lot of television may have problems at school.
   b. Some people today watch a lot of television every day.
   c. Television has negative effects on family life.

As with topics, the main idea should just fit the paragraph and should not be too general or too specific. The paragraph may or may not include a sentence that expresses the main idea. You may need to use information from several sentences to understand the main idea.

PRACTICE 4

A. *Read the paragraph and circle the best main idea.*

Television

     In the 1950s, when television was new, it seemed to bring families together. More than 50 years later, psychologists have a very different view of the effects of television. Many studies show that it can influence family life in quite negative ways. In fact, television stops most communication among family members. When families watch the television news during dinner, for example, their attention is on the television screen. They do not talk about the events of their day or about their problems or feelings. This lack of interaction may mean that there are fewer arguments at the dinner table. However, according to psychologists, arguments are better than no interaction at all in the family. The lack of interaction can lead to serious problems, including parent–child conflict, difficulty at school, and divorce.

   Main idea:

    a. Children who watch a lot of television may have problems at school.

    b. Some people today watch a lot of television every day.

    c. Television has negative effects on family life.

B. *Complete the diagram with the main idea sentence and the supporting facts and ideas.*

Main idea: _____

1. _____ 2. _____ 3. _____

C. *Compare your work with another student.*

Check the answers to this Practice activity on page 286.

EXERCISE 6

A. *Read each paragraph and circle the best main idea.*

Elephants

1. The elephant's trunk serves many purposes. It is a long nose with a strong sense of smell. It is also an upper lip used for drinking and eating. To drink, elephants suck the water up into their trunk and blow it into their mouths. They eat by pulling up grass or leaves with their trunks and putting the food into their mouths. Because of the muscles at the end, the elephant's trunk is also like a hand that can pick up and carry things. With its flexibility, elephants can use the trunk for all kinds of things, including scratching themselves and throwing things. Furthermore, the trunk plays a part in elephants' interactions with other each other. Elephants can use it to make a wide variety of sounds in order to communicate happiness, anger, or danger. They also use their trunks to touch each other and to show affection.

Main idea:

a. Elephants also use their trunks in interactions with other elephants.

b. The elephant uses its trunk to smell, eat, hold things, and interact.

c. On their heads, elephants have something called a trunk.

2. Elephants are the largest animals on land; whales are the largest animals in the sea. Apart from the fact that they are both large, these two animals share many characteristics. Some biologists, in fact, believe that they may be related. There is a lot of evidence to support this idea. The shape of an elephant's head, for example, is similar to a whale's. Both animals are also excellent swimmers. Whales live their whole lives in the sea, of course, while elephants have been known to swim up to 300 miles to get food on an island. Another similarity is the fact that both animals use sound to show anger or for other kinds of communication. Finally, their social organization is alike in some ways. Female elephants and whales stay close to other females in the group and help them when they give birth.

Main idea:

a. Elephants and whales are the largest animals in the world.

b. The social organization of elephants and whales is alike in some ways.

c. Elephants and whales share many characteristics.

3. Scientists and people who work with elephants have observed various kinds of behavior that shows how intelligent these animals are. One mark of intelligence is the ability to use tools. Elephants sometimes use sticks to scratch themselves in places they cannot reach with their trunks. Another mark of intelligence is the ability to plan ahead. Indian farmers who keep elephants as work animals have observed this ability. There is no fence that will keep their elephants out of an area where they want to go, such as a banana plantation. The only way the farmers can save their bananas is to tie bells around the necks of the elephants. Then the farmers will hear the elephants if they try to eat the bananas. However, some elephants have figured out a way to silence the bells. They roll in mud until the bells are filled with mud and no longer make any sound.

Main idea:

   a. People have seen elephants using a stick to scratch themselves.

   b. People who study or work with elephants believe they are very intelligent.

   c. Intelligent animals can use tools and plan ahead.

B.   *Compare answers with another student.*

Writing the Main Idea of a Paragraph

PRACTICE 5

A.   *Read the paragraph and write a main idea sentence.*

Bees

For insects that live together in large groups, such as honeybees, communication is very important. One way they communicate is by smell. This is possible because all the bees in a group or colony have a common smell. If a bee from outside the colony tries to enter a hive (the home of bees), it is immediately attacked by the bees that live there. Another way that bees communicate is through movement. When one bee finds a good source of food, it tells the other bees with a kind of dance. Through the dance, the bee can tell others which direction to go and if it is near or far.

   Main idea: _____

B.   *Complete the diagram with the main idea sentence and the supporting facts and ideas.*

   Main Idea: _____

   1. _____   2. _____

C.   *Compare your work with another student.*

Check the answers to this Practice activity on page 286.

EXERCISE 7

A. *Read each paragraph and write a main idea sentence.*

Maps

1. What happens when you ask someone to draw a map of the world? The results can be interesting. All kinds of mistakes are commonly made. Some of the mistakes are simply a matter of drawing ability. Not everyone can reproduce on paper what they see in their minds. But what people see in their minds is often not very accurate when it comes to geography. This is especially true in areas of the world that are far from their home country. For instance, many people do not know the relative size of continents. They tend to make their home continent larger and other continents smaller. Thus, a Brazilian tends to enlarge South America, while a Vietnamese enlarges Asia. Another common error also relates to point of view, but is common to people from all parts of the world. Everyone tends to draw Europe too large and Africa too small. This is true even for Africans.

Main idea: _____

_____

2. Why do people imagine Europe bigger and Africa smaller than they really are? One possible explanation is that many people grew up with maps that used the "Mercator projection." This technique for printing maps—which is no longer used—enlarged areas nearer the North Pole and shrank[1] areas near the equator.[2] Thus Europe became larger and Africa became smaller. However, there is a problem with this explanation because these maps also enlarged Greenland and Canada, but people generally do not draw them larger. There is another, more likely reason for the inaccurate ideas of the two continents. People are probably influenced by their sense of the economic and political power of the two continents. Europe seems important to people, so they make it larger, while Africa is considered less important, so it is drawn smaller.

Main idea: _____

_____

[1]**shrink** make smaller
[2]**equator** the line that separates the northern and southern halves of the Earth

3.   Until very recent times maps often contained errors. Old maps of Africa were particularly inaccurate because large parts of the continent were unknown to the Europeans who made them. In the 18th century, mapmakers began to add some details to maps of Africa, but many of these details were inaccurate. In the 1790s, for instance, an English explorer reported seeing mountains in west central Africa. Hearing this, an English mapmaker added a range of mountains to his 1798 map of Africa and called them the Kong Mountains. These mountains were featured in most maps of Africa for almost one hundred years. Finally, in 1887, a French explorer travelled through west central Africa and sent word back to Europe that the Kong mountains did not exist They soon disappeared from maps of Africa.

Main idea: _____

_____

B.   *On a separate piece of paper, draw a diagram for each paragraph to show the main idea sentence and the supporting facts and ideas.*

C.   *Compare your work with another student.*

Remember

- The titles of these exercises are general categories, not topics.
- Writers often mention the topic in the first or second sentence.

Following Ideas in Paragraphs

Once you have identified the topic and the writer's ideas about the topic, you need to follow those ideas through the text.

To do this, you need to use:

- the reading skills you have learned so far
- your knowledge about the topic
- your knowledge of English

The following exercises will give you practice using your skills and knowledge to follow ideas in paragraphs.

Notes:

- Work quickly in these exercises. If you work slowly, you will probably not be thinking in English.
- Do not look up new words the first time through an exercise. Try to skip them or guess the general meaning. You may look them up after you have checked your answers.
- In this type of exercise, your first guess is often the right one.

A. Read each paragraph quickly. Then circle the best ending.

1. Dogs were the first domesticated animals. In other words, they were the first animals that lived with people on a farm or in their home. Very early in human history, people realized that dogs could help with hunting and could protect them against dangerous wild animals. They also realized that dogs are good company, and so people began to keep dogs as pets. It is often said that a dog is man's best friend. We could also say that he is man's _____.

   a. worst enemy
   b. only friend
   c. latest friend
   d. oldest friend

2. Fog is a major cause of accidents on highways in some areas. This is true in many coastal areas, such as along the North Atlantic, and in low-lying valleys, such as the Po Valley in Italy. Every year many thousands of people lose their lives because fog dangerously reduces visibility for drivers. When there is fog, they cannot see very far ahead, so they _____.

   a. go faster to avoid accidents
   b. do not have time to avoid accidents
   c. have more time to read the signs
   d. do not have time to have accidents

B. Compare answers with another student.

Check the answers to this Practice activity on page 286.

EXERCISE 8

A. Read each paragraph quickly. Then circle the best ending.

1. When Europeans came to North America in the early 17th century, the forests were full of bears. Scientists estimate that there were more than half a million. Then the Europeans began to cut down the forests and hunt the bears. By 1900, there were very few left, except in Canada and Alaska. In recent years, however, the bear population has begun to multiply again. There are now at least 200,000 bears, thanks to better _____.

   a. hunting methods
   b. roads and communication
   c. laws to protect hunters
   d. laws to protect bears

2. Scotland is famous around the world for its golf courses and golf tournaments. Many Scottish people think of golf as a truly Scottish sport and believe that it started in Scotland. However, some historians believe that it may have started in ancient Rome or Persia. In any case, a game similar to modern golf was played in Holland in the 14th century. Not long after that, it moved across to the British Isles and became popular _____.

   a. in Scotland
   b. with rich people
   c. with the French
   d. as an Olympic sport

3. In the past, North American forests were full of chestnut trees, and people used chestnuts in cooking in many different ways. They also loved to cook chestnuts over a fire and eat them hot out of their shells. Then in the early 1900s, a disease killed almost all the trees. Now it is hard to find chestnuts in U.S. markets. Most chestnuts for sale there are _____.

   a. not healthy to eat
   b. roasted over a fire
   c. imported from Europe
   d. from North America

4. Chocolate is one of the most popular sweets in the world. It is eaten by itself, or in candy bars, cakes, cookies, and puddings. In some places, it is also eaten in a nonsweet form in dishes with meat or vegetables. The Mexicans, for example, make a chicken dish with a spicy chocolate sauce. This sauce does not include any _____.

   a. chocolate
   b. sweetener
   c. vitamins
   d. candy

5. Pigs have long been the most common animal for meat in many parts of the world. The reason for this is a simple matter of economics. The pig produces meat far more efficiently than any other animal. For every 100 pounds (45.5 kg) of feed that it is given, a pig produces about 33 pounds (15 kg) of meat. In comparison, for every 100 pounds of feed, beef cattle produce _____.

   a. more than 33 pounds of meat
   b. nearly twice as much meat
   c. only about 15 pounds (7 kg) of meat
   d. about the same amount of meat

B. **Compare answers with another student.**

EXERCISE 9

A. **Read each paragraph quickly. Then circle the best ending.**

1. Until recently the kiwi fruit was rare in most countries of the world. All the kiwis came from New Zealand, which meant they were transported a great distance and so were expensive. Now other countries, such as Israel, Italy, Spain, and the United States, all produce kiwis. Consequently, the supply of this fruit has greatly increased and the price has _____.

   a. gone down
   b. risen significantly
   c. not changed
   d. changed often

2. Vitamins are very important for good health. One vitamin that your body needs regularly is vitamin C. Certain fruits and vegetables contain good amounts of this vitamin, including oranges, lemons, melons, tomatoes, red peppers, and broccoli. It is a good idea to eat a variety of these fruits and vegetables, and at least some of them should be raw (uncooked), since the heat of cooking can _____.

   a. change the way they taste
   b. increase the amount of vitamin C
   c. destroy the vitamin C
   d. make them easier to eat

3. Some birds fly great distances every year. In the fall, they leave their homes in the north and fly thousands of miles south. Then, in the spring, they return to the north to exactly the same place. Scientists do not really know how this is possible. They believe that these birds have _____.

    a. a special way of flying   c. especially strong wings
    b. a kind of map in their heads   d. very good sight and hearing

4. We usually do not think of the night sky as a colorful scene. In fact, if you look at the stars with just your eyes, you will not see much color. However, scientists with special equipment now have a different picture of what is in the sky at night. A new series of photographs shows the night sky _____.

    a. without any colors   c. with bright colors
    b. with little color   d. without any equipment

5. Many people are very afraid of snakes. It is true that a bite from a poisonous snake can make you very ill or even kill you. But there are actually very few poisonous snakes. Most of them are harmless and, in fact, are usually afraid of people. If you find a snake in your garden, it will probably _____.

    a. bite you   c. come closer
    b. stay near you   d. move away

B. *Compare answers with another student.*

EXERCISE 10

A. *Read each paragraph quickly. Then circle the best ending.*

1. When people first began to travel by air in the late 18th century, they used hot-air balloons. These balloons stayed up in the air successfully, but there was a major problem: it was not possible to control the direction they traveled. They went wherever the wind was blowing. The idea of a flying machine with a motor that could be controlled remained a dream until the early 20th century. Then, in 1903, the Wright brothers _____.

    a. watched the birds flying   c. flew across the Atlantic Ocean
    b. built and flew the first airplane   d. invented a hot-air balloon

2. In a popular children's song, a star is compared to a diamond because of the way it looks against the dark night sky. Scientists now have reason to believe there may be real diamonds—or some kind of mineral similar to diamonds—among the stars of the universe. This is an interesting discovery for science. However, these diamonds are not likely to make anyone rich because they _____.

    a. are too far away   c. cannot be used in jewelry
    b. shine only at night   d. are not a pretty color

3. Many parents have exercise equipment in their home so they can keep in good shape. This is undoubtedly good for their health, but it may not be good for the health of their children. Every year, about 25,000 children in the U.S. are injured by exercise equipment, especially exercise bicycles. Many children have lost a finger or toe in the wheels of these bicycles. People with an exercise bicycle should _____.

   a. let their children use it
   b. let anyone use it
   c. not use it too often
   d. not let children near it

4. Long before airplanes were invented, people wanted to be able to fly. Even in ancient times, they studied birds' wings to see how they worked. Then they tried to build wings of wood or cloth and feathers, but these wings were not very successful. When they jumped off a high place and tried to fly, they never _____.

   a. hurt themselves
   b. fell to the ground
   c. stayed up in the air
   d. opened their wings

5. What would you do if you got lost in the desert? Your first and most important task is to find water. Deserts have few sources of water, so you will probably not find any lakes or rivers. One place where you can find water, however, is in desert plants. Certain kinds of desert plants, especially cactuses, often contain drinkable water. If you know the plants, have the right tools, and know how to open a cactus, you can get _____.

   a. very little good water
   b. a quart of water a day
   c. only undrinkable water
   d. lots of bottled water

B. **Compare answers with another student.**

EXERCISE 11

A. **Read each paragraph quickly. Then circle the best ending.**

1. The game of croquet was probably invented in France. In the 13th century, French villagers played something they called "paille-maille," with some sticks and a ball. From there, the game traveled to Ireland, where it was called it "crooky," and then to England, where it was known as "croaky." In the 19th century, the game became very popular in England and spread to other countries, including _____.

   a. several famous people
   b. western and northern England
   c. many English villages
   d. the United States and India

2. The U.S. penny (one-cent coin) has on it a picture of Abraham Lincoln, one of the country's greatest presidents. He came from a poor family, and as a young man he had to work very hard. This was the reason why the government decided to put Lincoln's picture on the smallest coin. It would remind everyone that in the United States, the highest positions were open to everyone, _____.

   a. even rich people
   b. even poor people
   c. especially young people
   d. especially the president

3. Many people hate going to the dentist and are afraid of dentists. There are a number of reasons for this. One is that the patient cannot see what the dentist is doing. Another is that the patient, who is lying back, may feel very helpless. They also may not like the look of the shiny metal instruments that dentists use. And finally, people are afraid that they will feel pain, even though most dentists today _____.

   a. can prevent pain
   b. use modern equipment
   c. cause a lot of pain
   d. charge high prices

4. The Japanese love to eat raw fish. Dishes of uncooked fish are prepared in various ways as sushi or sashimi and offered at most Japanese restaurants. Many different kinds of fish or shellfish are used for these dishes. But whatever the kind of fish, it should be very fresh. If it is not fresh, it will not taste good and may cause illness. To prove that a fish is fresh, some cooks like to show the fish to customers when it is _____.

   a. already dead
   b. still alive
   c. cooked
   d. in the sea

5. Children who are left handed tend to have more accidents than right-handed children. There are two theories to explain this fact. One is that left-handed children simply fall and bump into things more often. According to another theory, however, the problem is not with the left-handed children, but with the world around them. Most things, such as doors, toys, and cars are designed _____.

   a. by people without children
   b. by parents for their children
   c. for right-handed people
   d. for left-handed people

B. *Compare answers with another student.*

Focus on Vocabulary

Target Vocabulary

Check your knowledge of these words and phrases. (Do not look in the dictionary.)

Mark each one: ✔ *You are sure of the meaning.*
                ? *You have seen it before, but are not sure of the meaning.*
                X *You have not seen it before.*

____ solid	____ source	____ reaction	____ consideration
____ affect	____ conflict	____ avoid	____ ahead
____ vehicle	____ balance	____ measure	____ side effect
____ occur	____ sensitive	____ location	____ recover

EXERCISE 1

A. *Preview and then read the passage. Do not stop to look up new words.*

Suffering from Travel

Kate will never forget that two-hour cruise on a boat off the coast of Depoe Bay, Oregon. With about 25 other tourists, she was excited about sailing on the Pacific Ocean, but within half an hour, she felt unwell and soon she was very sick. Kate spent the next hour and a half lying down, counting the minutes until she could get back on solid ground. Seasickness made the cruise a very unhappy experience for her. She has never been out on the ocean since.

Kate is hardly alone. Ninety percent of the human race is affected by motion sickness of one kind or another. For some, boats are the only problem. Others cannot ride in the back of a car. Still others cannot read or look at a map in any kind of moving vehicle. People suffer from motion sickness on airplanes, motorcycles, amusement park rides, and even on camels.

Scientists have learned that motion sickness occurs when the brain cannot make sense of the messages it receives from different sources. That is, the information from your eyes is in conflict with what other parts of your body are telling your brain. That includes your ears, which send information about your balance, and your skin, which is sensitive to changes in air pressure. Your brain's reaction to this confusion is to send strong signals to your stomach that something is wrong.

Motion sickness discourages many people from traveling. But it is not necessary to avoid travel completely, since you can take preventive measures. First, you should eat lightly before the trip, and during travel, you should snack often on plain food, such as crackers. It is also important to avoid alcoholic and carbonated drinks, high-fat foods, and spices.

The location of your seat is another important consideration. In a plane, sit near the wings, where there is the least movement. In a car, sit in the front seat and keep the windows open. In a boat, if possible, stay outside. If you have to sit inside, choose a seat at the front. In a car or boat, you should try to keep your eyes looking ahead as much as possible.

People who still get sick in spite of these measures can take various medications. However, these may make you sleepy or have other side effects. One natural treatment for motion sickness is ginger, which has no side effects and can be found in drug stores or natural food stores.

If you are about to leave for a trip, you should consider taking measures even if you have never had motion sickness before. Apparently, people change over time and may become more or less likely to get sick as they age. If you do get motion sickness, on the other hand, there is hope that it may not last long. Some sailors find that they are seasick at the beginning of a trip and then recover.

B. *Read the passage again. Circle all of the words and phrases from the target vocabulary list. Underline all of the words and phrases you don't know in the passage.*

C. *For each underlined word or phrase, look at the context (the words and sentences around it). Make a guess about the meaning. Write your guess in the margin in pencil.*

D. *Check your comprehension. Write T (True) or F (False) after each sentence.*

1. Motion sickness affects only a small percentage of people. _____

2. One cause of motion sickness is bad food. _____

3. Your brain receives messages from different parts of your body. _____

4. There are measures you can take to prevent motion sickness. _____

5. Where you sit can make a difference in how you feel. _____

E. *Check the dictionary for the words and phrases you are not sure about. Compare the definitions with your guesses in Part C. Change your definitions if necessary.*

F. *Compare your work with another student.*

A. *Read the two sentences. Choose the best definition for the target word.*

1. Still others cannot read or look at a map in any kind of moving <u>vehicle</u>.
   A bicycle is usually considered a <u>vehicle</u>, but it does not have a motor.

   a. a kind of large car used in the mountains or the desert
   b. something such as a car or bus that is used for carrying people or things
   c. something such as a seat or sofa where you can sit down

2. Your brain's <u>reaction</u> to this confusion is to send strong signals to your stomach that something is wrong.
   This drug can cause a <u>reaction</u> in some people, but it is rarely serious.

   a. a change or effect (usually bad)
   b. a feeling of being hungry or thirsty
   c. something that you think or feel

3. But it is not necessary to <u>avoid</u> travel, since you can take preventive measures.
   Women should <u>avoid</u> walking alone in the evening after dark.

   a. to not do something because it is dangerous or bad
   b. to give someone something they prefer not to have
   c. to hate or dislike something or someone

4. But it is not necessary to avoid travel, since you can take preventive <u>measures</u>.
   New security <u>measures</u> will soon be in place at the airport.

   a. medicines or treatments
   b. things that prevent you from moving
   c. actions taken to deal with a problem

5. In a car or boat, you should try to keep looking <u>ahead</u> as much as possible.
   The government plans to go <u>ahead</u> with a new kind of power plant.

   a. around or to the side
   b. in front or forward
   c. back or behind

6. The <u>location</u> of your seat is another important consideration.
   The Green Room Restaurant opened at its current <u>location</u> ten years ago.

   a. a particular size or measure
   b. belonging to a particular person
   c. a particular place or position

7. The location of your seat is another important <u>consideration</u>.
   The committee will take into <u>consideration</u> both education and work experience.

   a. something to think about
   b. something to hold or keep
   c. something to pay for

8. Some sailors find that they are seasick at the beginning of a trip and then <u>recover</u>.
   After he fell off his bicycle, it took him almost a month to <u>recover</u> fully.

   a. to feel unwell when traveling
   b. to become better after an illness or accident
   c. to come down with a serious illness

B. *Compare answers with another student.*

EXERCISE 3

A. *Match each target word to its definition. There is one extra definition.*

1. source		a.	not liquid or gas
2. occur		b.	where something starts or comes from
3. conflict		c.	reacting to small changes
4. balance		d.	to choose a particular person or thing
5. affect		e.	to happen
6. solid		f.	an extra or unexpected consequence as a result of taking a drug
7. sensitive		g.	disagreement
8. side effect		h.	the ability to stand or walk without falling
		i.	to produce a change in something

B. *Compare answers with another student.*

EXERCISE 4

A. *Find the example that best fits each target word or phrase. (The first one is done for you.)*

Target word/phrase	Example
_g_ **1.** conflict	a. a rock
_____ **2.** vehicle	b. a headache
_____ **3.** location	c. the cost of something
_____ **4.** source (of water)	d. anger
_____ **5.** side effect	e. a van
_____ **6.** reaction	f. Coolidge Corner
_____ **7.** something solid	g. a fist fight
_____ **8.** consideration	h. a river

B. *Compare answers with another student.*

A. *Complete the passage with words from the box. Change the word to fit the sentence if necessary.*

> affect   avoid   conflict   vehicle
> ahead   balance   reaction

There are often problems in families when young people first get their driver's license. The new drivers come into _____ with their parents over use of the family car. Parents are afraid of accidents; teenagers want their freedom. According to experts, the best way to _____ arguments (and accidents) is to set clear rules.

One of the most important things parents should discuss with their children is drinking and driving. Young people need to understand how drinking can _____ driving ability. Teenagers may be aware only of the well-known fact that a drunk person cannot walk in a straight line. Yes, drinking does have an effect on _____. But it also changes the way you see things. Drunk drivers may not realize how close they are to other _____. Because of this, they are more likely to crash into cars _____ of them. Furthermore, drinking also has an effect on _____ time. After several drinks, you lose the ability to move quickly, which is essential when driving.

B. *Compare answers with another student.*

A. *Work with another student. Write different forms for each word. If you do not know a form, make a guess. Do not use the dictionary. (More than one answer is possible for some forms.)*

Noun	Verb	Adjective	Negative Adjective	Adverb
1.	avoid			X
2. balance				X
3. conflict			X	X
4. consideration				
5. location			X	
6. measure				
7.	occur	X	X	X
8. reaction			X	X
9.	recover			X
10.		sensitive		
11.		solid	X	

B. *Compare your work with another pair.*

Vocabulary Review

- In your vocabulary notebook, write all the words from this Focus on Vocabulary section that you want to learn. Include the parts of speech, the sentences, and the definitions (See Part 2, Unit 1).
- Review your notebook (See Part 2, Unit 2).
- Make study cards of 10–15 words that you have trouble remembering. Study them alone and then with another student.

Identifying the Pattern

Introduction

A pattern is a regular way that something is organized or done. Many things around us are organized into patterns. For example:

- Cities organize traffic so that drivers will not run into each other.
- Supermarkets organize products so people can find them on the shelves.
- College students organize their schedules so they can take the classes they want.

EXERCISE 1

A. *Look at the groups of numbers for one minute and try to memorize them. After one minute, close the book and try to write the lists of numbers in the same order on a separate piece of paper.*

a.	15	3	6	9	12
b.	2	1	17	1	9
c.	1	4	7	10	13
d.	19	2	5	6	11
e.	12	4	6	8	10

B. *Discuss these questions with another student:*

1. How many of the lists of numbers could you remember?
2. Which ones were the easiest to remember? Why?

In fact, the human brain prefers patterns. When it receives new information, it tries to fit the information into some kind of pattern. This is why people tend to find or make patterns all around them. Life is easier with patterns.

Writers also use patterns to organize and present their ideas. If you recognize these patterns when you are reading, you will understand the ideas better.

In this unit you will practice identifying five patterns that are commonly used in English writing.

Patterns Commonly Used in English		
Listing Sequence	Comparison	Problem-Solution Cause/Effect

With each pattern, writers tend to use certain words or phrases. These can act as signals that help the reader recognize the pattern and follow the ideas. For each pattern in this unit, there is a list of signal words and phrases that writers often use. However, writers do not always use them. They may use different signals or none at all.

In outlines in this unit, you will practice each pattern and notes to show how the ideas fit the patterns.

The Listing Pattern

In this pattern, the main idea includes a generalization and tells you to expect a list of facts or ideas. (These are the supporting facts and ideas.) The paragraph then gives the facts or ideas with some explanation or examples for each one.

Common Signal Words and Phrases for the Listing Pattern
For the main idea: *many, several, a lot of, lots of, some, a few, a number of, various, all kinds of* **For the supporting facts and ideas:** *first, third, one, other, another, in addition, last, finally, and, also, too, yet another, for example*

EXAMPLE

Paragraph with Listing Pattern

The Trobriand Islands

In the Trobriand Islands, the yam (a root vegetable) is important in several ways. First of all, this vegetable is one of their main foods. It is also part of their culture and religion. Every village has a "yam house" with a large yam hanging from the ceiling. It represents wealth and well-being for the village, life, and strength for the people. The yam harvest is the high point of the year, and the focus of many traditions. It is always carried out by groups of women. One tradition is that when the women are bringing the yams in from the fields, the men are supposed to stay away from them. Any man they meet will be chased, attacked, and treated as a fool.

Outline

Main idea: In the Trobriand Islands, the yam is important in several ways.	
Supporting	1. one of the main foods
facts and	2. part of the culture and religion
ideas	3. yam harvest is the high point of the year

EXERCISE 2

A. *Read these paragraphs. Then discuss the questions below with another student.*

Trash

1.   Where rich people see trash, poor people see all kinds of opportunities. For example, in the United States, some people make a living by picking up trash. They collect bottles and cans from the streets or trash cans and bring them to recycling centers for cash. In American and European cities, homeless people also sometimes make use of trash cans. They look in them for food and clothes that have been thrown out. They occasionally even sleep in large trash bins. In many developing countries, poor people collect trash directly at the city garbage dumps. In Cambodia, Nigeria, India, and Brazil, for example, these people—including many children—look through the trash for usable objects or materials such as plastic, glass, or metal. Then they sell the objects or materials to small companies that find ways to re-use or recycle them.

2.   Every year in the United States, 30 million computers are thrown away. These computers come to an end in various ways. A certain number are simply thrown into the trash, though this is against the law, and they end up in garbage dumps. When they break up, the computers release dangerous metals and chemicals into the soil and the air. Other computers are brought to recycling centers. However, the centers usually do not recycle the computers themselves. Sometimes they sell them to specialized companies that take them apart and sell the parts for re-use. Millions of other computers, however, are shipped off to developing countries. Only a small percentage of these can be fixed and or put to use in those countries. Most of them end up in garbage dumps, polluting the soil and air.

3.   Antarctica was once a perfectly clean wilderness of ice and snow. Now there are quite a few people—and their trash. Since people first began arriving on the continent, they have dealt with the trash in a number of ways. In the early years, many explorers and scientists often left things where they were. In fact, enormous metal pieces of old boats and equipment can still be seen near the research stations. Some visitors at least dug holes for their trash and covered it up again. However, this was not a good solution because it polluted the ground. According to international agreement today, everyone who visits Antarctica is supposed to take their trash away and bring it home with them. Most

visitors do this. However, according to scientists, a certain number of them dump their trash into the ocean on the way.

1. What is the main idea of each paragraph? Circle it.
2. What words in the main idea tell you to expect a list?
3. What are the supporting facts and ideas? Underline them.
4. What signal words or phrases are used? Circle them.

B. ***Work with your partner. Choose one paragraph from Part A. On a separate piece of paper, write an outline to show the main idea and supporting facts and ideas. Follow the example outline provided on page 174.***

The Sequence Pattern

In the sequence pattern, the main idea describes a sequence of events or steps that happen in a certain order.

The paragraph tells about each of the things in the sequence.

Common Signal Words and Phrases for the Sequence Pattern

For the main idea:
- A word or phrase that refers to a date, time, or period
  1945, life, was born, history, began, career, a long time
- A word or phrase that refers to a process
  how to, doing, prepare, process

For the supporting facts and ideas:
- A date, a time, or the age of a person
  yesterday, last week, a century ago, the age of six
- Phrases with time
  early in the morning, two o'clock, for an hour
- Phrases that tell about the order of events or steps
  first, second, before, soon, while, now, at last, finally, when, at first, then, now, next, last, after, during

---

EXAMPLES

1. **Paragraph with Sequence of Events**

Franklin D. Roosevelt

Franklin D. Roosevelt, the 32nd president of the United States, served his country for most of his life. He was born in Hyde Park, New York, on January 30, 1882, and he began his studies at Harvard in 1903. In 1905, he married Eleanor Roosevelt, a distant cousin, and they had six children. His first political position was New York State Senator in 1910. Then, from 1913 until 1921, he worked in Washington as Assistant Secretary of the Navy. In 1921, he became very ill with polio and lost the use of his legs. However, that did not end his career. Roosevelt ran for governor of New York State in 1928 and served for two terms. Then, in 1933, he was elected to the presidency. He served four terms and died in office on April 12, 1945.

Outline

Main idea: Franklin D. Roosevelt served his country most of his life.	
Supporting	_1._ January 30, 1882, born
facts and	_2._ 1903 began studies at Harvard
ideas	_3._ 1905 married Eleanor Roosevelt
	_4._ 1913-1921 worked in Washington
	_5._ 1921 became ill with polio
	_6._ 1928 ran for governor of New York
	_7._ 1933 elected to the presidency
	_8._ April 12, 1945 died

2. **Paragraph with Steps in a Process**

Doing the Laundry

Doing the laundry is not difficult. Some of us have done it hundreds of times, but if it is your first time, don't worry. It really is very simple. First, you sort all the clothes into piles. It is best to separate dark clothes and light clothes. When you have enough clothes to fill the washing machine, turn it on. Be sure to follow the directions. You can ruin your clothes if you make a mistake. When the washing machine is done, you can put your clothes in the dryer, if you have one. If not, you will have to use old-fashioned methods and hang up the clothes outside. When they are dry, you need to fold all the clothes, sort them out, and put them away. Then you are done—for now. Soon the time will come to do it again.

Outline

Main idea: Doing the laundry is not difficult.	
Supporting	_1._ sort clothes into piles
facts and	_2._ fill washing machine and turn on
ideas	_3._ put clothes in the dryer or hang outside
	_4._ fold clothes, sort, and put away

A. *Read these paragraphs. Then discuss the questions below with another student.*

Jackie Robinson: An African-American Sports Hero

1.   Jackie Robinson was born in Georgia in 1919. After his father left the family, the mother and five children moved to Pasadena, California, where there were very few other black families. Sports were always important for the Robinson boys. His older brother Matthew became a track star and won a silver medal behind Jesse Owens, another black athlete in the 1936 Olympics. Their medals were a major breakthrough against racial discrimination[1] in sports. Jackie Robinson played several sports in high school, including football, basketball, track, and baseball, and he was named most valuable player in 1938. At the University of California, he played on the university's top teams in all four sports. However, in 1941, he was forced to leave the university because he could not pay for it.

2.   In 1942, Robinson joined the United States Army, one of very few black officers. This was a difficult period for him. He soon found out that racial discrimination existed in the army too. At that time in Texas (and many other states), black people were supposed to sit at the back of city buses, separate from white people. On army buses this was not the rule. But one day, a bus driver on an army bus told Robinson to move to the back. He refused to do so. When the bus arrived at the army camp, he was arrested. Eventually, the army recognized that the bus driver was wrong and that Robinson should not have been arrested. By that time, the war was almost over.

3.   Robinson's career in baseball began in 1946 with the Montreal Royals, a minor league team. He had trouble in the beginning because he was the only black player in the white world of baseball. The other teams and people in other stadiums often shouted insults at him and some hotels would not allow him to have a room. Fortunately, his team and the Montreal fans supported him, especially since he was playing better and better. The next year, he moved to the major leagues—the Brooklyn Dodgers. After his first year there, he was awarded the prize for the best young player. From then until his retirement in 1956, he was the Dodger's most popular player—and one of the best loved athletes in the country.

---

[1]**racial discrimination** when a person or group is treated differently and unfairly

1. What is the main idea of each paragraph? Circle it.
2. What words in the main idea tell you to expect a sequence?
3. What are the supporting facts and ideas? Underline them.
4. What signal words or phrases are used? Circle them.

B. *Work with your partner. Choose one paragraph from Part A. On a separate piece of paper, write an outline to show the main idea and supporting facts and ideas.*

A. *Read these paragraphs. Then discuss the questions below with another student.*

1. **Giving a Book Talk**

When you are going to give a book talk, you need to prepare it carefully. First, you should choose a book that you enjoyed and that you understood well. You will give a better talk if you feel comfortable talking about it. After you have decided on the book, make notes about what you want to say. Use small note cards or pieces of paper. Then practice talking from the notes until you can talk without reading the notes and without many pauses. At this point, you should time yourself to make sure your talk is not too long or too short. If necessary, adjust your talk so that it takes the right amount of time. Finally, practice your talk with a friend or record it so you can listen to it.

2. **Recipe for Meat Broth**

To make a good meat broth, you need to have good ingredients (things you put in it). First you should buy several kinds of meat. You do not need to buy expensive cuts of meat. The important thing is to have meat that will give good flavor. For example, meat from an old hen is better for making broth than meat from a young chicken. You will need half a chicken (or hen), beef meat, and beef bones. The next step is to put all the meat in a large pot and fill the pot with water. Then add two carrots, two pieces of celery, and some fresh parsley (an herb for flavoring). At this point you should also add two or three teaspoons of salt. Now put the broth on the stove. When it is boiling, turn the heat down as low as possible and let it cook very slowly for three hours.

1. What is the main idea of each paragraph? Circle it.
2. What words in the main idea tell you to expect a sequence?
3. What are the supporting facts and ideas? Underline them.
4. What signal word or phrase is used for each one? Circle them.

B. *Work with your partner. Choose one paragraph from Part A. On a separate piece of paper, write an outline to show the main idea and supporting facts and ideas.*

The Comparison Pattern

In this pattern, the main idea presents two or more things, people, or ideas, and tells how they are similar, different, or both. The paragraph then gives various examples of the ways in which they are similar or different.

Common Signal Words and Phrases for the Comparison Pattern

For the main idea:

The main idea sentence usually includes the two things that will be compared.

Any of the signal words below may be included with the main idea.

For the supporting facts and ideas:

- Words that show similarity`
    alike, like, similar, similarly, same, also, both, too, in the same way, in common

- Words that show difference or contrast
    different, unlike, but, however, although, while, whereas, on the other hand, in contrast, rather, instead

Comparatives
    more (than), less (than), cheaper, more expensive, earlier than

---

EXAMPLE

2. **Paragraph with a Comparison Pattern**

Ukrainian and Japanese Cooking

In most ways, Ukrainian cooking is very different from Japanese cooking. For example, most Ukrainian meals have meat in them, whereas the Japanese often eat fish instead. Also, in the Ukraine, people eat a lot of potatoes, but not in Japan. Furthermore, the Ukrainians often eat dairy products, such as milk, cream, yogurt, and butter, but these are not common in Japan. On the other hand, there is one interesting similarity between Ukrainian and Japanese cooking. In both countries, people enjoy eating pastries filled with spicy meat. In the Ukraine, they are called *pilmeni*, in Japan *gyoza*. They are both made of pieces of flat pastry folded around a spicy meat filling. They look remarkably similar, though the flavors are different. Another similarity is that people usually eat these pastries with a sauce. The Ukrainians use sour cream and the Japanese use soy sauce.

Outline

Main idea: Ukrainian and Japanese cooking is different in many ways, though there are a few similarities.			
Supporting	*A. Differences:*		
facts	*1. Ukrainians mostly meat*	*Japanese often fish*	
and	*2. Ukrainians a lot of potatoes*	*Japanese no potatoes*	
ideas	*3. Ukrainians dairy products*	*Japanese not dairy products*	
	4. Ukrainian pastry different flavor	*Japanese pastry*	
	5. Ukrainian sour cream sauce	*Japanese soy sauce*	
	B. Similarities:		
	1. both eat pastry filled with spicy meat		
	2. both eat pastries with a sauce		

Note:

In the comparison pattern, along with comparison signal words and phrases, writers may also include listing or sequence signal words and phrases.

Examples:
Another similarity is the fact that people usually eat these pastries with a sauce.
For example, most Ukrainian meals have meat in them.
Also, in the Ukraine, people eat a lot of potatoes.

EXERCISE 5

A. Read these paragraphs. Then discuss the questions below with another student.

Universities in the United States and in Italy

1. Italian universities are quite different from most American universities. One difference is in the setting. Most American universities are on a campus—an area with just university buildings. However, Italian universities are usually in the middle of cities, and the university buildings are mixed in with other buildings. American universities also usually have some green space on campus, while Italian universities usually have no open or green space. Another important difference is that students at most American universities live in dormitories on campus. At Italian universities, on the other hand, there are few dormitories. Most students live at home with their families or in apartments around the city.

2. In both Italian and American universities, a certain percentage of students start but never graduate. In some cases, students stop attending courses because they cannot afford to pay for them. These students usually leave the university to go to work. This is true both in Italy and the United States, even though American universities cost much more. In both Italy and the United States, there are students who have trouble completing courses for other reasons. They may have made poor choices with regard to their university or their field of study. It may be too difficult for them, or they may simply not find it interesting. Then, there are always some students in any country who have psychological problems that prevent them from going ahead with their studies.

3. University programs in Italy and the United States are organized in different ways. In both countries, universities have requirements about the courses that students must take. However, in Italian universities, the required courses are all in the student's chosen field. For example, a medical student takes only courses required by the School of Medicine. Most American universities, on the other hand, require students to take courses outside their major (chosen field). A language major will have to take a science course, for example, and a science major will have to take a foreign language. Finally, one big difference between Italian and American universities is that Italian students are not required to attend all their classes. Instead, they often study at home for their exams. American students, however, are usually required to attend all their classes.

1. What is the main idea of each paragraph? Circle it.
2. What words in the main idea tell you to expect a comparison?
3. What are the supporting facts and ideas? Underline them.
4. What signal words or phrases are used? Circle them.

B. *Work with your partner. Choose one paragraph from Part A. On a separate piece of paper, write an outline to show the main idea and supporting facts and ideas.*

The Cause-Effect Pattern

In this pattern, the main idea states that something *causes* something else—or *is caused by* something else. The paragraph explains and/or gives examples of the causes and/or the effects.

EXAMPLES

<u>cause</u> → <u>effect</u>
1. Stress at work <u>can cause</u> loss of sleep.

<u>effect</u> ← <u>cause</u>
2. Loss of sleep <u>can be caused</u> by stress at work.

EXAMPLES

1. **Paragraph with One Cause and Several Effects**

Hurricane Katrina

When Hurricane Katrina hit the city of New Orleans in 2006, the consequences were dramatic. The high winds and high ocean waves caused water to go over the levees (walls) that were supposed to protect the city. As a result, some areas were badly flooded. The flooding was worst in some of the poorest neighborhoods because they were also the lowest. Tens of thousands of people fled their homes, many of which were completely destroyed. Altogether, 1,464 people were killed.

Outline

Main idea: When Hurricane Katrina hit the city of New Orleans in 2006, the consequences were dramatic.	
Supporting facts and ideas	Effects:
	1. water went over levees
	2. some areas badly flooded
	3. 1,464 people killed
	4. people fled their homes

2. **Paragraph with One Effect and Several Causes**

The Summit Hill Ice Cream Company

The Summit Hill Ice Cream company closed its shop in the center of town last week. The managers of the company had no choice. In recent years, other ice cream shops had opened in the area, and so there were fewer customers for Summit Hill Ice Cream. At the same time, increases in prices for supplies, electricity, and water had led to higher costs. Rent in the town center had also increased significantly. Because of all this, the shop had been losing money for some time.

Outline

Main idea: The Summit Hill Ice Cream company closed its shop in the center of town	
	last week
Supporting	Causes:
facts and	1. other ice cream shops opened in the area
ideas	2. higher prices for supplies, electricity, and water
	3. increased rent

Notes:

• Writers often use *may* or *can* with a verb when the cause or effect is possible but not certain.
Example: A diet that is high in fat *can contribute* to heart trouble.

• In cause and effect sentences, writers often use the passive tense.
Example: Loss of sleep *can be caused* by stress at work.

• Listing or sequence signal words or phrases may also be included in a comparison paragraph.
Example: *Another factor* in many health problems is lack of exercise.

EXERCISE 6

A. Read these paragraphs. Then discuss the questions below with another student.

The Spread of Disease

1. Traveling from one city or country to another can contribute to the spread of disease. When people arrive in a new place, they may bring in germs[1] that were not present before. The people there have no natural protection against these new germs, so they catch the disease more easily. Because it is unfamiliar, health workers may not identify it, and may not take any measures to stop it from spreading. People with the disease may continue to have contact with others. In this way, the germs travel from person to person through the population. This was what happened, for example, when soldiers traveled back home at the end of World War I, bringing with them the germs for the Spanish flu.

[1]**germs** very small living things that can make you sick (bacteria)

2. Heating and cooling systems are necessary in buildings, but they can also be a source of disease. For example, old air conditioners in windows are a common cause of health problems. They tend to collect dirt and water, which creates the perfect habitat for germs to grow. Then when the air conditioner is turned on, the germs are blown into the home or office and make people sick. The heating and cooling systems of large buildings can also cause illness. No problems arise in winter because the water is heated to temperatures

that kill any germs. However, at other times of year, germs tend to grow in the water of the cooling towers. They are then sent throughout the building with the air conditioning and can affect anyone in the building. Scientists first recognized this problem in July 1976, when 221 people became ill and 34 of them died.

3.   Pollution of the oceans can also be a factor in spreading disease. The pollution may be caused by chemicals used in farming that wash into rivers, and then into the ocean. Or it may be human waste that is dumped directly into the ocean with no processing. These pollutants result in the increased growth of tiny plants called algae. They can form a thick mass in the water, and they provide an ideal habitat for cholera, a deadly disease. When a ship passes through the algae, some of it may stick to the ship's bottom, along with some of the cholera germs. These germs then travel with the ship around the world. Cholera germs have traveled this way from India to South America, for example, causing an epidemic that killed thousands of people.

1.   What is the main idea of the paragraph? Circle it.
2.   What words in the main idea tell you to expect causes or effects?
3.   What are the supporting facts and ideas? Underline them.
4.   What signal words or phrases are used? Circle them.

B.   *Work with your partner. Choose one paragraph from Part A. On a separate piece of paper, write an outline to show the main idea and supporting facts and ideas.*

The Problem-Solution Pattern

In this pattern, the main idea presents a problem of some kind. The paragraph explains and gives details about the problem, and then explains or gives details about a solution to the problem.

> **Common Signal Words and Phrases for the Problem-Solution Pattern**
>
> **For the main idea:**
> • Words that indicate a problem: *problem, situation, trouble, crisis, issue, question, dilemma*
>
> • Words that indicate a solution: *solution, solve, resolution, resolve, decide*
>
> **For the supporting facts and ideas:**
>   The explanation of the problem may include elements of any of the other patterns. For this reason, writers may use any of the signal words that are common in those patterns.

Paragraph with a Problem-Solution Pattern

Stuck in a Snowstorm

Two German hikers found themselves in trouble last weekend. They were hiking in the Alps when an early snowstorm suddenly hit. It was snowing so hard and there was so much wind that they lost their way. The men were not dressed for snowy weather, so they were in serious danger of freezing to death. Fortunately, one of the men remembered a story he read as a child. He suggested that they dig a cave in the snow to protect themselves from the wind. They spent the night in their cave. In the morning, the snow had stopped and they were able to find their way down the mountain. The idea of digging a cave probably saved their lives.

Outline

Main idea: Two German hikers were hit by a snowstorm in the Alps and saved themselves by digging a cave in the snow.		
Supporting	A. Problems:	
facts		1. lost their way because of snow and wind
and		2. not dressed well so in danger of freezing
ideas	B. Solutions:	
		1. dug a cave in the snow
		2. spent the night in the cave
		3. went down the mountain in the morning

EXERCISE 7

A.   Read these paragraphs. Then discuss the questions below with another student.

Inventions for Developing Countries

1.   In many developing countries, homes do not have electricity, and people do not own refrigerators. Thus, they have no way to keep food fresh in hot weather. To help people in his area, a teacher in Nigeria, Mohammed Bah Abba, invented a new kind of cooler. His device is made of two clay pots, a smaller one inside a larger one, with wet sand between them and a wet cloth on top. As the water evaporates[1], it cools the pot so that food will stay fresh much longer. (It only works in a dry climate where the water will evaporate.) Since it does not require electricity or ice, and is easy and inexpensive to make, the cooler could be very useful in developing countries. Abba won a $75,000 Rolex Prize for his invention. He plans to make and distribute the coolers in Nigeria and other African countries.

[1]**evaporate**   when a liquid changes into a gas

2. The gases emitted by cooking stoves are a major cause of pollution and illness in developing countries. About three billion people use these stoves every day around the world. They burn large amounts of fuel—wood, coal, or dung[2]—and produce a lot of smoke and harmful gases. When the stoves are used indoors, these harmful gases are the direct cause of about 1.6 million deaths a year, many of them young children. The gases are also an indirect cause of deaths from lung cancer, pneumonia, and tuberculosis. Furthermore, the gases contribute to pollution that causes global warming. For all these reasons, scientists and inventors are working hard to develop stoves that will be more efficient, safer, and less polluting. This is not easy because the stoves also have to be cheap, easy to transport, and easy to use.

[2]**dung** solid waste from large animals

3. In many African countries, cell phone use has expanded dramatically in recent years. With their cell phones, people can now communicate with distant family members, do business, check markets, and transfer money. Sooner or later, however, cell phone batteries need to be recharged. But many Africans in small villages do not have access to electricity. One invention that could be helpful in this situation is the *Weza,* made by a British company called Lifeplay. *Weza* means power in the Swahili language. With this device it is possible for anyone to produce electric power by stepping many times on a foot pump. With the *Weza,* women are setting up small businesses recharging batteries for cell phones and lights. In this way, the families of the women increase their income, and villages gain access to electricity.

1. What is the main idea of the paragraph? Circle it (problem and solution).
2. What words in the main idea tell you to expect a problem/solution?
3. What are the supporting facts and ideas? Underline them.
4. What signal words or phrases are used? Circle them.

B. Work with your partner. Choose one paragraph from Part A. On a separate piece of paper, write an outline to show the main idea and supporting facts and ideas.

Recognizing Patterns

In these exercises, you will practice recognizing the patterns you have learned about. As you read each paragraph, think about the main idea and look for the signal words. Then decide which of the patterns the writer used:

Listing	Comparison	Problem-Solution
Sequence		Cause/Effect

Note: It may be possible to find more than one pattern in some paragraphs.

EXERCISE 8

A. *Write the pattern that best fits each paragraph.*

Sir Isaac Newton

1. Isaac Newton was born in Woolsthorpe, England, in 1642. He began his studies at Trinity College, Cambridge University, in 1661. In 1665, an outbreak of plague struck England, so Newton left the university and returned home. The next few years in Woolsthorpe were the most productive in his career. In fact, by age 26 he had already completed most of his best scientific work. However, his most famous book, *Principia,* was not published until 1682. He was made director of the English Mint[1] in 1699. Newton died in 1727 and is buried in Westminster Abbey.

[1]**mint** the official organization that manufactures a country's money

Pattern: _____

2. In the course of his career, Newton explored many different scientific fields. His most famous work was in physics, and in particular the discovery of two sets of natural laws. The first was the law of gravity, which he explained in his book, *Principia.* The second, equally important discovery was of the laws of motion, which formed the basis for modern mechanics. Outside of physics, Newton did important work in astronomy, and helped improve the telescope that Galileo had designed some years earlier. He also did experiments in chemistry and optics, and made discoveries about the nature of color. Finally, he wrote a number of books about philosophy, which was closely connected to science in his day.

Pattern: _____

3. In Newton's day, there were many theories about light, but no real understanding of the nature of light. Then Newton figured out how to make an experiment that would settle the question. In a room that was mostly dark, he allowed a white ray of sunlight to pass through a prism (a triangular piece of glass). The white light was divided by the prism into rays of primary colors (red, blue, green, yellow). He placed a prism so that the red light passed through it. It remained red and did not divide further. From this, Newton proved that light is composed of the four primary colors and that they cannot be divided.

Pattern: _____

4. Many historians and scientists have wondered why Newton did his best work during the years 1665 and 1668. How did he manage to produce so many brilliant ideas in such a short time? It is probably that he had begun to develop his theories earlier while he was at Cambridge. At that time, there were a number of important thinkers and scientists active at the university. Then, in the peace and quiet of Woolsthorpe, he was able to focus his thinking and do the experiments that led to his great discoveries. There may also have been personal reasons why he was so productive, but little is known about that period of his private life.

Pattern: _____

5. At first glance, Isaac Newton and Albert Einstein have several things in common. They both were geniuses who made fundamental discoveries in physics and they both did their most important work before the age of 26. But there the similarities end. Newton cared what people thought about him, and disapproved of improper behavior. Einstein, on the other hand, enjoyed being different and did not care what others thought. Furthermore, Newton spent his later years working as the director of the English Mint, a well-paid government job. However, Einstein remained a full-time scientist to the end of his life.

Pattern: _____

B. *Compare answers with another student. Discuss any differences.*

EXERCISE 9

A. *Turn back to the following exercises from Part 3, Unit 3. Reread each paragraph and write the pattern that fits best.*

1. Exercise 5 on page 155:

   a. Pattern: _____

   b. Pattern: _____

   c. Pattern: _____

2. Exercise 6 on page 157:

   a. Pattern: _____

   b. Pattern: _____

   c. Pattern: _____

3. Exercise 7 on page 159:

   a. Pattern: _____

   b. Pattern: _____

   c. Pattern: _____

B. *Compare answers with another student. Discuss any differences.*

Focus on Vocabulary

Target Vocabulary

Check your knowledge of these words and phrases. (Do not look in the dictionary.)

Mark each one:
    ✔   ***You are sure of the meaning.***
    ?   ***You have seen it before, but are not sure of the meaning.***
    X   ***You have not seen it before.***

____ intention	____ assume	____ contrast	____ access
____ actually	____ overcome	____ impression	____ intense
____ involved	____ limitation	____ complex	____ appearance
____ analyze	____ tend	____ regarded as	____ decline

EXERCISE 1

A.   ***Preview and then read the passage. Do not stop to look up new words.***

The Language of Online Love

Online dating used to be a bit embarrassing. It was something to be done late at night, at home, when no one could see. You also had to be careful about people with bad intentions who put up fake photos. And if you actually found love online, you would probably tell people instead that you met in a pub. But no longer. The Internet love industry has gone mainstream.[1] And now the academics are involved.

Lecturers and professors have probably been joining dating sites like match.com for years, but now they are also analyzing the contents. Dr. Jeff Gavin, a psychology lecturer at the University of Bath, has researched the social science behind the sites. His study focuses on online communications—how we talk and relate to people through computers and the Internet.

"A lot of theories assume that when people communicate online, they are missing important social cues," Gavin explains. "But people have found lots of ways to overcome the limitations of online communication by noticing other kinds of cues. For example, they look at people's email addresses, their spelling, and how and when they respond to messages. They also tend to ask more questions online, and give more personal answers."

---

[1]**go mainstream** become more common or ordinary

Gavin decided to compare the experiences of members of UK and Japanese online dating sites. The two cultures presented interesting contrasts because in Japan social context plays a much bigger part in communication. According to Gavin, "Japanese people tend to express themselves more with indirect things like body language and silence and social cues. A Japanese person who is too direct can give a negative impression. By contrast, communication in the West depends more on content—we express ourselves directly through what we say."

Gavin teamed up with a researcher from Sophia University in Tokyo to interview members of Japan's match.com site. He then compared the results with studies of similar sites in the United Kingdom. The findings revealed complex online rules about behavior.

"I found that Japanese online daters overcome the lack of social information online by developing their own cues. For example, dropping formal language means a closer relationship is developing. But dropping it too soon is regarded as a sign of social incompetence," Gavin explains. "Japanese people use the Internet very differently to the British. . . . They access it much more frequently from mobile phones. That means people tend to surf dating sites in public places like on the train, which has helped them become socially acceptable."

In Britain, he says, "There used to be a lot of horror stories about people building up very intense relationships online, and then discovering that the other person had lied about their appearance. I don't think that ever happened in huge numbers, but it has certainly declined now."

That doesn't mean today's online daters don't try to make improvements to their profiles. "It's natural that people want to put themselves in the best light, so most tend to describe themselves in a positive way, and upload photos that make them look better," Gavin says. "But I think that's just like making an effort before going to a nightclub . . . it's not dishonest."

[Adapted from "The Language of Online Love," by Lucy Tobin, *The Guardian Weekly,* June 25, 2010]

B. **Read the passage again. Circle all of the words and phrases from the target vocabulary list. Underline all of the words and phrases you don't know in the passage.**

C. **For each underlined word or phrase, look at the context (the words and sentences around it). Make a guess about the meaning. Write your guess in the margin in pencil.**

D. **Check your comprehension. Write T (True) or F (False) after each sentence below.**

1. In the past, people often hid the fact that they used online dating sites. _____
2. University professors are studying the way people relate online. _____
3. People who communicate online cannot tell anything about each other. _____
4. The Japanese and the British use online dating sites the same way. _____
5. People today do not usually lie about their appearance online. _____

E. **Check the dictionary for the words you are not sure about. Compare the definitions with your guesses in Part C. Change your guesses if necessary.**

F. **Compare your work with another student.**

A. *Match each target word to its definition. There is one extra definition.*

1. assume
2. contrast
3. decline
4. impression
5. intention
6. limitation
7. overcome
8. tend

a. a difference between people, ideas, or situation
b. to often do a particular thing
c. to think that something is true, although you have no proof
d. a plan or desire to do something
e. to deal successfully with a feeling or problem
f. to decrease in quantity or importance
g. the opinion or feeling you have about someone or something
h. to provide a place for something
i. a weakness or problem

B. *Compare answers with another student.*

EXERCISE 3

A. *Complete the passage with words from the box. Change the word to fit the sentence if necessary.*

actually	assume	impression	overcome
appearance	be regarded as	involved	tend

For many students, the first semester of college is not easy. It's a new situation, with new people, new rules, new demands. In the beginning, the courses are often not the main concern. In fact, some freshmen may pretend not to be very interested in their studies. They do not want to _____ "nerds"—people who are only
₁
interested in their studies or their computers and not in other people.

Those first weeks of classes, freshman usually want to be sure to make a good
_____. They are often especially concerned about their _____
₂   ₃
and they _____ to spend a lot of time wondering what other people think
₄
of them.

Many students also _____ that the others all know each other and
₅
know what they are doing. But _____, the truth is that everybody is in the
₆
same situation, with the same worries and fears. The best way to _____
₇
these worries and fears is not to think about them. Instead, students should focus on

their courses and should join a club, play a sport, or go watch a football (or soccer) game. In other words, they should get _____8_____ in all aspects of college life.

B. *Compare answers with another student.*

EXERCISE 4

A. *Find the word or phrase in each group that is NOT a possible synonym for the target word and cross it out.*

1. **access**	enter	reach	get into	meet
2. **actually**	in fact	now	truly	really
3. **analyze**	think about	examine	inform	study
4. **appearance**	looks	sight	application	view
5. **regarded as**	registered as	thought of as	considered as	viewed as
6. **complex**	expensive	complicated	difficult	with different parts
7. **intense**	strong	unhappy	serious	emotional
8. **involved**	included	connected	part of	open to

B. *Compare answers with another student.*

EXERCISE 5

A. *Choose a word from the box that fits with all the words or phrases in each group. You may use a dictionary.*

access	complex	intense	overcome
analyze	impression	intention(s)	

1. _____ + difficulties / feelings / limitations

2. _____ + data / results / contents

3. _____ + process / issue / rules

4. _____ + feelings / interest / relationship

5. no / free / limited + _____

6. wrong / first / negative + _____

7. every / bad / the best + _____

B. *Compare answers with another student.*

EXERCISE 6

A. *Work with another student. Write different forms for each word. Fill in as many as possible without a dictionary. Then look up the ones you are not sure about. (More than one answer is possible for some forms.)*

	Noun	Verb	Adjective	Negative Adjective	Adverb
1.		access			X
2.				X	actually
3.		analyze		X	
4.	appearance			X	
5.		assume	X	X	X
6.		X	complex	X	
7.	impression				
8.			intense	X	
9.	intention				
10.			involved		X
11.	limitation				X
12.		tend	X	X	X

B. *Compare your work with another pair.*

Vocabulary Review

- In your vocabulary notebook, write all the words from this Focus on Vocabulary section that you want to learn. Include the parts of speech, the sentences, and the definitions (See Part 2, Unit 1).
- Review your notebook (See Part 2, Unit 2).
- Make study cards of 10–15 words that you have trouble remembering. Study them alone and then with another student.

Reading Longer Passages

A longer nonfiction passage in English is like a paragraph in many ways:

- It is all about one thing, person, or idea—the topic.
- It includes the writer's idea about that topic—the overall idea of the passage.
- It contains other ideas that explain or develop the overall idea.
- It is structured in a way that helps the reader follow the writer's thinking.

In this unit, you will learn skills for understanding information and ideas in longer nonfiction passages. These skills are useful when you are reading textbooks, exam passages, magazine and newspaper articles, or online articles.

Structure of Longer Passages

Most nonfiction passages (except for informal writing such as blogs or email) are structured in a similar way, with three parts.

Introduction
The first paragraph(s) presents the *overall idea* of the passage. Readers in English usually look here to find out what the passage is about.

Development
The middle paragraphs explain and develop the overall idea. Each of these paragraphs has a main idea and supporting facts and ideas.

Conclusion
The last paragraph refers to the overall idea and may add an opinion or comment.

As with paragraphs (see Part 3, Unit 4), writers use patterns of organization to explain their ideas in longer passages. If you can identify these patterns, you will be able to follow the ideas better.

There is usually an overall pattern for the whole passage. The paragraphs within the passage may follow the same pattern or may have different patterns. Here are the patterns you learned about in Unit 4.

| Listing | | Problem-Solution |
| Sequence | Comparison | Cause/Effect |

Reading for Study

When you read longer passages for study or research, you can understand and remember better if you actively work with the text. In this unit, you will practice working with longer passages in three ways:

- By underlining and marking. This helps you decide which are the most important words, phrases, or sentences.
- By making an outline of the important facts and ideas in the passage. This helps you understand better how the ideas relate to each other. It also helps you remember them better.

Text Marking

Do you mark your texts in some way when you are reading for your courses—by underlining, highlighting, or writing symbols or notes in the margin?

Before you start marking a passage or a section of a textbook, you should first read through it quickly to understand the overall pattern of organization and the overall idea. Then go back and start marking.

PRACTICE 1

A. *Work with another student. Read the passage and notice the way it has been marked by a student.*

The Early Cinema

⁎ The cinema had its beginnings at the end of the 19th century in the United States. It grew out of several earlier forms of entertainment, including theater, and out of the technology developed for so-called "peep shows."

Peep Shows

⁎ In the 1890s peep shows were popular in many American cities. In a peep show, a film 1 was viewed through a small opening in a machine that was created for that purpose.

Among those who worked on peep shows was Thomas Edison, who invented a peep 2 show machine in 1894. He then opened several special shops for his machines, where 3 customers paid 25 cents to move from one machine to another and view short films.

New Technology

⁎ During these same years, however, other inventors began to work on developing film 1 projectors. They realized that there was a basic limit to the peep show machines: Only one person at a time could look at a film. These inventors wanted to improve the technology so they could show films to more people. Edison did not become involved 2 in this development because he believed he could make money with his peep show machines. As a result, he missed a major opportunity. By 1895, the first film projectors 3 were in use in theaters, halls and fairs.

Entertainment for Everyone

From the point of view of the producer, cinema had definite advantages over peep shows. ✳ It was more profitable than traditional theater or music hall productions because the _1_ material was recorded. Once the film was produced, there was no need for the actors, singers, lighting people, or makeup people. And unlike the theater, where audiences were limited, there were almost no limits to the number of viewers for a film. _2_

Audiences were immediately enthusiastic about these early films. Unlike the peep shows, the cinema experience could be shared with others. This was the real beginning of the ✳ mass entertainment of the 20th century.

Check the answers to this Practice exercise on page 287.

B. *Discuss these questions with another student:*
   1. **How is the overall idea of the passage marked?**
   2. **The main ideas? The supporting facts and ideas?**
   3. **Compare this with the way you usually mark a text. What is similar? What is different?**

C. *Look at the passage again. Decide on the overall pattern and the pattern for each paragraph.*

   Overall pattern: __sequence__

   Pattern of each paragraph:

   paragraph 1: _____

   paragraph 2: _____

   paragraph 3: _____

Notes:

- When you are marking a text, do not underline a lot. If you do, you will not be able to tell which facts or ideas are important.
- Put a mark or symbol in the margin to show where you can find the main idea of the whole passage and of each paragraph.
- Do not use a pen or a highlighter. Use a pencil so you can make changes later if your understanding of the passage changes.

Outlining

In Units 3 and 4, you learned how to outline paragraphs. Now you will learn about outlining longer passages. Before you try to make an outline, you should read and mark a passage. Then you can use your marking to help you decide what to put in the outline and how to format it.

Outlining is a more effective study method than just marking a text. You are much more likely to remember ideas and information after you have written them down in an outline.

A. *Work with another student. Complete this outline with the ideas and information from the example passage on page 195. Use the marking in the passage to help you.*

The Early Cinema

Introduction

Overall idea: _____

_____

Development

1. Main idea: _____

Supporting facts and ideas
  1. _____
  2. _____
  3. _____

2. Main idea: _____

Supporting facts and ideas
  1. _____
  2. _____
  3. _____

3. Main idea: _____

Supporting facts and ideas
  1. _____
  2. _____

Conclusion: _____

B. *Compare your work with another pair of students.*

Note: Different people may have somewhat different ways of marking or making outlines. Your marking should be clear to you, and it should include the important facts and ideas.

Check the answers to this Practice exercise on page 287.

Types of Passages

In these exercises, you will look at different types of longer passages to see how the structure can vary and how ideas are expressed. You will practice identifying the pattern, marking the text, and making an outline in these different passages.

News Articles (newspapers or websites)

These articles tell about recent events in the news. They may be short or long, depending on the importance of the event (and space in the newspaper or on the website). They generally contain lots of facts, including names, places, dates, numbers, and so on.

Readers of an English-language news report expect to find out immediately what it is about, so journalists always give that information at the beginning.

Introduction
The first sentences give the basic information about the event. This is the *overall idea*.
What happened? Who was involved? When and where did it happen? Why did it happen?

Development
The rest of the article explains and gives more details about the event.
It may include quotations (people's opinions) or statistics (numbers).
The paragraphs may be very short and may not have a clear pattern.
There often is no conclusion (because newspaper readers often do not read to the end).

Note: The writing of news articles is usually impersonal (not in the first person, "I") and usually does not include the writer's opinion.

EXERCISE 1

A. *Read the title and first two paragraphs of the article. Talk with another student about the title: What do you think "hit and run" means?*

Cyclist Accuses Officer in Hit and Run

B. *Read the article. Underline the main idea and put a star in the margin beside it. What is the overall pattern?* _____

A cyclist who was hit by the patrol car of police officer Louis Ramos has brought charges against him for driving away without reporting the accident. The officer was charged yesterday with assault,[1] reckless[2] driving, and leaving the scene of an accident where there had been an injury.

According to the authorities in Brooklyn, officer Ramos was driving with his lights flashing and his siren on, heading the wrong way on Jay Street, a one-way street in Brooklyn. He drove through a red light at Sands Street and struck the cyclist crossing Jay Street.

Witnesses at the scene say that the officer and his partner, Paris Anderson, got out of their police car after they hit the cyclist and pulled him over to the sidewalk. Then they gave him a tissue[3] and drove off without reporting the accident or calling an ambulance. Video cameras on the street corner filmed the accident.

Brought to Long Island College Hospital, the cyclist suffered cuts and bruises on his face, a broken nose, and a broken wrist. He was released after treatment.

Ramos, an officer with the New York Police Department for 19 years, pleaded[4] not guilty to the charges. He and officer Anderson were suspended[5] without pay last month. The New York City Police Department declined to comment.

The case comes at a time of conflict between New York police and cyclists. Two videos showing officers pushing cyclists off their bikes have been widely viewed online recently.

[1]**assault** a violent attack on someone
[2]**reckless** dangerous
[3]**tissue** a piece of soft paper for blowing your nose

[4]**pleaded** said
[5]**suspended** to officially stop someone from working for a period of time

C. *Now go back and mark the important facts and ideas (who, what, where, when, why or how).*

D. *On a separate piece of paper, make an outline of the article. Follow the example in the Practice exercise on page 197. Compare your work with another student.*

EXERCISE 2

1. A. *Read this title of an article from Unit 1, Exercise 9. Talk with another student. Do you remember what the article was about? If you do not remember, make a guess.*

Carver Children Safe after Night Out

B. *Turn to page 122. Read the article, underline the overall idea, and put a star in the margin. What is the overall pattern?* _____

C. *Now go back and mark the important facts and ideas.*

D. *On a separate piece of paper, make an outline of the article. Compare your work with another student.*

2. A. *Read this title of an article from Unit 1, Focus on Vocabulary, Exercise 1. Talk with another student. Do you remember what the article was about? If you do not remember, make a guess.*

> ## Police Arrest Hundreds in Italy

B. *Turn to page 125. Read the article, underline the main idea, and put a star in the margin. What is the overall pattern? _____*

C. *Now go back and mark the important facts and ideas.*

D. *On a separate piece of paper, make an outline of the article. Compare your work with another student.*

Feature Articles (newspapers, magazines, websites)

These articles are usually longer and give background information about people, places, issues, or scientific, medical, cultural, or social developments. Writers try to make them enjoyable and interesting to read, so there are usually fewer facts than in a news report.

Introduction
The first paragraph usually starts with something to catch the reader's attention (a description, comparison, quotation, etc.). The *overall idea* is usually at the end of the first paragraph or the beginning of the second paragraph.

Development
The middle part of the article explains and develops the overall idea. It may include description, quotation, narrative (what happened), or commentary. The paragraphs may be longer than in a news report.

Conclusion
The last paragraph usually mentions the overall idea again and often gives an opinion or recommendation about it.

Note: The writing may be more informal and personal (in the first person, "I") than in a news article. It may include the writer's own experience and opinion.

A. *Read the title and preview the passage quickly. Discuss it with another student. What do you know about this topic? What do you think the passage will say about it?*

The Cooking Wars

Over the centuries the French have lost a number of famous battles with the British, but they've always felt superior in the kitchen. France has for centuries had a reputation for culinary excellence, and Britain for some of the worst cooking in the world. But according to a recent poll, that reputation may no longer reflect reality.

The results of a new poll, which was carried out by a French magazine, Madame Le Figaro and the BBC food magazine, Olive, suggest that British home cooks spend more time cooking each week and also produce a greater variety of dishes than French home cooks.

In the survey, more than 1,350 Britons and about 2,000 French people were asked when, how often and what they cooked each day. Of the Britons, 71% said they cook at home every day, while only 59% of the French said they cook daily. The British also spent more time on their cooking than the French and tended to vary their ingredients more.

The reaction in London was predictably enthusiastic. According to Lulu Grimes, the food director at Olive magazine, British food has greatly improved since the 1990s. Once upon a time, the menu for many family meals would have been roast beef, potatoes and over-cooked vegetables, but not now. Home cooks are experimenting with the huge range of ingredients now available in British supermarkets and are preparing all kinds of new dishes, using the cookbooks that sell millions of copies every year.

Marilyn Jarmon, a marketing manager from Paris who has lived in London for 15 years has also noticed the improvement in British food and says that she eats very well in London – in homes and in restaurants. In her opinion, there's much more diversity in British food now, compared to French food, which tends to be very traditional.

Some French people say that the survey did not show the whole picture. Jeannine Loiret, a food writer, agrees that during the week French women don't cook as much as they used to because most of them work and don't have much time. They tend to buy ready-made or frozen dishes, but many of them make up for it on the weekend.

There's also a difference, says Jean-Paul Belmonde, a Parisian chef, between Paris and the countryside. "It's true that people in Paris don't cook much, but elsewhere, cooking is still at the heart of daily life. When I'm with my friends in Lyon (his native city), we spend the morning talking about what we'll make for lunch and then the afternoon about what we'll cook for dinner. We French like to talk about food—and wine."

For many French people, opinions about British food have not changed. When Bernard Blier, the food editor at Madame Le Figaro, was asked about British food, he replied: "I don't go out of my way to try it. It is not very refined. You can say that I'm not a fan at all."

B. *Read the article. Underline the main idea and put a star in the margin. What is the overall pattern?* _____

C. Now go back and mark the important facts and ideas.

D. On a separate piece of paper, make an outline of the article. Compare your work with another student.

EXERCISE 4

1. A. Read this title of the article from Unit 3, Focus on Vocabulary. Talk with another student. Do you remember what the article was about? If you do not remember, make a guess.

Suffering from Travel

B. Turn to page 166. Read the article. Underline the main idea and put a star in the margin. What is the overall pattern? _____

C. Now go back and mark the important facts and ideas.

D. On a separate piece of paper, make an outline of the article. Compare your work with another student.

2. A. Read this title of the article from Unit 4, Focus on Vocabulary. Talk with another student. Do you remember what the article was about? If you do not remember, make a guess.

The Language of Online Love

B. Turn to page 189. Read the article. Underline the main idea and put a star in the margin. What is the overall pattern? _____

C. Now go back and mark the important facts and ideas.

D. On a separate piece of paper, make an outline of the article. Compare your work with another student.

Chapters or Sections of Textbooks

Writers of textbooks want to help student readers find and understand the ideas in their books. For this reason, the ideas are usually explained clearly, and the text is well organized. The pages are also formatted to help students notice important terms and concepts, with headings, boxes, and special fonts (letter styles). There are also often many illustrations and photographs.

Introduction

The first paragraph of a section or chapter introduces the *overall idea*. It may come at the beginning, middle, or end of the paragraph.

Development

The middle part contains an explanation of the key concept and gives important facts or ideas relating to it. Definitions are usually included for new words relating to the key concept.

Conclusion

This may include more than one paragraph. It restates the key concept and summarizes the important terms, facts, and ideas.

Notes:

- The passages in Exercises 5 and 6 define and explain a term or concept. This is another pattern that is common in textbooks.
- The style is formal (third person) and academic (using the kind of language professors and researchers use to talk about ideas).
- In both passages, the conclusions are not included.

EXERCISE 5

A. *Read the title and headings of this passage from a psychology textbook. Discuss them with another student. What do you know about this topic? What do you think the passage will say?*

The Homeless

The homeless are among the extremely poor. They are, by definition, people who sleep in streets, parks, shelters,[1] and places that were never intended for living in, such as bus stations, lobbies,[2] or empty buildings.

According to Peter Rossi's study of the Chicago homeless, most are African American men in their mid-30s with an educational level similar to that of the general population. Most have never married; if they have, their marriages have failed. Most held their last steady job more than four years earlier, and the rest have worked only occasionally at jobs involving low skills and low wages.[3] Other studies have shown that many of the homeless are families with children, alcohol and drug abusers,[4] and people who are mentally ill.

Homelessness is not new. There have always been homeless people in the United States. But the homeless today differ in some ways from the homeless of the 1950s and 1960s. More than 40 years ago, most of the homeless were older men. Very few were

---

[1]**shelter** a place that protects you from the weather
[2]**lobby** a large hall inside the entrance of a building
[3]**wages** the amount of money you earn per hour
[4]**drug abusers** people who take illegal drugs

women and families with young children. Today's homeless people also are more visible
to the general public because they are much more likely to sleep on the streets or in other
public places. In recent years, however, most cities have cracked down on[5] the homeless,
removing them from the streets.

Homelessness today is the result of at least three social forces. One is the fact
that there is less inexpensive housing for poor families and poor single people because
the government no longer helps to pay for such housing. Another social force is the
fact that there is now less demand for unskilled labor. This has led to extremely high
unemployment among young men in general and African Americans in particular. A
third social force is the fact that the government has cut back on public welfare benefits[6]
over the last two decades. These three social forces have not directly caused homelessness.
But they have meant greater numbers of extremely poor people, thereby increasing the
chances of these people becoming homeless.

[Adapted from *Sociology: A Brief Introduction*, Alex Thio, Pearson, 2005, pp. 194–195]

---

[5]**cracked down on** to become more strict in dealing with a problem
[6]**welfare benefits** money paid by the government to people who are poor or not working

B. *Read the passage. Underline the main idea and put a star in the margin.*

C. *Now go back and mark the important facts and ideas.*

D. *On a separate piece of paper, make an outline of the article. Compare your work with another student.*

EXERCISE 6

A. *Read this title of a textbook passage from Unit 1, Exercise 10. Talk with another student. Do you remember what the passage was about? If you do not remember, make a guess.*

The Law of Demand

B. *Turn to page 123. Read the passage. Underline the main idea and put a star in the margin. What is the overall pattern? _____*

C. *Now go back and mark the important facts and ideas.*

D. *On a separate piece of paper, make an outline of the article. Compare your work with another student.*

Focus on Vocabulary

Target Vocabulary

Check your knowledge of these words and phrases. (Do not look in the dictionary.)

Mark each one: ✔   *You are sure of the meaning.*
               ?   *You have seen it before, but are not sure of the meaning.*
               X   *You have not seen it before.*

_____ in terms of	_____ specialized	_____ willing	_____ in the meantime
_____ serve as	_____ practical	_____ provide	_____ exception
_____ determine	_____ appreciate	_____ means	_____ experience
_____ goods	_____ trade	_____ purchase	_____ function

EXERCISE 1

A.   *Preview and then read the passage. Do not stop to look up new words.*

The Three Uses of Money

If you were asked to define money, you would probably think of the coins and bills in your wallet or the paychecks you receive for your part-time job. Economists define money in terms of its three uses. For an economist, money is anything that serves as a medium of exchange, a unit of account, and a store of value.

Money as a Medium of Exchange

A medium of exchange is anything that is used to determine value during the exchange of goods and services. Without money, people acquire goods and services through barter, or the direct exchange of one set of goods or services for another. Barter is still used in many parts of the world, especially in traditional economies in Asia, Africa, and Latin America. It is also sometimes used informally in the United States. For example, a person might agree to help paint a neighbor's house in exchange for vegetables from the neighbor's garden. In general, however, as an economy becomes more specialized, bartering becomes too difficult and time-consuming to be practical.

To appreciate how much easier money makes exchanges, suppose that money did not exist, and that you wanted to trade your CD player for a DVD player. You probably would have a great deal of trouble making the exchange. First, you would need to find someone who wanted to both sell the model of DVD player you want and buy your particular CD player. Second, this person would need to agree that your CD player is worth the same as his or her DVD player.

Now consider how much easier your transaction[1] would be if you used money as a medium of exchange. All you would have to do is find a buyer—someone willing to pay you $100 for your CD player. Then you could use that money to buy a DVD player from someone else. Because money makes exchanges so much easier, people have been using it for thousands of years.

Money as a Unit of Account

In addition to serving as a medium of exchange, money serves as a unit of account. In other words, money provides a means for comparing the values of goods and services. For example, suppose you see a jacket on sale for $30. You know this is a good price because you have checked the price of the same or similar jackets in other stores. You can compare the cost of the jacket in this store with the cost in other stores because the price is shown in the same way in every store in the United States—in dollars and cents.

Other countries have their own forms of money that serve as units of account. The Japanese quote prices in yen, the Russians in rubles, Mexicans in nuevos pesos, and so forth.

Money as a Store of Value

Money also serves as a store of value. This means that money keeps its value if you decide to hold onto—or store—it instead of spending it. For example, when you sell your CD player to purchase a DVD player, you might not have a chance to purchase a DVD player right away. In the meantime, you can keep the money in your wallet or in a bank. The money will still be valuable and will be recognized as a medium of exchange weeks or months from now.

Money serves as a good store of value with one important exception. Sometimes economies experience a period of rapid inflation, or a general increase in prices. For example, what if the United States experiences 10 percent inflation during a particular year. If you sold your CD player at the beginning of that year for $100, the money you received would have 10 percent less value, or buying power, at the end of the year. In short, when an economy experiences inflation, money does not function as well as a store of value.

[Adapted from *Economics: Principles in Action*, by Arthur O'Sullivan and Steven M. Sheffrin, 2003, Prentice Hall, pp. 244–245]

---

[1]**transaction** a business or financial operation

B. *Read the passage again. Circle all of the words and phrases from the target vocabulary list. Underline all of the words and phrases you don't know in the passage.*

C. *For each underlined word or phrase, look at the context (the words and sentences around it). Make a guess about the meaning. Write your guess in the margin in pencil.*

D. *Check your comprehension. Write T (True) or F (False) after each sentence.*

1. Barter is a way to use money to acquire goods and services. _____

2. No one uses barter in modern societies. _____

3. Using money to acquire something is often easier than bartering. _____

4. The unit of account in the United States is the dollar. _____

5. When there is rapid inflation, money does not keep the same value. _____

E. *Check the dictionary for the words you are not sure about. Compare the definitions with your guesses in Part C. Change your guesses if necessary.*

F. *Compare your work with another student.*

EXERCISE 2

A. *Read the two sentences. Choose the best definition for the target word.*

1. For an economist, money is anything that <u>serves as</u> a medium of exchange, a unit of account, and a store of value.
   The extra room on the ground floor <u>serves as</u> both a study and an extra bedroom.

   a. is included in
   b. is better or more than
   c. is used as

2. A medium of exchange is anything that is used to <u>determine</u> value during the exchange of goods and services.
   The study will help us <u>determine</u> the level of demand for a new product.

   a. to find out
   b. to grow bigger
   c. to inform people

3. Economists define money <u>in terms of</u> its three uses.
   <u>In terms of</u> pay, the job offer was excellent; the hours, however, were terrible.

   a. working for, earning
   b. talking about, considering
   c. looking for, searching

4. For example, when you sell your CD player to <u>purchase</u> a DVD player, you might not have a chance to purchase a DVD player right away.
   Students can <u>purchase</u> sports passes at the student affairs office.

   a. find
   b. buy
   c. sell

5. When an economy experiences inflation, money does not <u>function</u> as well as a store of value.
She has to take medication so her heart will <u>function</u> normally.

    a. get or win something
    b. increase or go faster
    c. work in a correct way

6. In other words, money <u>provides</u> a means for comparing the values of goods and services.
The article does not <u>provide</u> much information about the costs or conditions.

    a. gives something or makes it available
    b. shows that something is true
    c. compares facts or ideas

7. In other words, money provides a <u>means</u> for comparing the values of goods and services.
Facebook is now an important <u>means</u> of communication among young people.

    a. amount of something good or something you want
    b. sum of money that is used to pay for things
    c. method or system that you use to achieve a result

8. <u>In the meantime</u>, you can keep the money in your wallet or in a bank.
They plan to wait until gas prices go down and, <u>in the meantime</u>, drive less.

    a. within a very short period of time
    b. in a period of time from now until a future event
    c. sometime in the very distant future

B. **Compare answers with another student.**

EXERCISE 3

A. **Match each target word to its definition. There is one extra definition.**

1. goods	a.	likely to succeed and be effective
2. specialized	b.	to be involved, influenced, or affected by something
3. practical	c.	of any possible type
4. exception	d.	products
5. appreciate	e.	relating to one particular purpose, type of work, or product
6. trade	f.	prepared to do something
7. willing	g.	to understand the value or good qualities of something
8. experience	h.	someone or something that is not included in a rule
	i.	give something to someone for something else

B. **Compare answers with another student.**

A. *Complete the paragraph with words or phrases from the box. Change the words to fit the sentence if necessary.*

> provide   trade   serve as   specialized   in terms of   practical

  The Mason College of Business is well-known in this country and abroad for its program in international _____ and finance. In this program,
               1
students follow courses taught by well-known economists and experts. The courses _____ students with an excellent background in business
         2
theory and practice. Furthermore, the college gives students opportunities to gain _____ experience. The program includes a semester-long internship at a
   3
_____ firm here or abroad. The internships often _____
  4   5
a way for students to gain entry into the business world. In fact, the college has an excellent record _____ job placement for graduating students.
             6

B. *Compare answers with another student.*

A. *Choose the word from the box that can be used with all the words or phrases in each group. You may use a dictionary.*

> determine   experience   means   practical   provide   specialized

1. _____ + suggestion / advice / experience
2. _____ + training / skills / economy
3. _____ + pain / a change / inflation
4. _____ + of survival / of transportation / of communication
5. _____ + meals / advantages / the means
6. _____ + value / the level / policy

B. *Compare answers with another student.*

A. **Work with another student. Write different forms for each word. If you do not know a form, make a guess. Do not use the dictionary. (More than one answer is possible for some forms.)**

	Noun	Verb	Adjective	Negative Adjective	Adverb
1.		appreciate			X
2.		determine			X
3.	exception	X			
4.		function			
5.			practical		
6.		provide		X	
7.		serve			X
8.			specialized		
9.			willing		

B. **Compare your work with another pair.**

Vocabulary Review

* In your vocabulary notebook, write all the words from this Focus on Vocabulary section that you want to learn. Include the parts of speech, the sentences, and the definitions (See Part 2, Unit 1).
* Review your notebook (See Part 2, Unit 2).
* Make study cards of 10–15 words that you have trouble remembering. Study them alone and then with another student.

Skimming

When you skim, you read something very quickly to get the general idea. As with scanning, you need to move your eyes quickly over the text. You also usually have a question in mind, though not about specific information as in scanning. Instead, in skimming you usually skim to get the gist— the general idea.

Skimming is useful:

- to preview a text (as you learned in Part 3, Unit 1).
- to find out quickly what a reviewer thinks about a book, movie, product, etc.
- to get the main idea from an article in a newspaper or online.
- to decide if a text will be useful for a research assignment.

Which of these uses of skimming have you tried? Which could be most useful for you?

The key to skimming—as with all other kinds of fast reading—is *skipping* text. You skim by reading some parts of the text and skipping the rest. The more text you skip, the faster you can skim. It is also true, however, that the more you skip, the less you will understand and remember. This is especially true for language learners and slow readers in general.

Even good readers do not try to skim all the time. They only skim when they do not need a detailed or complete understanding of a text. And they change the way they skim—skipping more or less text—according to what they are skimming and why.

How do you know which parts to read and which to skip when you skim? In fact, there is no simple answer. Every text is different, and each reader has different thoughts and questions about the text.

For all readers, however, skimming requires concentration and active thinking about the text.

Guidelines for Skimming

- Look at the title. Ask yourself questions about it.
- Look at the passage as a whole and decide what type it is (a news article, a background article, an opinion essay, etc.).
- Keep asking questions as you look at the parts of the passage that are likely to have the most information and ideas. (See Part 3, Unit 5.) These may include:
  - the first paragraph(s).
  - the first sentence(s) of other paragraphs. If they are very short, or do not seem interesting, you can skip some paragraphs completely.
  - the last paragraph (except in news articles).
- Keep asking yourself questions as you look.
- Remember: You only want the *important* ideas. You can usually skip the details and examples.

These exercises in this unit are timed to encourage you to skim faster as you look for the general ideas. You should aim to skim the passages at least 50% faster than you normally read (as measured in the timed reading passages in Part 4).

The passages in these exercises are all about 400 words long. You should be able to skim them in the same amount of time or less than it takes you to read the 600-word passages in Part 4.

Write your most recent reading time from Part 4. This is your normal reading time: _____

Skimming News Articles

People often skim articles in newspapers or magazines. This allows them to save time and to skip parts that are not interesting. When skimming news articles, ask yourself questions with *Wh-* words, such as, "*Who* is this article about?" "*What* happened?" Use the title to think of questions, as you do when previewing.

EXERCISE 1

A. *Work with another student. Read the title of the article. Talk about it with another student. What do you think happened?*

September 13, 2010

News Reporter Missing in White Mountains

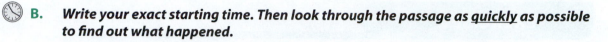

B. *Write your exact starting time. Then look through the passage as <u>quickly</u> as possible to find out what happened.*

Starting time: _____

CONWAY, N.H.—Rescue teams searched the White Mountains woods all night and into the morning, searching for Boston radio and television reporter Sam Murphy, who failed to return from a hike on Sunday. The 60-year-old reporter for WGBH left yesterday morning for a hike alone on trails about 10 miles west of the Maine border, according to New Hampshire officials and studio managers.

When he did not return by evening, Murphy's wife, Sally, called WGBH to say that he was missing. She notified the Carroll County, N.H., sheriff's office, which contacted the New Hampshire Fish and Game Department. Several volunteers joined the search.

Rescue officials, lead by Lieutenant Paul Rinaldo used six dogs to help in the operation. The rescuers were expected to suspend their search early this morning and resume at daylight.

WGBH managers, who held a press briefing yesterday afternoon, said Murphy had no health problems they knew of and that he stayed in good physical condition.

Colleagues of Murphy said that they were optimistic that he would be found. They noted that the weather was good and that Murphy was in good shape. Several mentioned that he often went hiking in New Hampshire and knew the trails well.

The trails in the area where he has disappeared near the Maine border are not especially steep or rocky, and there are no dangerous cliffs or gullies where he might have fallen. However, they are lightly traveled, especially after the summer season.

Rinaldo said there could be dangers of another kind as well. "The lack of rocky terrain doesn't necessarily make it an easy place to hike. The foot trails in that area are little used and hard to stay on. Also, there are a lot of trees damaged by ice that could fall at any time."

It was the second time in eight days that a hiker has disappeared in the White Mountains. A search for Abraham Hauer of Brooklyn, N.Y., ended tragically when his body was found last Tuesday near Franconia. Though an accident was blamed at first, doctors have confirmed that Hauer probably died of a heart attack while hiking alone.

Rinaldo said that Murphy had been dressed appropriately for a hike, though apparently not for staying out overnight in the mountains. "He probably should have been better equipped", said Rinaldi. According to weather reports, the low temperature early yesterday would have been in the 40s (5–9°C).

Finishing time: _____

C. *Write your finishing time and calculate your reading time: _____*
(Finishing time – Starting time = Reading time). How does this compare to your normal reading time?

D. *Work with your partner. Can you tell what happened? Do not look back at the article.*

E. *Check your understanding by reading the article again more carefully.*

A. *Work with another student. Read the title of the article. Talk about it with another student. What do you think happened?*

September 14, 2010

Murphy Found, Safe and Sound

B. *Write your exact starting time. Then look through the passage as <u>quickly</u> as possible to find out what happened.*

Starting time: _____

CONWAY, N.H.—A team of rescuers, including New Hampshire police and volunteers, had just taken up their search again around 9:30 a.m. when they met WGBH news reporter Sam Murphy about 2 miles from the start of the Moat Mountain Trail. Missing since Sunday evening, he had not returned from a solo hike in this little travelled area. The rescuers had spent all night searching a hilly 50-square-mile section of the White Mountain National Forest.

Murphy appeared suddenly in the woods and came up to the group, asking if they were looking for him. He was wearing a baseball cap, a fleece sweater, and a light jacket. He had drunk all his water, but still had half a peanut butter sandwich in his pocket.

He was very tired, thankful, and very embarrassed about going off on a hike far beyond his skills. When found, he admitted that he had no idea where he was. Apparently he had been walking in circles most of the night.

Murphy walked back with the group to the road where his wife Sally was waiting. She had a few sharp words to say to him about putting her through an emotionally difficult time.

"Quite honestly, this is an embarrassing incident," said Murphy. "I should have listened to my common sense—and my wife—and then you wouldn't have had to go through all this. This should have been just a Sunday hike, not a news story."

Basically, Murphy said, he had underestimated the difficulty of the route. After hiking a short and easy section of the Moat Mountain Trail several weeks ago with his son Jason, Murphy had decided to do it alone, thinking he could complete the hike in 6 ½ hours. He brought along a bottle of water, two peanut butter sandwiches, and four cheese sticks.

The route climbs to about 3,000 feet (914 m) along the Moat Mountain Trail all the way to Bear Notch Road, a Class III hike (the most difficult category), which veterans say would take even an experienced hiker some 11 hours.

Sally Murphy said, "I think people sometimes don't understand their limits and don't have enough respect for the woods and mountains. I told him it wasn't a good idea to go out alone, I gave him the whole argument, but he kept saying that thousands of people go hiking up here every year and don't have any trouble."

Finishing time: _____

C. *Write your finishing time and calculate your reading time:* _____

How does this compare to the reading time you wrote on page xxx?

D. *Work with your partner. Can you tell what happened? Do not look back at the article.*

E. *Check your understanding by reading the article again more carefully.*

Skimming Reviews

In newspapers, magazines or online, you can find *reviews,* where writers give their opinion of restaurants, movies or books. The next two exercises include book reviews. When skimming the reviews, ask yourself, "What does this writer think about the book?" and "Why?"

EXERCISE 3

A. *Work with another student. Read the title of the book review. Talk about it with another student. What can you tell about the book?*

> Go Ask Alice: A Real Diary

B. *Write your exact starting time. Then look through the review as <u>quickly</u> as possible to find out the main points.*

Go Ask Alice was written almost forty years ago, but it remains a powerful story of adolescent unhappiness and destruction that is still very relevant today.

The reader enters the life of the writer near the time of her fifteenth birthday. It seems an ordinary life in many ways—arguments with parents, boredom with school, concern about what others think of her—but she loves her family, and they care about her. She does well in school when she wants to and she has friends she enjoys being with. And then the family moves because of her father's job, and her life falls apart.

How she struggles and fails to get her life back together again is the story we follow in this diary. We never learn the name of the writer ("Alice" refers not to the author, but to *Alice in Wonderland*), but after just a few pages, we feel we know her well. We probably all know someone like her: an unhappy, insecure teenager who suffers terribly from real or imagined offenses of her parents and her classmates.

When she changes schools, she also has to deal with all the difficulties of being a new student. Her new classmates are uncaring, even cruel at times, and this does not help her self-confidence. Then, over the summer, new friends play a trick on her, adding some drugs to her Coke. The friends push her to try it again, and soon she begins to experiment with other kinds of drugs. Before long, she is an addict and drugs have taken over her life, alienating her from family, friends, and school. She runs away from home, lives for a time as a prostitute, and ends up on the streets, filthy, hungry and ill. There are moments of hope when she manages, with the help of her family, to break out of the drug habit and make a new start. But each time, she is unable to stay away from the drugs.

Through all this, she writes in her diary, recording events and feelings. The language is that of a teenager, but so vivid that we are drawn into her life and participate in her emotional highs and lows. As a diary, it does not offer any solutions or any general truths about the problem of teenage drug addiction, but it does help us understand one person's choices and the consequences for her.

Finishing time: _____

C. **Write your finishing time and calculate your reading time: _____ How does this compare to your skimming time in Exercise 2?**

D. **Work with your partner. Can you retell the main points of the review? Did the reviewer have a positive or a negative opinion? Do not look back.**

E. **Check your understanding by reading the review again more carefully. Then discuss these questions:**

1. Have you ever read any autobiographies or memoirs (when a person writes about their own life)? If so, who were they about?
2. Do you know any teenagers who have had problems like hers?
3. Does this book interest you?

A. *Work with another student. Read the title of the book review. What can you tell about the book?*

> Ice Bound: A Doctor's Incredible Battle for Survival at the South Pole—by Dr. Jerri Nielsen

B. *Write your exact starting time. Then look through the review as <u>quickly</u> as possible to find out the main points.*

Starting time: _____

This is a story of ordinary people doing extraordinary things under some of the most difficult conditions on the planet. Jerry Nielsen went to the Antarctic to escape a series of family problems ending in a bitter divorce. What she found during her 11 months there was a near-death experience, another kind of family and a new outlook on life.

As a doctor, Nielsen's job at the polar scientific station was to keep the scientists and workers healthy during the long winter. The most serious medical problem that she had to face, however, turned out to be her own.

The drama began in July when Nielsen suspected she might have breast cancer. She performed a biopsy (a test for cancer) on herself, using ice as the anesthetic, which showed she had a particularly dangerous form of breast cancer.

Her situation was desperate. She was trapped in the middle of the polar winter, without any specialized medical supplies and no other doctor within 600 miles. Her only connection to the outside world was through email, which only worked when a communication satellite passed overhead.

In any circumstances, the survival rate for women with her type and stage of breast cancer would not be more than 50%. Nielsen's circumstances certainly did not help her. In the station, 41 people were crowded into a space designed for 17. The temperatures were so cold that landing aircraft was out of the question, so planes could only fly by and drop cancer-fighting drugs and other medical supplies.

With instruction from doctors in the United States, two men at the station learned how to give her the anti-cancer drugs. While continuing with these weekly treatment sessions, Nielsen also kept up her job at the station, treating people for various injuries and minor illnesses.

By October 16, when a plane was finally able to land, Nielsen had to be carried out. She was rushed back to the States, to further treatment and eventually, full health. At the South Pole, she left behind a very close group of friends—the closest she'd ever made—whom she calls modern-day heroes.

As a whole, *Ice Bound* is a good read, though at times the writing feels rushed and repetitive—perhaps a better editor was needed. Still, the book is full of fascinating details of life at the South Pole and a very realistic and moving account of cancer survival.

Finishing time: _____

C. *Write your finishing time and calculate your reading time: _____ How does this compare to your skimming time in Exercises 2 and 3?*

D. *Work with your partner. Can you retell the main points of the review? Did the review have a positive or negative opinion? Do not look back.*

E. *Check your understanding by reading the review again more carefully. Then discuss these questions:*

1. How is this autobiography different or similar to *Go Ask Alice*?
2. Do you know any other dramatic stories of survival from difficult conditions or from illness?
3. Does this book interest you?

Skimming for Research

When you are doing research for an assignment, skimming can help you find information quickly. It can also help you decide if a text will be useful for your research or not. Ask yourself, "What is it about?" or "Will it be useful?"

EXERCISE 5

A. *Work with another student. Read the title of the article. What is it about? Will it be useful to do research for a report about natural disasters?*

THE NEW YORK STAR   **January 13, 2010**

Devastating Earthquake Hits Haitian Capital

by Sandra Shaw and Nick Dormer

B. *Write your exact starting time. Then skim the article as <u>quickly</u> as you can to find out what it's about and if it will be useful.*

Starting time: _____

PORT-AU-PRINCE — A powerful earthquake struck Haiti late yesterday afternoon, causing major damage in the capital. Many buildings collapsed, including a hospital, the presidential palace, the headquarters for the United Nations peacekeeping force, and thousands of homes.

The earthquake, at 7.0 magnitude, was the worst to hit the country in over 200 years. According to the U.S. Geological Survey, it lasted around a minute and was quickly followed by two strong aftershocks.

As night fell in Port-au-Prince, the city was dark, except where fires burned in the downtown area. Telephones were also not working and relief workers had great difficulty making their way around the rubble in the streets. It was impossible for officials to determine the number of casualties, but they fear that deaths could be in the tens of thousands.

Most of the capital's three million people live in cheaply constructed concrete houses on hillsides.

Haiti, a former French colony, occupies half of the island of Hispaniola. It is the poorest nation in the Caribbean, and has been hit by frequently by hurricanes in the past decade. The lack of political stability has encouraged violence and prevented economic development.

Witnesses have reported seeing buildings of all sizes collapsed, and people trapped inside who could be heard screaming for help. In the streets, the scene was total chaos, with people running in all directions.

In the hours after the quake, the sky was grey with dust. Survivors remained outside, sitting in the streets. Many were in shock, with nowhere to go. Those with homes still standing are afraid to return to them.

With no sign of rescue workers, people are trying to dig under the rubble by flashlight to free those trapped under buildings.

The United States and other countries have given significant humanitarian support to Haiti, and funded a large United Nations peacekeeping force. According to reports, there had been significant progress in controlling crime and violence. There had also been some progress in raising the country's very low health and education levels.

After emergency meetings in Washington, President Obama stated that administration officials were closely monitoring the situation and "stand ready to assist the people of Haiti." The President said his "thoughts and prayers" were with the Haitians.

As news of the quake spread through the Haitian-American community last night, people were desperately trying to contact family members in Port-au-Prince, but communication with the city has not yet been established.

Finishing time: _____

C. *Write your finishing time and calculate your reading time: _____ How does this compare to your skimming time in other exercises?*

D. *Work with a partner. Retell the main points of the article.*

E. *Check your understanding of the article by reading it again more carefully. Then discuss these questions with your partner:*

1. How strong was the earthquake in scientific terms?
2. How serious was it in terms of damage to people and places?
3. Is there scientific information in the article?
4. Is there information about people's reactions?

A. *Work with another student. Read the title of the article. What is it about? Will it be useful to do research for a report about natural disasters?*

THE NEW YORK STAR   **February 27, 2010**

Chile Quake Displaces Millions

by Rosana Pineido and Sam Thorndike

B. *Write your exact starting time. Then skim the article as <u>quickly</u> as you can to find out what it's about and if it will be useful.*

Starting time: _____

SANTIAGO — Yesterday's 8.8-magnitude earthquake, which struck at 3:34 a.m. in central Chile, left hundreds of people dead and a section of the country in ruins. It was centered roughly 200 miles southwest of Santiago at a depth of 22 miles.

More than 1.5 million people have been displaced, according to local news services and the death toll, now estimated at about 200, is expected to rise.

The second-largest city, Concepción, was only about 70 miles from the quake's center and was hit hardest, with damage to highways and bridges and communications. Several buildings collapsed, trapping more than 100 people, and a biochemical lab at the university caught fire. Streets were filled with damaged cars, telephone wires and power cables.

In Talca, many older buildings were severely damaged and residents slept on the streets near open fires built with wood from destroyed homes. Large parts of the local hospital were in ruins, according to the local news network.

In Chillán, the wall of a prison collapsed, allowing 300 prisoners to escape. The police captured 60 of them, but more than 200 were still at large.

President Michelle Bachelet, speaking at a news conference on Saturday night, called the quake "one of the worst tragedies in the last 50 years" and declared a "state of catastrophe."

While this earthquake was far stronger than the 7.0-magnitude Haitian quake in January, the damage and casualties are likely to be far less devastating.

Whereas the Haitian quake was close to the earth's surface, causing violent to extreme shaking, the Chilean, which was much deeper (21 miles) caused only "severe" shaking, according to the U.S. Geological Survey. The Chile quake was also centered in an area with lower population density than the Haitian one.

Chile and the entire Andean ridge is subject to frequent earthquakes. The last major one, a 9.5 magnitude quake in 1960 killed nearly 2,000 people. After that disaster the country established strict building laws to regulate materials and construction methods. In yesterday's quake, most newer buildings survived the shocks. Damage was most extensive in older buildings.

In Haiti, by contrast, there is no building code. Furthermore, the people there had not experienced an earthquake in the past 200 years and were not trained in how to react as were Chileans.

The U.S. President Obama has expressed concern for the victims of the earthquake and has offered aid, though Chile's government has not yet requested assistance.

Finishing time: _____

C. *Write your finishing time and calculate your reading time:* _____ *How does this compare to your skimming time in the other exercises?*

D. *Work with a partner. Retell the main points of the article.*

E. *Check your understanding of the article by reading it again more carefully. Then discuss these questions with your partner:*

1. How does this earthquake compare to the one in Haiti in scientific terms?
2. How does it compare in terms of damage to places?
3. How does it compare in terms of casualties?
4. Why was the earthquake in Haiti more devastating than the one in Chile?
5. Were there any differences in the way people reacted to the two earthquakes?

Reflect on Your Learning

Discuss these questions with a partner.

1. Which of the text types in this unit was the easiest to skim? Why?
2. Which was the most difficult to skim? Why?
3. When you skipped part of the text, what was the reason?
   - It did not have important information or ideas.
   - You understood enough about the ideas already.
   - It was not interesting.
   - It was not necessary for the task.
   - Another reason: _____

Focus on Vocabulary

Target Vocabulary

Check your knowledge of these words and phrases. (Do not look in the dictionary.)

Mark each one: ✔ *You are sure of the meaning.*
                       ? *You have seen it before, but are not sure of the meaning.*
                       X *You have not seen the it before.*

____ injury	____ arise from	____ insensitive	____ range from
____ dominate	____ pressure	____ essential	____ substance
____ lead to	____ merely	____ potential	____ relief
____ damage	____ process	____ harm	____ release

EXERCISE 1

A. *Preview and then read the passage from a psychology textbook. Do not stop to look up new words.*

The Experience of Pain

If you are in severe pain, nothing else matters. An injury or a toothache can dominate all other sensations. And if you are among the one-third of Americans who suffer from constant or frequent pain, the experience can be debilitating[1] and can sometimes even lead to suicide.[2] Yet pain is also part of the way your body responds to conditions that could damage it.

Unlike other sensations, pain can arise from various kinds of causes, such as a very loud sound, a heavy pressure, a knife wound, or an extremely bright light. But pain is not merely the result of something outside the body. Many people who were born without a limb[3] or have had a limb amputated[4] feel painful sensations that seem to come from the missing part, often called a *phantom limb*. Neurological studies show that the painful phantom sensations do not come from damaged nerves[5]. Rather, the sensations arise in the brain itself. To understand pain, then we must understand not only painful sensations but also the way the brain processes pain.

---

[1]**debilitating** affecting your body in a way that prevents you from doing much
[2]**suicide** the act of killing oneself
[3]**limb** an arm or leg
[4]**amputated** cut off someone's arm, leg or finger in a medical operation
[5]**nerves** a long thin part of your body through which feelings and messages are sent to the brain

Dealing with Pain

Wouldn't it be nice to get rid of pain altogether? In reality, that could be deadly. Some people have a genetic condition that makes them insensitive to pain; they do not feel what is hurting them. Their bodies become scarred[6] and their limbs broken from injuries that a normal person could avoid. Because of their failure to notice and respond to the warning signs of pain, these people tend to die young. In general, pain serves as an essential defense signal that warns us of potential harm, and tells us to get treatment for sickness and injury.

What can you do if you are in severe pain? Pain-killing drugs, ranging from aspirin to prescription drugs such as morphine, are widely used and effective. These act in a variety of ways. Morphine, for example, acts much like substances your own body produces. However, all such drugs—especially the more powerful ones—can have unwanted side effects. These include addiction[7] or damage to organs.

Many people can learn to control pain by psychological techniques, such as hypnosis and deep relaxation. Others find relief by taking a *placebo*, a fake drug given in the place of real drugs. Its effectiveness, of course, depends on the person believing that they are getting real medicine. How is this possible? Apparently, the expectation of pain relief is enough to cause the brain to release its own painkilling substances.

[Adapted from *Psychology: Core Concepts*, 5th ed., by Philip G. Zimbardo, Robert L. Johnson, Ann L. Weber, Allyn and Bacon/Pearson, 2006, pp. 202- 203]

---

[6]**scar** to have a permanent mark on the skin after a cut or a wound
[7]**addiction** the inability to stop taking a drug or harmful substance

B. *Read the passage again. Circle all of the words and phrases from the target vocabulary list. Underline all of the words and phrases you don't know in the passage.*

C. *For each underlined word or phrase, look at the context (the words and sentences around it). Make a guess about the meaning. Write your guess in the margin in pencil.*

D. *Check your comprehension. Write T (True) or F (False) after each sentence.*

1. Very few Americans suffer from pain often. _____

2. Pain can come from outside the body or within the brain. _____

3. People who cannot feel pain usually do not live long. _____

4. There is no way to find relief from pain. _____

5. There are psychological ways to control pain. _____

E. *Check the dictionary for the words you are not sure about. Compare the definitions with your guesses in Part C. Change your guesses if necessary.*

F. *Compare your work with another student.*

A. *Match each target word to its definition. There is one extra definition.*

1. pressure (n)   a. not able to feel or react to small changes
2. potential   b. to be larger or more noticeable
3. harm (n)   c. a feeling of comfort or happiness when something bad has ended
4. range from   d. the force or weight put on something
5. relief   e. not yet real, but possible in the future
6. process (v)   f. to deal with, react to
7. insensitive   g. damage, injury or trouble
8. dominate   h. a subject or situation
                  i. to include one thing and another thing and anything in between

B. *Compare answers with another student.*

A. *Cross out the word or phrase in each group that is NOT a possible synonym for the target word.*

1. **injury**	wound	harm	damage	accident
2. **lead to**	drive	cause	produce	result in
3. **substance**	material	chance	thing	stuff
4. **release**	let go	set free	give out	make up
5. **essential**	different	basic	important	necessary
6. **arise from**	result from	order from	follow	come from
7. **merely**	only	simply	widely	just
8. **damage**	harm	hurt	injure	feel

B. *Compare answers with another student.*

A. Choose a word from the box to complete each sentence. Change the word to fit the sentence if necessary.

range from	damage	relief	process
release	substance	injury	pressure

1. The failure of one big bank can do great _____ to the whole economy.

2. In order to _____ the application, we need your signature on the form.

3. The company sells a variety of products, _____ sportswear to camping equipment.

4. The most common _____ for a skier is a broken leg.

5. If you cut yourself badly, you should apply _____ with a clean towel.

6. As part of the process of photosynthesis, plants _____ oxygen into the air.

7. When he saw Jody, Brett felt great _____. He had feared she might be lost.

8. Some kinds of fish can produce a black _____, like ink.

B. Compare answers with another student.

EXERCISE 5

A. Choose the word from the box that can be used with all the words in each group. You may use a dictionary.

injury	substance	potential	release
essential	relief	process	damage

1. _____ + needs / services / part

2. _____ + emotions / chemicals / prisoners

3. _____ + conflict / harm / sales

4. _____ + food / information / data

5. head / back / serious + _____

6. extensive / major / minor + _____

7. illegal / chemical / sticky + _____

8. disaster / pain / great + _____

B. *Compare answers with another student.*

EXERCISE 6

A. *Work with another student. Write different forms for each word. If you do not know a form, make a guess. Do not use the dictionary. (More than one answer is possible for some forms.)*

	Noun	Verb	Adjective	Negative Adjective	Adverb
1.		damage			X
2.		dominate		X	X
3.		X	essential		
4.	harm				
5.	injury				X
6.				insensitive	
7.		lead		X	X
8.			potential	X	
9.		process			X
10.		range	X	X	X
11.	relief			X	X
12.	substance				

B. *Compare your work with another pair.*

Vocabulary Review

- In your vocabulary notebook, write all the words from this Focus on Vocabulary section that you want to learn. Include the parts of speech, the sentences, and the definitions (See Part 2, Unit 1).
- Review your notebook (See Part 2, Unit 2).
- Make study cards of 10–15 words that you have trouble remembering. Study them alone and then with another student.

Reading Fluency

Introduction

Why Read Faster?

There are three important reasons for learning to read faster:

1. You can be a more efficient reader.
2. Your knowledge of English can improve.
3. Your comprehension can improve.

1. You can be a more efficient reader.

This will help you with homework, class work, and tests. It will also make reading books, magazines, and newspapers more enjoyable—so you'll probably read more.

2. Your knowledge of English can improve.

If you read faster, you will be able to read more. This way you will get more language input from your reading. You will see and think about more words and phrases, and you will have more practice getting meaning from sentences and longer passages. This will help you:

- learn more vocabulary
- understand how sentences work
- learn what words are used together
- become a better writer

3. Your comprehension can improve.

How is this possible? The answer is very simple: when you read slowly, you read one word at a time. Your eyes and your brain take in each word separately. This is like reading a text with extra spaces between the words.

EXAMPLE

Try reading these sentences with separated words. Is it easier or harder to read this way?

> What   really   happens   when   we   read?   Many   people
> think   we   read   one   word   at   a   time.
> They   think   we   read   a   word,   understand   it,
> and   then   move   on   to   the   next   word.

You probably found it harder to read this way. The separate words are separate pieces of information that your short-term memory must try to hold on to. With short sentences, this does not matter. But with longer sentences, it is a problem. You may not be able to keep the words in your memory long enough to make sense of the sentences.

When you read faster, on the other hand, you no longer take in the words one by one. You take in small groups of words that form ideas. Your brain can work more efficiently this way to make sense of the sentences and of the passage as a whole.

In fact, your brain automatically tries to group words together in a way that makes sense. (See Part 2, Unit 5: Collocations.)

You can hear how words are grouped together when you listen to fluent speakers, especially when they are reading aloud or giving a lecture or speech. They often make pauses between groups of words to allow listeners to understand better.

EXAMPLE

Read the sentences while your teacher reads them aloud. What groups of words do you hear?

What really happens when we read? Some people think we read one word at a time. They think we read a word, understand it, and then move on to the next word.

Different readers may group words somewhat differently, depending on how they interpret the text. Readers who are more fluent also tend to group more words together than slow readers. Here is the way a reader might group the sentences you read above:

What really happens / when we read? / Some people / think we read / one word at a time. / They think / we read a word, / understand it, / and then move on / to the next word.

When you read faster, you group words together naturally. This can help you better understand what you read.

Notes:
- With certain types of text, it is necessary to read slowly and carefully. This is true, for example, with directions, cookbook recipes, poetry, or technical explanations.
- You should not try to read faster all the time. Instead, you should be flexible in your reading, speeding up or slowing down as necessary.

Guidelines for Reading Faster

1. **Check your reading habits.**

   Some habits can slow you down when you are reading. Think about your own reading habits:

   ➤ *Do you try to pronounce each word as you read?*
   You will probably understand less this way. If you are trying to say and understand the words, your brain has to do two things at the same time. (You can practice saying the sentences <u>after</u> you read them silently.)

   ➤ *Do you move your lips when you read silently?*
   If you do, you are probably thinking each word to yourself. You will have the same problems as someone who pronounces the words.

   ➤ *Do you point at the words with your finger or a pencil?*
   If you do, your eyes will follow your finger or pencil word by word across the lines. However, your eyes need to be free to follow your thinking. You may want to go back and check a word or you may want to skip ahead.

   ➤ *Do you try to translate into your native language while you are reading in English?*
   If you do, you will have to stop often to think about the translation. This will make

it harder to think about the story or the ideas. It also means you will be thinking in your language, not in English.

2. Skip or guess unknown words.

➤ *Skip words that are not necessary for understanding the passage.*
It is not necessary to know the meaning of every word. You may be able to follow the story or understand the main idea even when there are words you do not know. (See Part 1, Unit 1, Exercise 1, page 4.)

➤ *Guess the general meaning of the words you need to understand the passage.*
From the words or sentences around it (the context), you can learn a lot about a word. It is often possible to understand the general meaning. This will allow you to continue reading and understanding the passage. (See Part 2, Unit 3 for more about guessing meaning.)

3. Practice reading faster by timing yourself.

Reading rate (speed) is partly a matter of habit (what you are used to doing). If you are used to reading at a certain rate, you continue to read at that rate.

Timed readings can help you break the habit of slow reading. When you read against the clock, you push yourself to read faster. This helps you change the way you read.

In the practice exercises, you will find out how fast you read now and how to time yourself. In the exercises in Units 1–3, you will work on improving your reading rate.

Read the guidelines before you start to work on the practice passages.

Guidelines for Timed Reading

1. Before you start, write down the *exact* time shown on your watch or clock (minutes and seconds).
2. Preview each passage quickly before reading it.
3. Read the passage and write down the exact time you finish.
4. Answer the questions without looking back at the passage. Do not look back at the passage. Then check your answers with your teacher.
5. Read the passage again. Look for the answers to the questions that you answered incorrectly.
6. Find your reading time (finishing time minus starting time) and find your reading rate on the Reading Rate Table on page 233.

   Example: *Finishing time:* 10:14:30 *(14 minutes and 30 seconds after 10 o'clock)*
   Starting time: 10:10:45
   Reading time: 4:15 *(4 minutes and 15 seconds)*

7. Write your reading rate and your comprehension score (the number of correct answers) on the progress charts on pages 234–236.
8. After reading four or five passages, check your progress.
9. If your reading rate has stayed the same, you should push yourself to read faster.
10. If you have more than two incorrect answers on any passage, you might be trying to read too quickly. Slow down a little and read more carefully.

A. *Write your starting time: _____ Preview and then read the passage.*

The Great Lisbon Earthquake

The first of November is an important Catholic holiday—All Saints' Day. On the morning of that day in 1755, the people in Lisbon, Portugal, were getting ready to celebrate the holiday. At 9:40 a.m., an earthquake hit the city. The ground shook for about five minutes. Buildings collapsed (fell down) and enormous cracks appeared in the earth.

5 Many people were trapped or killed by the collapsing buildings. Some of the survivors rushed down to the harbor. They felt safer in the open area by the sea. But the sea began to do strange things. The water was slowly pulled back further and further until they could see the harbor floor. Then in less than an hour, the sea came back in an enormous tsunami (giant wave). It filled the harbor and all of the downtown area, carrying away boats, people, horses,

10 carts—everything in its way.

In the parts of the city that were not flooded, fire broke out. It burned for five days. Many buildings that were still standing were then destroyed by the flames. These included the simple homes of poor people, as well as the palaces of the rich, including the Royal Ribeira Palace, home of the king.

15 The king and his family, however, were safe in their country home, where they had gone for the holiday. Afterwards, the king was afraid to return to Lisbon, and had a large tent city built outside the city for the royal family. The prime minister, the Marquis of Pombal, had also escaped death. He was a more practical person, and wasted no time on prayers or tears. The situation was dramatic. As many as 100,000 people had died, out of a population of 275,000.

20 Eighty-five percent of the city was in ruins.

The Marquis sent firefighters to try to control the fire. He organized teams to remove the bodies of dead people. Though it was against the Catholic religion, thousands of bodies were quickly buried at sea, to prevent the spread of disease. All healthy men were required to help clear the city of bodies and rubble (ruined buildings). To prevent disorder, people who stole

25 from abandoned buildings were punished by death.

In less than a year, the city was free of rubble (ruined buildings) and reconstruction had already started. The new city was more orderly and spacious, with large squares and wide streets. The new buildings were the first in the world designed to stay up in earthquakes. The marquis had wooden models built and tested them by marching soldiers and horses around

30 them. The new downtown, known as the *Baixa Pombalina*, remains one of the city's main attractions.

Apart from his modern ideas about cities, the Marquis was also modern in his interest in the earthquake. To gather information, he sent a questionnaire to every city and town, asking about the effects. One of the questions even asked about the behavior of animals just before the

35 earthquake. In fact, in Lisbon, there were reports that animals had behaved strangely and had run to higher ground before the tsunami.

The Lisbon earthquake had serious consequences for Portugal, bringing to an end a period of expansion overseas. It had consequences of a different kind in Europe, which had never seen a disaster of this size. Many philosophers were deeply affected, especially in their ideas about

40 religion. How could a whole city be destroyed, along with all its churches, and on a religious holiday, too? This was a time when science was leading people to question religious belief. For Voltaire and other important thinkers, the earthquake was proof that God did not exist.

B. *Write your finishing time: _____ Then turn the page and answer the questions.*

C. *Circle the best answers. Do not look back at the passage.*

1. Where did some survivors go right after the earthquake?
   a. to the royal palace
   b. into their homes
   c. to the harbor

2. The harbor and the downtown area were hit by _____.
   a. a tsunami
   b. a storm
   c. a fire

3. The fire after the earthquake _____.
   a. burned only the buildings of poor people
   b. did not damage many buildings
   c. destroyed buildings that were still standing

4. The new buildings after the earthquake _____.
   a. were exactly like the old ones
   b. were built outside the city
   c. were designed to be stronger

5. Which of the following was NOT mentioned in the passage?
   a. Bodies were buried at sea.
   b. The royal palace was rebuilt.
   c. Healthy men had to help clear the city.

6. We can infer from this passage that the Marquis of Pombal _____.
   a. was not strongly influenced by the Catholic religion
   b. believed strongly in the Catholic religion
   c. did not believe at all in the Catholic religion

7. Afterward, the Marquis wanted to know more about _____.
   a. the religious feelings of the people
   b. the effects of the earthquake
   c. the economy of the country

8. What fact about the earthquake influenced European thinkers?
   a. It took place on a Catholic holiday.
   b. The ground shook for five minutes.
   c. It was followed by a fire.

D. *Read the passage again. Try to read faster this time. Then look at the questions again and change your answers if necessary.*

E. *Calculate your reading time: Finishing time – Starting time = Reading: _____. Find your reading rate on page 233. Write it in the progress chart on page 234.*

F. *Check your answers to the questions with your teacher. Write your comprehension score (number of correct answers) in the progress chart.*

Check the answers to this Practice exercise on page 287.

Reading Rate Table

All of the passages are about 600 words long. To find your reading rate, find the reading time that is closest to yours. Then look across at the reading rate column.

Reading time (minutes)	Reading rate (words per minute)
1:00	600
1:15	480
1:30	400
1:45	343
2:00	300
2:15	267
2:30	240
2:45	218
3:00	200
3:15	184
3:30	171
3:45	160
4:00	150
4:15	141
4:30	133
4:45	126
5:00	120
5:15	114
5:30	109
5:45	104
6:00	100
6:15	96
6:30	92
6:45	89
7:00	85

Faster Reading Progress Charts

Under the exercise number, write your comprehension score (number of correct answers). Then check (✓) your reading rate. Write the date at the bottom of the chart.

Introduction

Unit 1

Exercise →	Practice	1	2	3	4	5	6	7	8
Comprehension Score →									
600									
480									
400									
343									
300									
267									
240									
218									
200									
184									
171									
160									
150									
141									
133									
126									
120									
114									
109									
104									
100									
96									
92									
89									
85									
Date									

Reading rate

Unit 2 Progress Chart

Under the exercise number, write your comprehension score (number of correct answers). Then check (✓) your reading rate. Write the date at the bottom of the chart.

Exercise →	1	2	3	4	5	6	7	8
Comprehension Score →								
600								
480								
400								
343								
300								
267								
240								
218								
200								
184								
171								
160								
150								
141								
133								
126								
120								
114								
109								
104								
100								
96								
92								
89								
85								
Date								

Reading rate

Unit 3 Progress Chart

Under the exercise number, write your comprehension score (number of correct answers). Then check (✓) your reading rate. Write the date at the bottom of the chart.

Exercise →	1	2	3	4	5	6	7	8
Comprehension Score →								
600								
480								
400								
343								
300								
267								
240								
218								
200								
184								
171								
160								
150								
141								
133								
126								
120								
114								
109								
104								
100								
96								
92								
89								
85								
Date								

Reading rate

Harry Houdini: The Life of an Escape Artist

A. *Write your starting time:* _____ *Preview and then read the passage.*

Arrival in Appleton

When Harry Houdini made his name at the beginning of the 20th century, there was, of course, no Internet. Television was still many years away, and even the radio was not yet sending music or voices over the air. All entertainment was "live." Real people performed—singing, dancing, acting, doing tricks—in real time in front of an audience.

The pop stars of the day were the performers who could bring crowds to the theaters. This was what Houdini dreamed of when he was a boy named Ehrich Weiss. He wanted to see his name in big letters outside a theater, his picture beside big headlines in the newspaper.

And he did. He became The Great Houdini, known around the world. Success did not come to him easily. He went through many years of hard times, but he was good at what he did, and he knew it. He did not give up. In the end, he became richer and more famous than he could ever have imagined.

According to his official life story, he was born in Appleton, Wisconsin. This was not true, however. He was actually born in Budapest, Hungary, in 1874. His father, Mayer Samuel Weiss, was a rabbi (a Jewish religious leader) and a well-educated man, with several university degrees. In Budapest, however, he was not able to make a good living. The family was poor, so two years after Ehrich was born, his father decided to go to America.

At that time, Jews in Hungary and other eastern European countries were often treated badly. Many were leaving for America. They had heard stories about the great riches in America. Though they may not have believed these stories, they did hope for better lives for themselves and their families. They thought there might be more opportunities in America for Jewish people.

From Budapest, Ehrich's father went straight to Appleton, Wisconsin. A group of families he knew had moved there and were looking for a rabbi. Two years later, his wife, Cecelia, and their five sons joined him in Appleton.

The family remained there for four years. Houdini remembered that time as the happiest years of his life. Appleton was a small market town surrounded by farms. The family lived over a shop on the main street. From their windows, they could watch the townspeople and farmers below. But the apartment was small, so most of their free time was spent playing outside in the park or in the fields.

The high point of each year was when the circus came to town. In the 19th century, these traveling circuses brought entertainment to small towns all around America. To advertise their shows, they would first parade through the streets. Then they would set up a big tent and perform for a day or two—with wild animals, clowns, acrobats, magicians, and more.

Like many other children, Ehrich loved going to the circus. He also loved pretending he was a circus performer. He especially liked doing acrobatic tricks on the trapeze (a bar hung by ropes from a high place). Unlike other children, however, he never got tired of these games. He practiced and practiced until he got very good.

Unfortunately, this happy life did not last. Ehrich's mother was a good housewife, but she could barely feed the family with her husband's pay. Then, after four years, he lost his job. The Jewish families in Appleton decided they wanted a rabbi who could speak English. Ehrich's father could speak German, Hungarian, Yiddish, and Hebrew. But he could not speak English, and he was not learning it fast enough.

B. *Write your finishing time:* _____ *Then turn the page and answer the questions.*

C. *Circle the best answers. Do not look back at the passage.*

1. What was the dream of Ehrich Weiss (Houdini)?

   a. to work for a newspaper
   b. to sing on the radio
   c. to perform in a theater

2. Ehrich Weiss (Houdini) was born in _____.

   a. Budapest, Hungary
   b. Appleton, Wisconsin
   c. New York City, New York

3. Why did Rabbi Weiss go to America?

   a. to work
   b. to study
   c. to start a family

4. We can infer from the passage that Jews in Eastern Europe _____.

   a. were treated the same as other people
   b. had few opportunities
   c. had great riches

5. Which of the following is NOT true about Appleton, Wisconsin?

   a. It was a small town.
   b. It did not allow Jewish families.
   c. It was home to some Jewish families.

6. When Ehrich (Houdini) was older, he said he _____.

   a. liked living in Appleton
   b. was unhappy in Appleton
   c. wanted to leave Appleton

7. We can infer from the passage that there were _____.

   a. traveling circuses only in Wisconsin
   b. many traveling circuses in America
   c. circuses only in big cities

8. Which of the following is NOT mentioned in the passage?

   a. Ehrich spent a lot of time practicing circus tricks.
   b. Ehrich enjoyed watching circus performances.
   c. Ehrich got tired of circus tricks after a while.

D. *Read the passage again. Try to read faster this time. Then look at the questions again and change your answers if necessary.*

E. *Calculate your reading time:* _____
Find your reading rate on page 233. Write it in the progress chart on page 234.

F. *Check your answers to the questions with your teacher. Write your comprehension score in the progress chart.*

A. *Write your starting time:* _____ *Preview and then read the passage.*

The Runaway

From Appleton, the Weiss family moved to Milwaukee, Wisconsin. But Ehrich's father did not have much luck finding work there, either. The only way he found to earn money was by giving Hebrew lessons. However, he could not earn very much this way.

Meanwhile, two more children were born and the Weiss family often had trouble paying
5 the rent and putting food on the table. The older Weiss boys left school to help support the family. When Ehrich was only eight years old, he worked after school selling newspapers and shining shoes.

In later life, Houdini preferred not to talk about those years in Milwaukee. But there were a few bright moments. When he was nine, friends in the neighborhood organized a children's
10 circus. They charged five cents, and each child did some tricks.

Ehrich's mother made him a costume, and he performed on the trapeze. He called himself "Eric, Prince of the Air" and his best trick was to pick up pins with his teeth. He also performed as a contortionist (a person who twists his body into strange positions). This early training on the trapeze and as a contortionist was useful for him later in life. It helped prepare
15 him for the kinds of tricks that made him famous.

Though Ehrich continued to work after school, he was earning very little. He wanted to earn more to help his family, so he decided to go to Texas. He had heard it was a good place to find a job. Since he knew his parents would not allow him to leave, he ran away. This was not a very well-planned escape. He took little food, clothes, or money. He also got on the wrong
20 train, so that he ended up in Kansas City, Missouri.

In Kansas City, he sent his parents a postcard. He told them not to worry. He was going to Texas to make some money and he would be back in a year. His mother kept the postcard, and after she died, he kept it. He never threw away anything with his signature on it.

He did not get to Texas. Instead, he walked out of Kansas City, hoping to find work on a
25 farm. But all he could find were small jobs and a free meal now and then. Walking and riding wagons, he made his way through the states of Missouri and Illinois.

One day, tired and hungry, he knocked on a farmhouse door in southern Wisconsin. A woman named Mrs. Flitcroft took one look at him and brought him inside. She gave him a good meal and a bath and sewed a hole in his pants. Ehrich remained there all winter. He
30 became good friends with her son Al. Along with helping on the farm, he also earned some money in the nearby town, which he sent home to his parents. For the rest of his life, he remembered how kind Mrs. Flitcroft had been.

While he was with the Flitcrofts, he got a letter from his mother telling him that his father had gone to New York City. He was hoping to find work as a rabbi there, since there was such
35 a large Jewish community. Ehrich left the Flitcrofts and moved east to be with his father.

Once again, Ehrich's father was unable to find any work except giving Hebrew lessons. For a boy like Ehrich, however, New York was full of opportunities. He quickly got work as a messenger for a department store. In a year, he and his father had saved enough money to bring the rest of the family to New York.

B. *Write your finishing time:* _____ *Then turn the page and answer the questions.*

C. *Circle the best answers. Do not look back at the passage.*

1. In Milwaukee, Ehrich's father _____.
   a. did not find a good job
   b. studied Hebrew
   c. worked as a rabbi

2. Which of the following is NOT true about the years in Milwaukee?
   a. The older boys worked.
   b. The family was poor.
   c. Ehrich was happy.

3. Who performed in the neighborhood circus?
   a. the parents
   b. the children
   c. professionals

4. Ehrich's practice with circus tricks as a child was _____.
   a. not good for his body
   b. a waste of time
   c. good for him later

5. Which of the following can be inferred from the passage?
   a. It was against the law for children to work.
   b. It was not unusual for children to work.
   c. All children were required to work.

6. Why did Ehrich run away from home?
   a. to get away from his family
   b. to see the country
   c. to help his family

7. Which of the following is NOT true about Mrs. Flitcroft?
   a. She felt sorry for him.
   b. She let him stay there.
   c. She sent him away.

8. In New York, Ehrich _____.
   a. had trouble finding work
   b. soon found a job
   c. returned to school

D. *Read the passage again. Try to read faster this time. Then look at the questions again and change your answers if necessary.*

E. *Calculate your reading time: _____*
Find your reading rate on page 233. Write it in the progress chart on page 234.

F. *Check your answers to the questions with your teacher. Write your comprehension score in the progress chart.*

A. *Write your starting time:* _____ *Preview and then read the passage.*

New York City

A photograph shows Ehrich Weiss at the age of 13 when he was a messenger boy for a department store in New York. He is a good-looking boy with a ready smile. At this age, he already seems to know how to get people's attention. Ehrich was then living with his family on East 69th Street. When he was 16, his father became ill and unable to work. Ehrich and
5   his brothers worked long hours at any job they could find. From the department store, Ehrich moved to a necktie factory.

At the factory, Ehrich worked nine or ten hours a day. That did not leave him much free time, but he made good use of every minute. He joined the Pastime Athletic Club and competed in swimming and running. Another photograph from this period shows him with
10   athletic medals pinned to his running shirt. He is clearly very proud, a young man who would not accept anything but first place.

Most of his free time, however, was spent practicing magic tricks. One of his brothers, Theo, had learned how to do a few magic tricks and taught them to Ehrich. At the factory, he made friends with Jacob Hyman, who was also interested in magic. They learned more tricks
15   and practiced together whenever they could. Ehrich also found out about magic tricks through books. He often stopped to look through the used books that were sold on the streets in those days. In fact, throughout his life, he loved books and reading. At the time of his death, he had an enormous collection of books on magic.

One day he found a book that changed his life—*The Memoirs of Robert-Houdin.* Until now,
20   Ehrich had never thought of magic as a possible profession. In this book, Robert-Houdin, a French magician, told the story of how he had started out poor and gained wealth and fame as a magician. Soon after reading this book, Ehrich left the necktie factory and convinced Jacob to leave too. They, too, would become famous magicians.

But first they needed a good stage name. In memory of the Frenchman, Ehrich decided
25   to call himself Houdini. The extra letter at the end made it sound better in English. For a first name, he took the nickname his friends used for him—Ehrie—and changed it to Harry. From then on, he was Harry Houdini. He and Jacob Hyman became the Brothers Houdini. He also copied Robert-Houdin's costume—a formal jacket and white shirt—not the long magician's robe that had been popular before.

30   Why did he give up his job and risk everything to become a magician? As an intelligent and ambitious young man, Ehrich wanted to make something of his life. A career on the stage was one way he could escape from poverty. As a Jew at that time, many professions were closed to him. A career in business might have been possible, or even in medicine (like one of his brothers), but it would not have been easy. He had had to leave school early, and his family was
35   unable to help him get started.

In any case, Ehrich/Harry was not interested in those careers. He was a born showman who loved an audience. Furthermore, on stage as a magician, he became more powerful. He was the one in control, who could make people believe whatever he wanted. On stage he also stood above the audience physically. This was important to him since he was quite short—only
40   5' 4" (162 cm). All his life, he stood very straight and tried to make himself seem taller.

B. *Write your finishing time:* _____ *Then turn the page and answer the questions.*

C. *Circle the best answers. Do not look back at the passage.*

1. Where did Ehrich work after he left the department store?

   a. on the streets
   b. at a tie factory
   c. in an Athletic Club

2. Which of the following is NOT mentioned in the passage?

   a. Ehrich enjoyed competing in sports.
   b. He enjoyed getting attention.
   c. He enjoyed wearing nice clothes.

3. Ehrich learned magic tricks _____.

   a. from his father
   b. anywhere he could
   c. at the necktie factory

4. Which of the following is NOT true about Ehrich?

   a. He liked reading and books.
   b. He liked doing sports.
   c. He liked playing music.

5. The book that changed his life was about _____.

   a. a very rich man
   b. a professional athlete
   c. a famous magician

6. Why did Ehrich change his name?

   a. Because he did not like his name.
   b. Because he did not want to be recognized.
   c. Because he needed a good stage name.

7. Which of the following can be inferred from the passage?

   a. Jews could have careers as performers.
   b. Jews were not allowed to perform on stage.
   c. Jews could not become businessmen or doctors.

8. On stage, Harry Houdini felt taller and _____.

   a. more handsome
   b. more powerful
   c. more educated

D. *Read the passage again. Try to read faster this time. Then look at the questions again and change your answers if necessary.*

E. *Calculate your reading time: _____*
Find your reading rate on page 233. Write it in the progress chart on page 234.

F. *Check your answers to the questions with your teacher. Write your comprehension score in the progress chart.*

A. Write your starting time: _____ Preview and then read the passage.

Dime Shows, Beer Halls, and Amusement Parks

New York, 1891. On the one hand, there was Fifth Avenue and the huge, elegant homes of people like the banker Henry Pierpont Morgan. On the other hand, there were thousands of poor immigrant families packed into apartments on dirty streets. This was the city where The Brothers Houdini started out.

5 They did their show anywhere and everywhere—street corners, beer halls, and amusement parks. Their show was simple: card tricks and disappearing tricks with coins, flowers, or other small things. Their only pay was the "throw money" that landed in their hat when people liked the tricks. Sometimes they were invited to perform in "dime museums." Inside these small museums, there were cages with strange animals and cases of unusual minerals. There was also a
10 small stage for performances by magicians, contortionists, or acrobats.

When they were not working, Harry and Jacob practiced their tricks. But after a year, even though they were getting much better, they were still earning less than in the necktie factory. Jacob decided to go back to the factory, so Harry got his brother Theo to come to work with him instead.

15 At this point, Houdini realized he needed to make their show more interesting. He got a new idea from a book about spiritualism (talking with the spirits of dead people). At the time, many people believed that it really was possible to speak with the dead. "Spiritualists" sometimes held performances that helped them believe this. They asked someone to tie them to a chair with a rope. Then, with the lights out, they untied themselves. Moving around the
20 room, they made strange sounds that people thought were spirits. Then they tied themselves up again before the lights were turned on.

Spiritualism did not interest Houdini, but he was very interested in rope escapes. Soon he also learned how to escape from handcuffs (metal rings used by the police) and how to open all kinds of locks. At about this time, he bought a magician's trunk (a large box used for traveling).
25 It looked like a regular trunk, but it could be opened from the inside. With the trunk and the ropes, he invented a new trick. In this trick, Theo tied Harry up with ropes, covered his head with a bag, and locked him in the trunk. Then he pulled across a curtain. In less than a minute, the curtain was pulled back again—by Harry. Theo was now tied up in the trunk.

With this trick, the Houdini Brothers were invited to a popular vaudeville theater. These
30 theaters offered eight to ten short shows—singing, dancing, magic, acrobatics, and clowning. This was inexpensive entertainment for ordinary families. The Houdini Brothers did some tricks with cards and coins, and then the trunk trick. For the first few nights, all went well and the audience was enthusiastic. But one night Theo made a mistake and the trick failed. After that, the director of the theater did not want them and they were back in the beer halls and dime shows.

35 In 1892, after a long illness, Harry's father died. Before dying, he made Harry promise to take good care of his mother. Harry kept that promise and remained very close to her until she died.

Not long after this, there was another big change in his life. While he and Theo were working in Coney Island, New York, he met a young woman named Wilhelmina Beatrice Rahner. Known to everyone as Bess, she was working in a song and dance act called the Floral
40 Sisters. Harry and Bess got married after they had known each other for just two weeks.

B. Write your finishing time: _____ Then turn the page and answer the questions.

C.   *Circle the best answers. Do not look back at the passage.*

1. When The Houdini Brothers started out _____.

   a. they did not earn any money
   b. people paid for tickets to see them
   c. people put money in a hat for them

2. Which of the following were NOT shown in dime museums?

   a. magicians and acrobats
   b. strange animals and minerals
   c. photographs and paintings

3. Why did Jacob decide to go back to the necktie factory?

   a. He did not earn enough money with magic.
   b. He liked working in the factory.
   c. He did not like working with spiritualists.

4. Which of the following can be inferred from the passage?

   a. Spiritualism did not have many followers.
   b. Spiritualism was popular in those days.
   c. Spiritualism was mostly for rich people.

5. From the spiritualists, Houdini learned _____.

   a. how to make strange sounds
   b. how to talk with dead people
   c. how to escape from ropes

6. What was special about the trunk trick?

   a. He changed places very quickly with Theo.
   b. He was locked in handcuffs and escaped.
   c. He talked with the spirits of dead people.

7. Which of the following was NOT true about vaudeville?

   a. There were lots of different short shows.
   b. It offered free beer and food.
   c. It was a cheap form of entertainment.

8. Soon after Harry's father died _____.

   a. Harry got married
   b. Harry's mother also died
   c. Harry started a song and dance act

D.   *Read the passage again. Try to read faster this time. Then look at the questions again and change your answers if necessary.*

E.   *Calculate your reading time: _____*
   Find your reading rate on page 233. Write it in the progress chart on page 234.

F.   *Check your answers to the questions with your teacher. Write your comprehension score in the progress chart.*

A. Write your starting time: _____ **Preview and then read the passage.**

On the Road

When they were married, Harry was 19 and Bess was 18. She was from an Irish-Catholic family, but the difference of religion did not seem to matter to them. By then, he was a handsome, strongly built young man. She was very pretty, and also very small, only 5' tall (152 cm). This helped make Harry seem taller on stage. Just as important, she could get in and out of the trunk more easily than Harry's brother. She soon took Theo's place on stage with Harry and the show was renamed The Houdinis.

Though they hardly knew each other before they married, their marriage was a happy one. They remained together, working and traveling side by side, until his death. Many other men—especially good-looking showmen like Houdini—might have run after other women. But he remained faithful to Bess, and she to him. No children were ever born, but if this caused unhappiness, they kept it to themselves.

Now that Bess was in the show, they were offered a job at a vaudeville theater. Harry hoped this was their big opening, but no other offers came along after that. They had to go back to dime museums and beer halls. Since the couple could not afford an apartment of their own, they lived with Harry's mother on 69th Street. Finally, they got an offer from the Welsh Brothers Circus in Pennsylvania. The pay was not much—$25 a week—but they also got meals and a place to sleep. This was not what they had been dreaming of, but it was a job.

And indeed, they worked very hard. They did magic shows and the trunk trick, as well as all kinds of other shows: singing, dancing, fortune telling, and anything else Mr. Welsh wanted. Harry even performed as a Wild Man who could only roar like an animal.

While they were traveling with the circus, they worked long hours. But they also made good friends, including a young couple named the Keatons who did a comedy act with their young son. Houdini gave him the nickname Buster that he used later in his films. Another friend was an elderly Japanese acrobat. He taught Harry a skill that he probably used later for his escape acts: how to swallow things, keep them in his throat, and then bring them back up to his mouth.

This was also when Houdini realized how to get free publicity. The first time was in Rhode Island. He invited a reporter to go to the police station with him. There he challenged the police chief to lock him up. The police chief put six pairs of handcuffs on him, locked him in a jail cell (locked room), and went away laughing. Minutes later, Houdini was laughing—and free. The next day there was an article in the newspaper and crowds of people to see his show.

But these were small-town shows. A year passed, then another year. Houdini was getting better and better at escaping from ropes, handcuffs, and jail cells. But he was still not famous. He and Bess could not even get regular work in the vaudeville theaters. They were still doing show after show every day and staying in the cheapest hotels.

By the fall of 1898, they were getting tired of this life. Houdini's brother-in-law offered him a job with a lock company, and he almost accepted it. He felt he had failed as a magician. In fact, he was so sure that his career was over that he offered to sell his magic secrets. Fortunately, no one wanted to buy them.

B. Write your finishing time: _____ **Then turn the page and answer the questions.**

C. *Circle the best answers. Do not look back at the passage.*

1. Which of the following was NOT mentioned in the passage?

   a. Bess was quite small.
   b. Bess was Catholic.
   c. Bess liked to read.

2. Which of the following can be inferred from the passage?

   a. Many showmen did not like young women.
   b. Many showmen did not get married.
   c. Many showmen did not have happy marriages.

3. After Bess started working with Harry _____.

   a. they did not get many jobs
   b. they got lots of jobs in theaters
   c. they moved into their own apartment

4. Harry and Bess got their first regular job _____.

   a. at a theater
   b. in a dime museum
   c. with a circus

5. Which of the following is NOT true about Harry's job at the circus?

   a. He had to sing and dance.
   b. He had to clean the animal cages.
   c. He played the part of a Wild Man.

6. While they worked for the circus, Harry learned _____.

   a. how to hide things in his throat
   b. how to do Japanese acrobatics
   c. how to do comedy films

7. How did Houdini get publicity?

   a. by going to Rhode Island
   b. by breaking out of a jail cell
   c. by writing an article in the newspaper

8. What did Houdini do when he thought his career was over?

   a. He went to work for a lock company.
   b. He decided to write a book.
   c. He tried to sell his secrets.

D. *Read the passage again. Try to read faster this time. Then look at the questions again and change your answers if necessary.*

E. *Calculate your reading time: _____*
Find your reading rate on page 233. Write it in the progress chart on page 234.

F. *Check your answers to the questions with your teacher. Write your comprehension score in the progress chart.*

A.   Write your starting time: _____ **Preview and then read the passage.**

Good Luck at Last

Before he gave up on his magic career, Houdini wanted to do one last tour in the Midwest. He decided that he would try once again to challenge the police, but this time he would do it in a big city. He went with reporters to the police in Chicago. They thought he was joking. But of course, for Harry Houdini, getting out of their handcuffs and cell locks was easy.

5   There was a huge crowd afterwards at his show in a dime museum. Houdini now invited people from the audience to lock him up. That evening a policeman came forward and put handcuffs on him. Houdini realized quickly that these cuffs were a problem. Though he worked on them for an hour, he could not open them. In fact, they had been jammed with metal so they could not open. The crowd was disappointed and left. The newspaper reporters
10   made fun of him.

At this point, Houdini wanted to go home, but the tour was not finished. They went on to Minneapolis, thinking this was the end of the road. In Minneapolis, however, Houdini finally had some good luck. It happened one night after the show. A well-dressed older man asked Harry and Bess out for dinner. He told them that Houdini was a talented showman, but they
15   were trying to do too many things too quickly. Audiences did not have time to enjoy the show. They should drop all the little tricks and do just the more unusual and spectacular ones. For a show like that, he offered them $60 a week. This was Martin Beck, manager of the biggest chain of theaters in the West and Midwest.

So Harry revised the show and they went out to San Francisco. Now they only did three
20   tricks: an escape trick, the trunk trick, and the Indian Needle-Swallowing Trick. This involved "swallowing" (eating) twenty or more needles (for sewing), "swallowing" a piece of thread, and then pulling the thread slowly from his mouth with all the needles attached.

How did he do this? He never told anyone. Why did audiences love it? Because of the way he did it. He was very dramatic and sometimes quite funny. For example, he said that he
25   swallowed the eyes of needles first (the eye is the hole in the needle), so the needles could "see on their way down."

In San Francisco, Houdini used reporters and the police to get attention again. Now he had no more trouble at his shows, and they were a huge sensation. He and Bess moved on to Los Angeles, and then to other cities. Beck raised their pay to $90 a week, then to $125. At
30   last, Harry and Bess did not have to worry about money. They could afford better costumes for the show and they could stay in nicer hotels.

However, by the summer of 1900, they had played at all the theaters managed by Beck. Houdini wanted to work in New York, of course, but Beck could not help him there. Instead, he advised Harry to go abroad. If he could become famous in Europe, he would have no
35   trouble getting work in New York. Harry and Bess got their passports and sailed for London.

In London, as usual, Houdini invited reporters to watch him challenge the police. This was Scotland Yard, the best of the best—or so they believed. They used their strongest handcuffs and locks on him, but that made no difference. In minutes he was free, and before long he was on the stage of the Alhambra Theater for $300 a week.

B.   Write your finishing time: _____ **Then turn the page and answer the questions.**

C. *Circle the best answers. Do not look back at the passage.*

1. Why did Houdini challenge the police in Chicago?

   a. to get the attention of the newspapers
   b. to make the policemen laugh
   c. to show they had bad locks

2. The show in Chicago failed because _____.

   a. not many people came
   b. the police closed the show
   c. he could not open the handcuffs

3. Which of the following is NOT mentioned in the passage?

   a. After Chicago, Houdini thought his career was over.
   b. Houdini did not want to go to Minneapolis.
   c. The police told him to leave Chicago.

4. Martin Beck told Houdini he should _____.

   a. do fewer tricks
   b. do more tricks
   c. dress differently

5. In Harry's new trick in San Francisco he _____.

   a. unlocked himself in the trunk
   b. pretended to swallow needles
   c. sewed something on stage

6. Why did people love the needle-swallowing trick?

   a. Because it did not always work.
   b. Because it was quite frightening.
   c. Because it was dramatic and funny.

7. Which of the following can we infer from the passage?

   a. People in New York followed fashions and trends in the West.
   b. People in New York did not care about fashions and trends.
   c. People in New York followed fashions and trends in Europe.

8. What was the result of his challenge to Scotland Yard in London?

   a. He got a job at the Alhambra Theater.
   b. He was unable to open the handcuffs and locks.
   c. The newspaper reporters laughed at him.

D. *Read the passage again. Try to read faster this time. Then look at the questions again and change your answers if necessary.*

E. *Calculate your reading time: _____*
Find your reading rate on page 233. Write it in the progress chart on page 234.

F. *Check your answers to the questions with your teacher. Write your comprehension score in the progress chart.*

A. *Write your starting time: _____ Preview and then read the passage.*

Houdini in Europe

Audiences at the Alhambra loved the Houdinis. Harry was entertaining, surprising, mysterious, thrilling. For six months, his shows were sold out. By then, news of the American escape artist had reached the continent. Soon he had bookings in Germany.

His first stop was Dresden. To get attention there, he decided to try something new. With heavy chains and handcuffs on him, he jumped off a bridge into a river. This meant he had to unlock handcuffs underwater, which was much more difficult.

But whenever Houdini did a new trick, he was always well prepared. He was a strong swimmer, first of all, and he had been practicing holding his breath underwater in the bathtub. In London, he had also collected European locks and handcuffs so he could study them carefully.

In Dresden, the police refused to give him permission to jump off the bridge. Houdini did it anyway—with newspaper reporters watching him of course. Once he was underwater, he stayed there for a very long time, probably more time than necessary to undo the locks. He was a showman after all, and he knew all about creating suspense. Several minutes passed and everyone was sure he had drowned. When he came to the surface at last, laughing and free of the chains, the crowd went wild.

News of the jump spread quickly. All over Germany, theater managers wanted Houdini. After Germany, he moved on to France, Holland, and then to Russia. He repeated the bridge jump many times, and continued to challenge the police wherever he went. He took off all his clothes when they locked him up, to show them he was not hiding anything (though they did not look in his throat, of course). He also had himself locked up in all kinds of different places. In Moscow, for example, he was locked into a Siberian prison van.

For the next four and a half years, he filled theaters around Europe. Now he could afford to bring over his mother and Theo from New York. He also could pay an assistant. Bess still helped in many ways, but she was happy not to be in his shows, especially the dangerous ones.

However, there was another side to success. Now and throughout his career, people accused him of fraud (not being truthful or real). They said he had a special key and that was how he got out. His answer to these people was always to challenge them—and then to escape.

There was no doubt that he could escape from almost anything. How did he do it? Lots of practice and training were probably part of the answer. He was in excellent shape physically until the day of his death. Did he have a tool hidden somewhere, perhaps in his throat? We will never know for sure. Houdini did not give away his secrets and neither did Bess, the only one who knew everything. In any case, the audiences did not care. They wanted drama, and he gave it to them.

By 1905, when Houdini was again in London, he was earning $2,000 a week. This was an enormous amount of money at that time. He was a rich man now. During a quick visit to New York, he bought a large house on West 113th street and invited his mother and brothers to move in. Then later that year, he got the offer he had been waiting for: $5,000 to perform in a New York theater. At last, he could return home in grand style and show America what he could do.

B. *Write your finishing time: _____ Then turn the page and answer the questions.*

C. *Circle the best answers. Do not look back at the passage.*

1. What did Houdini do in his new trick?

   a. He took off handcuffs on a bridge.
   b. He took off handcuffs underwater.
   c. He swam to a bridge with handcuffs.

2. Which of the following is NOT mentioned in the passage?

   a. Houdini prepared by jumping off lots of bridges.
   b. Houdini studied European locks and handcuffs.
   c. Houdini practiced holding his breath in the bathtub.

3. To create suspense, Houdini _____.

   a. stayed underwater longer than necessary
   b. pretended to die underwater
   c. waited a long time before jumping

4. What did Houdini do in Germany when he challenged the police?

   a. He hid a key in his clothes.
   b. He offered some money.
   c. He took off all his clothes.

5. Which of the following can we infer from the passage?

   a. Houdini's Jewish background was not a problem in Europe.
   b. His Jewish background was often a problem in Europe.
   c. His Jewish background was a problem only in Germany.

6. Which of the following is NOT mentioned in the passage?

   a. Houdini was in very good shape physically.
   b. He prepared his tricks carefully.
   c. He used a special key to escape.

7. Houdini did not want people to _____.

   a. see him with no clothes
   b. find out how he escaped
   c. read about his escapes

8. Why did Houdini return to New York?

   a. He was offered a lot of money.
   b. He wanted to be closer to his mother.
   c. He was not successful in London.

D. *Read the passage again. Try to read faster this time. Then look at the questions again and change your answers if necessary.*

E. *Calculate your reading time: _____*
Find your reading rate on page 233. Write it in the progress chart on page 234.

F. *Check your answers to the questions with your teacher. Write your comprehension score in the progress chart.*

A. *Write your starting time:* _____ *Preview and then read the passage.*

The Great Houdini

In America, Houdini soon realized he could not just repeat what he had done before. He had been welcomed back as The Great Houdini, and he had to prove that he was indeed great. Now he also had competition. Other magicians and escape artists were trying to steal some of his fame.

To keep ahead of them, his challenges became more and more spectacular. At the United
5 States Jail in Washington, D.C., for example, he got out of a locked cell on "Murderers' Row," got dressed, opened eight other locked cells, moved the murderers to different cells, and locked them up again—all in two minutes. When he wanted to work quickly, he could.

As for his other escapes, they became more difficult and dangerous. He jumped into the Detroit River when there was ice on it. In New York, he had himself locked into a box and
10 then thrown into the East River. For some stage performances, he was locked into a giant milk can filled with water. In a new kind of trick, he was hung up by his feet high off the ground in a straitjacket (a tight jacket used on violent mentally ill people). Thousands of people would gather below him to watch this. Bess refused to watch, but these tricks kept his name in the newspapers.

15 In 1908, he found yet another way to bring attention to himself—in an airplane. Flying was still very new and dangerous when Houdini bought an airplane and taught himself how to fly. Then in 1910, he took it with him on a tour to Australia. He made the first successful flight in Australia, staying up in the air for three and a half minutes. After this, however, Houdini gave up flying. It may have been too dangerous, even for him.

20 During the First World War, Houdini stayed in America. He performed around the country, sometimes as an escape artist and sometimes as a magician, making things disappear. In one famous performance in New York City, he somehow managed to make a live elephant named Jeannie disappear from the stage.

After the war, Houdini became interested in a new form of entertainment—the cinema.
25 Over the next few years, he made a number of films, all written especially for him with dramatic escape scenes. For example, *The Man from Beyond,* showed Houdini rescuing the heroine as her canoe rushed toward Niagara Falls. People liked these scenes, which he did himself. However, the movies had little else to offer and were not very successful financially, so he returned to the stage.

30 How much longer could he have continued with his difficult escapes? He was still rich and famous and still in excellent physical shape, but he was getting older. And then, very suddenly, his career and life came to an end when he was 52.

It did not happen during one of his escapes, as Bess had feared. His death was caused by appendicitis. On stage, Houdini often invited people to punch him in the stomach, so they
35 could feel his strong muscles. One evening after a show in Montreal, a student punched him before he was ready. This may have caused his appendix to burst (break open).

Houdini did not feel well the next day, but he did not cancel his show. Against the advice of doctors, he traveled to Detroit and even managed to do a show there. But then he collapsed. The burst appendix had caused a massive infection. In those days before antibiotics, there was
40 nothing doctors could do at that point. He died on October 31, 1926—on Halloween.

B. *Write your finishing time:* _____ *Then turn the page and answer the questions.*

C. *Circle the best answers. Do not look back at the passage.*

1. Why did Houdini need to make his tricks more dramatic?

   a. to get more work in New York
   b. to earn enough money for his family
   c. to compete with other magicians

2. On "Murderer's Row" in Washington DC, Houdini _____.

   a. stayed far away from the murderers
   b. showed he was not afraid of murderers
   c. let all the murderers leave the jail

3. What did Houdini do in one of his most dangerous tricks?

   a. He climbed a high tower.
   b. He was hung upside down.
   c. He jumped into a swimming pool.

4. Why did Houdini learn how to fly planes?

   a. to fly over crowds
   b. to get publicity
   c. to have fun

5. Which of the following is NOT mentioned in the passage?

   a. Houdini jumped into a frozen river.
   b. Houdini escaped from an airplane.
   c. Houdini made an elephant disappear.

6. Why did Houdini start making movies?

   a. Because he wanted to move to Hollywood.
   b. Because he wanted to stay popular.
   c. Because he liked watching movies.

7. Which of the following is NOT mentioned in the passage?

   a. He was still very famous when he died.
   b. His career was ending before he died.
   c. He was still in good physical shape when he died.

8. Which of the following can we infer from the passage?

   a. Houdini knew he was very ill in Montreal.
   b. Houdini often missed shows because of illness.
   c. Houdini did not like to disappoint his audience.

D. *Read the passage again. Try to read faster this time. Then look at the questions again and change your answers if necessary.*

E. *Calculate your reading time: _____*
Find your reading rate on page 233. Write it in the progress chart on page 234.

F. *Check your answers to the questions with your teacher. Write your comprehension score in the progress chart.*

UNIT 2 — Making a Living

EXERCISE 1

A. *Write your starting time:* _____ *Preview and then read the passage.*

Delivering Lunches in Mumbai (India)

No other city in India or in any country has a system like this. The men who make it work are called *dabbawallas*. In Hindi, *dabba* means box and *walla* is a person who holds or carries something. The 5,000 dabbawallas carry lunch boxes—about 175,000 per day—to offices around the city.

Dabbawallas are almost all men. They come from poor families in villages outside Mumbai, and most of them have not had much schooling. Many cannot read or write at all. But their system works almost perfectly, thanks to good timing, strong teamwork, and a special code with numbers and colors. Business schools in England and the United States have studied the system. According to these studies, the lunch boxes are delivered to the right place 99.9999 percent of the time.

The system was started in the late 19th century by a man named Mahadeo Havaji Bacche. He noticed that lunch was often a problem for workers in government offices in Mumbai. It took too long for them to go home for lunch, but there were few good, inexpensive restaurants. In any case, most Indians preferred a home-cooked meal to a restaurant meal. So Mahadeo hired 100 young men and started a lunch delivery service.

Since then, it has grown and is continuing to grow. One reason is that it costs very little, only 300 rupees or $7.00 per month. The other reason is that most Indians still prefer a home-cooked lunch. They cannot bring it themselves because they often have a long trip to work and leave very early in the morning before lunch can be prepared.

How does it work? Each lunch box is usually handled by three or four different dabbawallas. The first one picks up 30–40 lunch boxes, mostly from homes, though occasionally these days, they are ordered from hotels or restaurants.

One by one, the dabbawalla picks up the lunch boxes and hangs them on his bicycle. Each of the round metal boxes has a long handle for this purpose. The bicycle is a very important piece of equipment for the job. It must be a good strong bicycle, since each lunch box can weigh two to three pounds. In fact, to start the job, a dabbawalla must have two bicycles—in case of mechanical problems—as well as the traditional white uniform (clothes for work). The total cost of this equipment is about 5,000 rupees, or $120. That is about what the dabbawalla will earn in a month, much more than they could earn in their villages.

By 9:00 a.m., the lunch boxes must all be at the nearest train station. Time management is an important part of the system. A worker who cannot be perfectly on time will not last long in this job. At the train station, a second dabbawalla sorts through all the lunch boxes. Each has a code with colored numbers painted on the top. They are put into large wooden boxes and then onto trains that will bring them to the station nearest the customer's office. On each train, a third dabbawalla travels with the crates.

A fourth dabbawalla picks up the lunch boxes when they arrive and delivers them to the offices, by bicycle or with a cart. By 12:30 each person has received their home-cooked meal. In the afternoon, the empty lunch boxes are brought back to the homes the same way. Each dabbawalla gets to know his area and his part of the system very well, and the service goes on in every weather, even the worst of the monsoon rains.

B. *Write your finishing time:* _____ *Then turn the page and answer the questions.*

C. *Circle the best answers. Do not look back at the passage.*

1. A dabbawalla is a person who _____.
    a. works in an office
    b. delivers lunches
    c. cooks meals

2. Which of the following is NOT true about the dabbawallas?
    a. They are not well educated.
    b. They come from villages outside Mumbai.
    c. They take special courses to train for the job.

3. Why are business schools interested in the dabbawalla system?
    a. It works very well.
    b. It is not expensive.
    c. It uses a special code.

4. The dabbawalla system was started _____.
    a. in 1999
    b. 30–40 years ago
    c. more than a hundred years ago

5. Which of the following is NOT mentioned in the passage?
    a. People want to help the dabbawallas.
    b. The dabbawalla system is not very expensive.
    c. Most Indians prefer home-cooked meals.

6. Which of the following can be inferred from the passage?
    a. In most Indian families, people eat out often at restaurants.
    b. In most Indian families, both men and women work in offices.
    c. In most Indian families, someone stays at home and cooks meals.

7. What do all dabbawallas need for the job?
    a. knowledge of English
    b. two bicycles
    c. a cell phone

8. Which is most important for a dabbawalla?
    a. being on time
    b. being polite
    c. being careful

D. *Read the passage again. Try to read faster this time. Then look at the questions again and change your answers if necessary.*

E. *Calculate your reading time: _____*
Find your reading rate on page 233. Write it in the progress chart on page 235.

F. *Check your answers to the questions with your teacher. Write your comprehension score in the progress chart.*

A. *Write your starting time*: _____ *Preview and then read the passage.*

Dog Sitting in New York City (United States)

In some ways, it is easier than babysitting. The dogs do not cry and ask for their mothers. The sitters do not have to help with homework or read bedtime stories. But it is probably more tiring physically. Walking the dogs is a large part of the job. Rain or shine, snow or ice, the dogs need to get out, and the dog sitters have to take them.

Some dog sitters take out groups of dogs together. This is a common sight in Central Park—the dog sitter with four or five dogs trotting along at the end of their leashes (the ropes attached to the dogs' collars). But this only works for experienced dog walkers, and only with well-trained dogs. Otherwise the dogs are soon pulling in all directions.

Most of the time, dog sitters take out one dog at a time. It is easier for the dog sitters, better for the dogs, and preferred by the owners. Before a sitter starts with a new dog, there is always a meeting with the owner. The pet owners are like parents choosing a babysitter. They need to be sure that this is the right person. Like parents, too, many pet owners feel bad about being away at work all day. They wish they could spend more time with their pets. They are often willing to pay extra to make sure their pets have good care.

This is especially true when the owners go away for work or vacation. They may ask the dog sitter to come to their home for an hour in the morning and evening. Or they may ask for overnight sitting. While the owners are away, the sitters will keep in touch with them by email. They send reports on the day's activities, along with pictures of the dog. Owners on vacation may also ask the sitter to take care of other pets in their home, including cats, fish, and birds. These animals do not need to go out for walks every day, but they do need food and attention.

All kinds of people work as dog sitters. Some who are students in high school or college do it only part time. For others it is a full-time profession. There are men and women, young and middle-aged dog sitters. The one thing they all have in common is their love for animals. They enjoy spending hours with them day after day. These pet professionals also are able to understand what the dogs need, what makes them happy. And they have a lot of patience.

As a profession, dog sitting is not very well known. In fact, most dog sitters have gone into it by chance. They may have heard about it from a friend or seen an advertisement. Then they thought, "There's the job for me." People who used to work in offices enjoy spending time outdoors. They also like working independently, with no boss checking on them all the time. They are not completely free, however. The dogs need to go outside at regular hours. Arriving late to walk a dog may mean unpleasant surprises.

There are certainly times when the job is not fun. Cleaning up after the dogs can be tiresome. (It is the law in New York City.) There can be difficulties with some dogs. They may bark, pull at the leash, or make a mess in the wrong places. Some can even become aggressive (angry) with the dog sitter or with other people or dogs. But these bad moments are rare. Most dogs just want to be loved and are easy to love in return.

B. *Write your finishing time*: _____ *Then turn the page and answer the questions.*

C. **Circle the best answers. Do not look back at the passage.**

1. What is dog sitting compared with in the passage?
   a. babysitting
   b. owning pets
   c. cleaning homes

2. What takes up the most time for a dog sitter?
   a. feeding the dogs
   b. talking to the dogs
   c. walking the dogs

3. Before starting a new job a dog sitter _____.
   a. meets with the owner
   b. checks the Internet
   c. takes a walk with the dog

4. Which of the following is NOT true about the dog owners?
   a. They care about their pets.
   b. They all earn a lot of money.
   c. They feel bad about staying away.

5. Dog sitters sometimes use email to _____.
   a. tell owners on vacation about their dogs
   b. keep in touch with other dog sitters
   c. find good places for walking dogs

6. What do the dog sitters like most about their job?
   a. They earn a lot of money.
   b. They spend a lot of time with animals.
   c. They meet the owners of the dogs.

7. Which of the following is NOT mentioned in the passage?
   a. Dog sitters like being independent.
   b. Many retired people work as dog sitters.
   c. Dogs need to go outside regularly.

8. In New York, people _____.
   a. have to clean up after their dogs
   b. never clean up after their dogs
   c. always let their dogs make a mess

D. **Read the passage again. Try to read faster this time. Then look at the questions again and change your answers if necessary.**

E. **Calculate your reading time: _____**
   Find your reading rate on page 233. Write it in the progress chart on page 235.

F. **Check your answers to the questions with your teacher. Write your comprehension score in the progress chart.**

A. *Write your starting time:* _____ *Preview and then read the passage.*

Okada Driving in Lagos (Nigeria)

Lagos is an enormous city—over 15 million people at the last count. Getting around can be a problem. One solution is to take an *okada*, a motorcycle taxi.

The name came from Okada Airlines, which used to fly between cities in Nigeria. It was not known for comfort, but it was popular. The planes usually got to places more or less on time. When the first motorcycle taxis appeared in the late 1980s, some of the drivers started using that name. They liked to think they were flying over the roads. The airline stopped flying, but people continued to use the name for the motorcycle taxis. Now there are many thousands of *okadas* in Lagos, as well as in other Nigerian cities.

The *okada* drivers are all young men. They usually have little education or training. If they were not driving an *okada*, they would probably be jobless. As *okada* drivers, they can at least earn a living. There is plenty of work for all of them. However, they are never able to save much money because of all their expenses. The biggest expense is the rent for their motorcycles. These days, it is possible to buy Chinese motorcycles quite cheaply in Nigeria. However, they still cost too much for many drivers. They usually have to rent a motorcycle from a company. The prices charged by these companies can be quite high.

Then there are other expenses. The driver has to pay for gas and repairs to the motorcycle. Many drivers also have to rent space somewhere for the motorcycles. In Lagos, things cannot be left outside on the streets at night. Even a locked motorcycle will probably be gone in the morning. Another expense for the drivers is buying helmets. Two are now required for each driver—one for him and one for the passenger. A good helmet can cost $25–50, or several weeks of earnings. Drivers and passengers are fined if they are caught without helmets. Many *okada* drivers, however, just pretend to wear a helmet. It may really just be a piece of plastic or an empty gourd (vegetable like a pumpkin).

Safety is not a big concern in Lagos, but it should be. The traffic is terrible, with lines of stopped cars, trucks, and busses that hardly move for hours. This has helped the *okada* business, since the motorcycles can usually get around the traffic. But when the traffic is moving, accidents are more and more common. Almost 70 percent of them involve *okadas*. All too often, drivers or passengers are hurt or killed.

One reason for all the accidents is poor driving. Nigerian drivers in general do not follow the rules of the road. The *okada* drivers are even worse. They drive very fast. And to get around a traffic jam, they drive through lines of cars, onto sidewalks, or even on the wrong side of the road. Many Nigerians think the government should make it more difficult for all drivers, and especially *okada* drivers, to get a driver's license. They are required to get a license now, but all they have to do is pay for it. They do not have to take courses in road safety or have training on the road. In fact, many *okada* drivers have had very little experience on motorcycles before they start carrying passengers.

Another reason for the accidents is probably the condition of the roads. In fact, the roads are full of holes, and they are often blocked by broken-down trucks, parked cars, or outdoor markets. To make matters worse, traffic lights often do not work.

B. *Write your finishing time:* _____ *Then turn the page and answer the questions.*

C. *Circle the best answers. Do not look back at the passage.*

1. The first motorcycle taxis were called *okadas* because _____.
   a. they had wings like airplanes
   b. they were comfortable to ride on
   c. they could get places on time

2. Which of the following is NOT true about *Okada* drivers?
   a. They used to drive regular taxis.
   b. They are not well educated.
   c. They are young men.

3. Which of the following can be inferred from the passage?
   a. Bus tickets are expensive in Lagos.
   b. Many people in Lagos travel by *okada*.
   c. Many *okada* drivers later buy a car.

4. Why do most *okada* drivers rent motorcycles?
   a. They cannot afford to buy one.
   b. The rent is very cheap.
   c. The rental companies pay for gas.

5. Which of the following is NOT mentioned in the passage?
   a. Motorcycles cannot be left outside in Lagos.
   b. They have to pay for repairs to their motorcycles.
   c. Gas and motorcycle parts are not expensive in Nigeria.

6. What are *okada* drivers required to do?
   a. take a course on the rules of the road
   b. wear helmets and have helmets for passengers
   c. have experience riding motorcycles

7. As traffic gets worse in Lagos, the *okada* drivers are _____.
   a. getting more passengers
   b. not finding as many passengers
   c. not getting any work

8. To get an *okada* license now, drivers have to _____.
   a. attend a course
   b. take a road test
   c. pay some money

D. *Read the passage again. Try to read faster this time. Then look at the questions again and change your answers if necessary.*

E. *Calculate your reading time:* _____
Find your reading rate on page 233. Write it in the progress chart on page 235.

F. *Check your answers to the questions with your teacher. Write your comprehension score in the progress chart.*

A. *Write your starting time:* _____ *Preview and then read the passage.*

Street Performing in Paris (France)

At any time of year, the streets of Paris are full of tourists. They come from around the world to see the museums and the sights, and their pockets are full of euros. That is why the streets are also full of performers. They are hoping the tourists will give them some euros after a performance.

5   Paris has a long tradition of street entertainment. Performers have been on the streets of the city for hundreds of years. In the past, whole families often worked together on their outdoor shows. These shows included music, performing animals such as monkeys or bears, juggling (throwing and catching things), and acrobatics (jumping, bending, gymnastics). A highlight in many shows was the tightrope walking. A rope was tied
10 between two high points, and a member of the group would climb up and walk out on the rope. Good tightrope walkers could dance on the rope and juggle things.

    Back then, the performances were welcomed by the common people. These street shows were free, and were almost the only entertainment for poor people. Many of the performers were foreign. They often did not have real homes and they were usually very
15 independent-minded, like artists and performers everywhere. For all these reasons, they were not loved by the rich people in Paris. To them, the street performers were no better than beggars (people who ask for money). So the police would arrest them regularly and put them in prison or send them away. But the performers always came back to the streets.

20   These days, too, there is often tension in Paris between the street performers and the police. The city laws allow street performances in some places, but only under certain conditions. The performers should not make too much noise, and they should not occupy too much space. But how much is too much? The laws are not very clear about this. On one day, a policeman will allow a performance. On another day, a different policeman will
25 not. The performers are never sure what they are allowed to do.

    But this is not enough to keep them off the streets. Today's street performers tend to be more specialized than in the past. There are musicians, each playing a different kind of music: classical, jazz, rock, Senegalese, Brazilian, Irish, or Balkan. Some play alone on a street corner—a solo violin, a guitar, or a one-man band. Others play in groups in a square
30 or in front of a museum. This is how some musicians in the past started their careers, including the famous French singer Edith Piaf. Some of the young musicians today may dream of fame. Others are probably just hoping to earn enough so they can stay in Paris for a while longer.

    Other performers do "circle shows." This is when the audience is invited to make a
35 circle around the performer or performers. Then the show begins—juggling, acrobatics, clowning, dancing, magic tricks, or miming (storytelling without words). Good performers try to involve the audience. They want to surprise people or make them laugh. They often ask people in the audience, especially children, to take hold of things or help in some way.
40   In Paris today, you are not likely to see the king of performers—the tightrope walker. Some of the most famous tightrope walkers of the past have been French. And they have done some dramatic walks in Paris. In 1972, for example, Philippe Petit walked between the towers of Notre Dame (with no safety net). But back then, people worried less about safety. Something like that would probably not be allowed today.

B. *Write your finishing time:* _____ *Then turn the page and answer the questions.*

C. *Circle the best answers. Do not look back at the passage.*

1. Why are there so many street performers in Paris today?

    a. There are lots of rich tourists in Paris.
    b. The streets are wide in Paris.
    c. There are no laws against them.

2. Which of the following is NOT mentioned in the passage?

    a. In the past, street performers performed in theaters.
    b. In the past, animals were included in street performances.
    c. In the past, families of street performers worked together.

3. What kind of people watched the street performers in the past?

    a. foreign people
    b. rich people
    c. poor people

4. The rich people did not like the street performers because _____.

    a. they were foreign and independent-minded
    b. they used animals in their shows
    c. they did things that were dangerous

5. Today, street performers are _____.

    a. sometimes allowed to perform
    b. never allowed to perform
    c. allowed to perform only on weekends

6. Which of the following can you infer from the passage?

    a. Street performers today do not make much money.
    b. Many of today's street performers will become famous.
    c. Some street performers today earn enough to live in Paris.

7. Which French performer is NOT mentioned in the passage?

    a. Edith Piaf
    b. Marcel Marceau
    c. Philippe Petit

8. Why will you probably not see tightrope walking in Paris today?

    a. People think it is too dangerous.
    b. No one knows how to do it anymore.
    c. No one is interested in it now.

D. *Read the passage again. Try to read faster this time. Then look at the questions again and change your answers if necessary.*

E. *Calculate your reading time: _____*
Find your reading rate on page 233. Write it in the progress chart on page 235.

F. *Check your answers to the questions with your teacher. Write your comprehension score in the progress chart.*

A. *Write your starting time:* _____ *Preview and then read the passage.*

Painting in Lishui (China)

The Chinese government called the project the *Lishui Barbizon*. They wanted to give it some of the importance of the French Barbizon painters of the 19th century. These painters were the first to work outdoors and to paint real scenes of farms and villages.

5 Lishui, China, is not at all like the French countryside. It is a medium-sized industrial city in southwest China. Like many Chinese cities today, it is full of new buildings, mostly factories. It might not be the first choice for young Chinese artists. They would probably prefer to live in Beijing or another big city. But when the government offered free rent in an old building by the river, artists soon arrived. Now there are 12 galleries (art shops). Some are small, a room with a single artist or a couple working together. Others are much bigger, with 20 or 30 artists.

10 These galleries are not like galleries in most other places. There are paintings on the walls, but showing the art is not so important here. In fact, people rarely come to look at the paintings. Instead, the galleries are used mainly as workspaces for the artists.

About once a month, the gallery owners or artists travel to the nearby city of 15 Guangzhou. There they go to the big art market and sell their paintings to Chinese buyers. In turn, these buyers send the paintings to online companies or galleries, who sell them to customers in France, Germany, Russia, Australia, United States, or other countries. Like the factories in Lishui, the painters work almost entirely for foreign customers.

20 What kinds of pictures do these customers want? Scenes from Europe are very popular, such as St. Mark's Square in Venice, the Eiffel Tower in Paris, or a canal in Amsterdam. Working from postcards or photographs, the artists may do 20 or 30 pictures of the same scene in a year. They also paint pictures of waves breaking on rocks, or mountain villages under snow, or farms and fields. In general, the customers like scenes 25 that are colorful and realistic, and that remind them of happy vacations. Sometimes, however, people have special requests. They send photographs and ask for paintings of their houses or the main street of their town.

When working on these scenes, the artists have to be careful to get the details right. Famous buildings have to look real, for example, and the language on street or shop signs 30 has to be correct. This is sometimes a problem for the artists, who do not speak French or Italian or Dutch. If there are serious mistakes, the pictures may be sent back. This is one reason why the artists do not mind painting the same scene many times. They are less likely to make mistakes on familiar scenes. They can also get the pictures done sooner.

Painters with some experience can work quite quickly. They can finish a medium-35 sized painting in just two days. This is possible because they waste no time trying to be creative. They do not try to build on Chinese or on Western artistic traditions. Most of them have some training in art, at high school or college. But they do not think of themselves as artists. People around the world like their paintings and buy them, and that is enough.

40 Would these artists like to visit the places they are painting? Perhaps someday. At the moment, however, they are making a good living—a very good living compared to a factory worker. Their goal is to save up some money so they can move to Guangzhou or Beijing.

B. *Write your finishing time:* _____ *Then turn the page and answer the questions.*

C. *Circle the best answers. Do not look back at the passage.*

1. Why did the Chinese government call the project the *Lishui Barbizon*?
   a. That was the name of the city.
   b. They wanted French painters.
   c. It sounded French and important.

2. Artists moved to Lishui mainly because _____.
   a. they wanted to paint outdoors
   b. they were given free rent
   c. they liked French art

3. Which of the following is NOT mentioned in the passage?
   a. Some galleries are owned by artists.
   b. Not many people come to the galleries.
   c. Some galleries also sell photographs.

4. Most of the paintings are sold to people _____.
   a. outside China
   b. in other Chinese cities
   c. in Lishui

5. What kinds of painting are popular?
   a. pictures of the Chinese countryside
   b. pictures of famous people around the world
   c. pictures of popular European tourist places

6. Paintings are sometimes sent back when _____.
   a. the artist makes a mistake in a scene
   b. the picture is the wrong color
   c. the price is too high

7. Which of the following is NOT true about the artists?
   a. Most of them have some art training.
   b. Many of them can work very quickly.
   c. The artists are interested in Chinese art.

8. Which of the following can you infer from the passage?
   a. The artists do not enjoy painting pictures.
   b. The artists care most about earning a living.
   c. The artists want to learn more about European art.

D. *Read the passage again. Try to read faster this time. Then look at the questions again and change your answers if necessary.*

E. *Calculate your reading time: _____*
Find your reading rate on page 233. Write it in the progress chart on page 235.

F. *Check your answers to the questions with your teacher. Write your comprehension score in the progress chart.*

A. *Write your starting time*: _____ *Preview and then read the passage.*

Butterfly Farming in the Kakamega Forest (Kenya)

The women used to sell boiled eggs at the bus station, or they grew vegetables that they sold at the market. The men worked in the forest, cutting trees or hunting animals. Their earnings were never more than a few dollars a week. Then they found out about butterfly farming.

5   Since they started their farms and started selling butterflies, everything has changed. With the money they are now earning, they can put food on the table. They can send their children to school or to the doctor. At the same time, they no longer have to do back-breaking work in the fields or forest. No more digging, planting, or pulling weeds (unwanted plants) under a hot sun.

10   Farming butterflies does not require great strength. It also does not require much land or a lot of money to get started. All a farmer needs is a small piece of land with wild plants growing on it. Around these plants, the farmer builds a large cage. Getting the material for this cage is the only real expense for the farming. The only other piece of equipment they need is a butterfly net.

15   Once the cage is built, the farmer goes into the forest with the net to catch a few female butterflies. These are kept in the cage until they lay their eggs—a month or less. The eggs are collected and cared for until the farmer wants to sell them—as eggs, caterpillars (the young butterflies), pupae (in between caterpillars and butterflies), or butterflies.

The work is not physically demanding, but it does require knowledge and skill. To be
20   successful, the farmers have to learn a great deal about butterflies. They have to know which kinds live in the nearby forest and how to catch them. They have to learn what to feed them and how to keep them healthy. And they also have to know what kinds of butterflies they can sell.

Selling the butterflies is another part of the job. There is a big demand for butterflies in
25   Kenya and in other countries. Some people want them alive, while others want them dead and preserved. Scientists buy them for research purposes. Collectors buy them for their collections. Others buy them to decorate their homes, or for special occasions like weddings or parties. Hotels and tourists buy them as souvenirs of Africa. European designers buy them to study the colors and patterns for the textile (cloth) and fashion industries.

30   Then there are the pupae, the young insects before they become butterflies. These, too, are in demand by the scientists. The fashion industry also uses some pupae to make a special kind of silk cloth. Even the eggs can be sold to people who want to grow their own butterflies. In Nairobi, Mombasa, and other African cities, raising and trading butterflies is now a popular hobby.

35   Many farmers form groups to work together and help each other, especially with the marketing and sales. They also get help from international organizations that work to save the forests in Africa. In fact, butterfly farming is good not only for the people, but also for the forest. In the past, large forests covered parts of Kenya. Most of these have been cut down by now, but the remaining forests are still home to a huge variety of plants and
40   animals, including butterflies.

Butterfly farming provides people with a way to earn a living without destroying the forest. It also teaches them to care for the forests. People who start farming butterflies soon realize that the success of their business depends on preserving forests and the wildlife in them.

B. *Write your finishing time*: _____ *Then turn the page and answer the questions.*

C. *Circle the best answers. Do not look back at the passage.*

1. What kinds of jobs did the butterfly farmers do before?

   a. jobs that paid well
   b. jobs that paid poorly
   c. jobs that were dangerous

2. Which of the following is NOT true about butterfly farmers?

   a. They need a small piece of land.
   b. They need a butterfly net.
   c. They need to be very strong.

3. The farmer starts the farm by _____.

   a. buying some female butterflies
   b. catching some female butterflies
   c. killing some female butterflies

4. To be successful, a butterfly farmer has to _____.

   a. buy lots of butterfly nets
   b. catch lots of butterflies
   c. learn a lot about butterflies

5. Which of the following is NOT mentioned in the passage?

   a. People buy butterflies for medicine.
   b. People buy butterflies for research.
   c. People buy butterflies for their collections.

6. The pupae are the _____.

   a. young insects before they become butterflies
   b. plants that are eaten by the butterflies
   c. special kind of clothes made from butterflies

7. Which of the following can you infer from the passage?

   a. Butterfly farmers with more education will probably do better.
   b. Women butterfly farmers are more successful than men.
   c. Many butterfly farmers have trouble selling the butterflies.

8. Why do international organizations help the farmers?

   a. Because butterfly farming brings tourists to the area.
   b. Because butterfly farmers help research scientists.
   c. Because butterfly farmers take good care of the forest.

D. *Read the passage again. Try to read faster this time. Then look at the questions again and change your answers if necessary.*

E. *Calculate your reading time: _____*
Find your reading rate on page 233. Write it in the progress chart on page 235.

F. *Check your answers to the questions with your teacher. Write your comprehension score in the progress chart.*

A. *Write your starting time*: _____ *Preview and then read the passage.*

Caring for Nails in Richmond, Virginia (United States)

People who take care of fingernails or toenails are called manicurists. Most of them are women, though there are a few men. As for the customers, they are mostly women, too. These days, American men buy more hair and skin products than in the past. But not many men want to spend money taking care of their fingernails or toenails.

5   Still, manicurists have plenty of work. Even when women are worried about their jobs or their bank accounts, they go to the manicurist. They may decide not to buy a new car, a new washing machine, or a new winter coat. They may go out less to restaurants or to the movies. But to feel better about their lives, they continue to spend money on certain small pleasures—a bar of chocolate or a manicure.

10   In fact, a simple manicure does not cost much—only about $15. Of course, nail salons also offer all kinds of other services that cost more. Customers can have their hands and/or feet treated with baths, massages, and creams. They can make their hands more beautiful with fake (not real) nails and colorful nail polish. These days, manicurists will decorate nails with almost anything, including jewels—fake or real. However, these

15   special services aren't for everyone, as they can cost hundreds of dollars.

A good manicurist can do quite well financially. It is not surprising that the streets of American cities are full of nail salons (shops). Some are quite fancy, with beautifully decorated rooms and websites advertising their prices and services. Others are much smaller and simpler, with just one room and a sign in the window with the prices.

20   It is an easy business to get into. After a six-month course, the manicurist can get a license and start working. Many begin their careers by renting a small space in a hair salon. Women can then get their nails done while they are waiting for their hair to dry. It is a good way for manicurists to make themselves known to people.

Later, when they have enough customers, they can open their own nail salons. This

25   requires less money than opening a hair salon. The manicurist does not need a lot of space, equipment, or products to sell. It is important, however, to make the salon pleasant for customers. Comfortable chairs, pretty colors for the walls and furniture, and nice lighting are all necessary.

However, the success of the salon depends mostly on the manicurist. She has to be

30   good at her job, first of all. Customers will only come back if they like the way their nails look. But the manicurist also has to make the visit a pleasant experience. She needs to know how to build up a comfortable relationship with the customers. Some may enjoy a little light conversation. Others may want to sit back, close their eyes, and rest.

Not all manicurists work in salons. In fact, they can work almost anywhere. This is

35   another reason why some people go into this profession. For example, they can set up a little nail salon in a corner of their living room at home. This is convenient for those who have young children or who only want to work part time.

Other manicurists who are already well known may start going out to their customers. Some also work for agencies that offer this service. Going to the home of the

40   customer takes time and is more trouble than working in a salon, especially when there is bad weather. But the traveling manicurist can charge quite a lot more.

B. *Write your finishing time*: _____ *Then turn the page and answer the questions.*

C. **Circle the best answers. Do not look back at the passage.**

1. Among the customers of manicurists there are _____.

   a. mostly women
   b. equal numbers of men and women
   c. mostly men

2. What do women do in times of economic difficulties?

   a. They only buy necessary things like clothes.
   b. They go out to eat and to the movies more often.
   c. They buy small and inexpensive things like chocolate.

3. Which of the following is NOT mentioned in the passage?

   a. Only rich people can afford a manicure.
   b. Some manicurists use jewels to decorate nails.
   c. A simple manicure is not very expensive.

4. Which of the following can you infer from the passage?

   a. People from poor backgrounds can become manicurists.
   b. People who work as manicurists usually have a college education.
   c. Manicurists are usually people who could not afford to become hairdressers.

5. What is required to become a manicurist?

   a. a college degree
   b. a course and a license
   c. experience on the job

6. Which of the following is NOT mentioned in the passage?

   a. It is hard to find a good manicurist in American cities.
   b. Manicurists often start off working in a hair salon.
   c. A nail salon usually offers a variety of services.

7. An important part of a manicurist's job is _____.

   a. advertising prices
   b. keeping the salon clean
   c. relating to the customers

8. Some women become manicurists _____.

   a. so they can work in the evening
   b. so they can meet famous people
   c. so they can work at home

D. **Read the passage again. Try to read faster this time. Then look at the questions again and change your answers if necessary.**

E. **Calculate your reading time:** _____
   Find your reading rate on page 233. Write it in the progress chart on page 235.

F. **Check your answers to the questions with your teacher. Write your comprehension score in the progress chart.**

A.   Write your starting time: _____ *Preview and then read the passage.*

Making Coffee at a Highway Rest Stop in Modena (Italy)

The work is nonstop in these bars on the highway. This is the main highway between Milan and Rome and there are always a lot of cars in the parking lot. The restaurant slows down in between meal times, but the bar stays busy.

Italian bars are not like the bars in some countries that serve mainly alcoholic drinks. In Italy, bars serve mainly coffee, tea, and cold drinks, as well as pastries, pieces of pizza, and sandwiches. The bars at the highway rest stops also sell candy, magazines, and gifts.

People come to the rest stops for many reasons. They may need to fill up their cars with gas or use the bathrooms. They may need to take a rest from driving. But if they go into the bar, they usually want coffee. Drivers everywhere drink coffee to help them stay awake on the road. Italian drivers do, too. For many Italians, however, coffee is more than just a way to stay awake. It is an important part of their day—on the road or off.

In fact, their daily routine includes a series of coffees, starting with one for breakfast, another at mid-morning, a third after lunch, and yet another in the afternoon. Some may make their morning coffee in the kitchen at home, but many prefer to drink it at a bar. They say that coffee from a big espresso machine tastes better than coffee made at home. Even housewives or retired people often go out for coffee during the day.

In fact, going to a bar often involves more than just drinking coffee. It is a chance to take a break from work, to talk to someone. Many people have their mid-morning coffee with their co-workers, so they can catch up on news or gossip. If they are alone, they may get into a conversation with bar workers or other customers about local politics, Sunday's soccer match, or the latest crime story.

At the highway bars, this does not happen. The bars are often crowded and the men and women who work at them are too busy. Here, as at all Italian bars, the bar workers have to be quick on their feet. They also have to have a good memory. They may get ten orders for coffee one after another, and each one will be a little different.

Each Italian, it seems, likes coffee prepared in a certain way. One person wants a "short" black espresso (strong coffee made with little water). Another wants a "tall" espresso (with more water), with a drop of milk. A third person wants warm—but not hot—milk with a little coffee in it (a caffe latte). Then there are all the different ways to make cappuccino. Some Italians like more milk and some less milk. Some like a little chocolate on top. Others do not. And finally, all of these—espresso, caffe latte, and cappuccino— can also be prepared with decaffeinated coffee.

At a regular Italian bar, the bar workers usually get to know some of their customers and their preferences for coffee. That makes the job easier and more enjoyable. At a highway bar, this is not possible. People come and drink their coffee and then disappear forever.

Not surprisingly, many bar workers do not stay long at these jobs. Those who remain are the ones who work fast and do not get confused. They can keep up or even stay ahead of the orders. They are quick with the espresso machine, they do not let the dirty cups pile up, and sometimes they even have a smile for customers.

B.   Write your finishing time: _____ *Then turn the page and answer the questions.*

1. The rest stop bars _____.
   a. are often quiet
   b. close between meals
   c. usually have customers

2. What is the most popular thing at Italian bars?
   a. coffee
   b. beer
   c. pizza

3. Which of the following is NOT mentioned in the passage?
   a. Some Italians do not drink coffee at all.
   b. Many Italians drink several coffees per day.
   c. Most Italians enjoy going to a bar for coffee.

4. Many Italians who are at home most of the day _____.
   a. drink less coffee than Italians who work
   b. prefer to make their coffee at home
   c. like to go out for a coffee

5. Why do Italians prefer to go out for coffee to a bar?
   a. Because they cannot make an espresso at home.
   b. Because then they can also talk to someone.
   c. Because the coffee is cheaper at a bar than at home.

6. The most difficult thing about working at an Italian bar is _____.
   a. operating and cleaning the coffee machine
   b. remembering the way customers want their coffee
   c. learning how to make the different kinds of coffee

7. Which of the following can you infer from the passage?
   a. Italians have strong opinions about what they eat and drink.
   b. Italians generally work less than people in other countries.
   c. Italians drink less coffee than they used to.

8. Unlike other bar workers, rest stop bar workers _____.
   a. do not get to know their customers
   b. have to make many different kinds of coffee
   c. can relax in between meals

D. *Read the passage again. Try to read faster this time. Then look at the questions again and change your answers if necessary.*

E. *Calculate your reading time: _____*
Find your reading rate on page 233. Write it in the progress chart on page 235.

F. *Check your answers to the questions with your teacher. Write your comprehension score in the progress chart.*

UNIT 3 Better Lives in a Better World

A. *Write your starting time:* _____ *Preview and then read the passage.*

Donkey Power for Women Farmers in Africa

Hunger is a major problem worldwide, but the continent where the most people suffer from hunger is Africa. This is also the continent with the most poverty, the highest population growth, and the most wars. But experts from the Food and Agricultural Organization (FAO) of the United Nations say that another important cause of hunger is low productivity on farms. If Africans could produce more food for themselves and local markets, there would be less hunger.

Why are African farms unproductive? Of course, there are some highly productive farms in Africa, mostly large farms, often owned by international food companies. They produce cash crops, such as coffee, sugar, or bananas, which are sent to the developed countries. The farms that produce food for Africans are mostly small. Furthermore, the work is done mainly by women—70 percent according to the FAO. Women have always had an important role in agriculture in Africa, but in recent years, their share of the farming has grown, as many men have moved to cities to work.

Thus, women are the key to reducing hunger in Africa. Food production will never increase unless the women get some help on their farms. They are certainly in need of help. First of all, they are usually overloaded with other jobs. They have to prepare meals and care for children, and they often have to carry water from miles away. Secondly, they have to do all the work in the fields themselves, with just a hoe (digging tool). This is back-breaking work, but most women have no other choice. Tractors are far too expensive for most small farmers in Africa—women or men. In recent years, some African men have begun farming with work animals such as oxen. Studies have shown that using oxen does increase productivity. But women are not allowed to own or use oxen in many parts of Africa. In any case, oxen are quite expensive and the plows used to break up the soil are very heavy.

There is another animal, however, that could help women with their farm work: donkeys. There are a number of reasons for promoting the use of donkeys among women farmers. One is that there are no traditions anywhere in Africa against women using donkeys. Second, donkeys are much cheaper than oxen. They are also less expensive to keep, since they do not need special food, but can live on the grass and leaves that they find. Unlike oxen, donkeys rarely get sick, and they do not mind hot, dry weather. Finally, donkeys are smaller and lighter, so they are easier to handle and to train.

At the same time, though much smaller than oxen, donkeys are surprisingly strong and tough. They are not strong enough to pull a plow deeply through heavy soil, but they can do other kinds of plowing and they can be used to remove unwanted plants between rows in fields. Furthermore, the donkeys can help with transport. This is no small matter. Instead of carrying water or vegetables in heavy containers on their heads, women can put things on the back of the donkey, or in a cart pulled behind the donkey.

In Zimbabwe, some women are already using donkeys on farms. Researchers from the FAO talked with these women and found that the donkeys made a real difference in their lives. With the donkeys to help, women were able to produce more food for their families. Also, with a lighter workload, women had more time and energy for other things. They could take better care of their families and even start small businesses in their villages.

B. *Write your finishing time:* _____ *Then turn the page and answer the questions.*

C. *Circle the best answers. Do not look back at the passage.*

1. We can infer from the passage that farm productivity is _____.
   a. higher in Africa than in other parts of the world
   b. lower in Africa than in other parts of the world
   c. not a problem in Africa or in other parts of the world

2. Many of the large farms in Africa produce _____.
   a. food for Africans
   b. special food for oxen
   c. crops for developed countries

3. Which of the following is NOT mentioned in the passage?
   a. Women traditionally do most of the farming.
   b. Women like working outdoors on farms.
   c. Many men have left farms to work in cities.

4. African women do most farm work _____.
   a. with oxen
   b. with a tractor
   c. with a hoe

5. Which of the following is NOT mentioned in the passage?
   a. African women farmers cannot afford to buy tractors.
   b. In some areas of Africa, women are not allowed to use oxen.
   c. Many African women are afraid of oxen and other large animals.

6. Which of the following is NOT true about donkeys?
   a. They are harder to train than oxen.
   b. They are easier to care for than oxen.
   c. They are much less expensive than oxen.

7. Donkeys can help women with many kinds of work, including _____.
   a. carrying heavy loads
   b. plowing in heavy soil
   c. bringing children to school

8. What did the women farmers say in the FAO study?
   a. They wanted to work with oxen like the men.
   b. The donkeys were a big help to them and their families.
   c. They could start businesses if they had more money.

D. *Read the passage again. Try to read faster this time. Then look at the questions again and change your answers if necessary.*

E. *Calculate your reading time:* _____
Find your reading rate on page 233. Write it in the progress chart on page 236.

F. *Check your answers to the questions with your teacher. Write your comprehension score in the progress chart.*

A. *Write your starting time*: _____ *Preview and then read the passage.*

Food for the 21st Century: Insects

Insects for dinner? This idea may not appeal to everyone, but insects are a regular part of the diet in many areas of the world. Now scientists working for the Food and Agriculture Organization (FAO) of the United Nations are studying insects as a food source. Insect farming is already common in some countries, such as Thailand, and the scientists hope to
5 expand it.

The reason is simple: millions of people around the world get just enough food to survive, usually rice or corn. However, they do not get enough nutrients (things your body needs), such as protein, vitamins, and minerals. Insects are a very good source of these nutrients. They contain as much protein as meat or fish. They also contain large amounts of
10 vitamins and minerals, especially calcium (necessary for your bones).

Before focusing on insects, the FAO experts considered other food sources that might be developed. One was fish. In developing countries, fish used to be an important food source for families living near rivers, lakes, and oceans. But these days, fishermen with small boats are catching less and less fish. In fact, wild fish are disappearing from the waters around the
15 world because of pollution and overfishing by huge factory ships. In developing countries there are now many fish farms. In fact, this farmed fish is taking the place of wild fish in the supermarkets of developed countries. But people in developing countries do not benefit from the fish farms. The fish is too expensive, and the fish farms are highly polluting.

Meat was another food source considered by the scientists. In recent years, demand for
20 meat has increased dramatically, and so has production. However, in developing countries, meat is too expensive for most of the population. Moreover, most farmers in developing countries are too poor to buy the land or animals to produce meat, so they cannot benefit from the increased demand. Instead, meat production is mostly in the hands of big landowners and international food businesses.

25 Another problem with meat production is environmental. Animals such as cows, sheep, and pigs produce ammonia (a chemical) which pollutes rivers, lakes, and groundwater. These animals also produce large amounts of global-warming gases, such as methane and nitrous oxide. According to scientists, 20 percent of the global-warming gases from human activities comes from farm animals.

30 Furthermore, to increase the production of meat, farmers need more land. To get more land in developing countries, such as Brazil, farmers have cut down forests. Large areas of the Amazon forest, for example, have been cut down for this reason. But forests are important for the planet in many ways, especially because they help reduce global-warming gases.

Compared with farming for meat, insect farming has many advantages. First of all, it
35 is easier for farmers to get started, since they do not need much land or equipment. Insect farming is also much less harmful to the environment. Unlike warm-blooded animals, insects do not produce ammonia and they produce only small amounts of global-warming gases. Since insect farming does not require much land, farmers also would not need to cut down trees in forests.

40 The FAO scientists say that their knowledge about insects for farming is still very limited. They are working with the Thai farmers to develop farming methods that can be taught to farmers in other countries. The scientists are also working with people who traditionally eat forest insects to learn more about those insects. Finally, they are studying the methods used by people who raise insects for other purposes, such as bees for honey or silk
45 worms for silk.

B. *Write your finishing time*: _____ *Then turn the page and answer the questions.*

Circle the best answers. Do not look back at the passage.

1. The FAO is looking for a food source that is healthy, inexpensive, and _____.
   a. good for business
   b. popular in developed countries
   c. not harmful to the environment

2. What can you find in insects?
   a. calcium, protein, and other nutrients
   b. less protein than meat or fish
   c. some harmful chemicals

3. Which of the following can we infer from the passage?
   a. Fish will probably not be an important food source in developing countries.
   b. Fish is an important food source these days in developing countries.
   c. Fish will soon become an important food source in developing countries.

4. Many people in developing countries do not eat meat because _____.
   a. they think it is unhealthy
   b. they do not like it
   c. they cannot afford it

5. Which of the following is NOT mentioned in the passage?
   a. Raising animals for meat causes water pollution.
   b. Cows produce more global-warming gases than pigs.
   c. Farm animals produce global-warming gases.

6. Why do some farmers who raise animals for meat cut down forests?
   a. to get more land
   b. to sell the land
   c. to sell the wood

7. Which of the following is NOT mentioned in the passage?
   a. Insect farming is better for the environment than raising animals for meat.
   b. Insect farming requires more land and equipment than raising animals for meat.
   c. It is less expensive to raise insects than to raise animals for meat.

8. The FAO experts are learning about insect farming from _____.
   a. people who raise bees and silk worms
   b. scientific studies of insects raised on farms
   c. farmers who raise animals for meat

D. **Read the passage again. Try to read faster this time. Then look at the questions again and change your answers if necessary.**

E. **Calculate your reading time:** _____
   Find your reading rate on page 233. Write it in the progress chart on page 236.

F. **Check your answers to the questions with your teacher. Write your comprehension score in the progress chart.**

A. *Write your starting time:* _____ *Preview and then read the passage.*

Green Roofs and Gardens

Where do you go for your salad greens? Most likely, you go to the supermarket. But soon it may be possible to go up to the roof. More and more cities are encouraging building owners to cover their buildings with green roofs—with or without gardens.

Not all green roofs have vegetable gardens or any kind of garden. There are two types, in fact. The first is called intensive. It has a deep layer of soil (garden dirt), and can be planted with vegetables or flowers and trees. These require regular watering and care. They are also quite expensive to build since the layer of soil is heavy and needs strong support.

The other kind of green roof is the extensive green roof. This type is actually more common. It has a thinner layer of very light soil and only low-growing plants, such as grasses or sedums—desert plants that can grow in thin soil and with little water. These roofs are less expensive to build and require less care afterward.

In North America, Toronto is the leader of the green roof movement, with laws that require green roofs on many new buildings. Chicago is promoting green roofs as well. There is now a green roof park on City Hall, where workers can go at lunchtime. A green roof on top of the Uncommon Ground restaurant in Chicago is planted with vegetables that are served downstairs in the restaurant. In St. Louis, the children's hospital has created a green roof with a pond and walkways for patients and families.

In other parts of the world, green roofs are also becoming common. In Tokyo, Japan, laws have been passed that require green roofs on all larger new buildings. Some cities in Europe have gone even further, particularly in Switzerland. In Basel, Zurich, and Luzern, all new buildings with flat roofs—large or small—must have plants on top.

Green roofs cost more to build than regular roofs, but in the long term, they allow building owners to save money. In most cities, people have to use air conditioning to stay comfortable in the summer. Building owners pay huge electricity bills to run that air conditioning. With a green roof, much less air conditioning is needed. Studies have shown that a regular black roof can reach 180° F (82° C) on a summer day, while a plant-covered roof will stay much cooler, not more than 85° F (30° C). This makes a big difference in the temperature inside the building.

Green roofs also benefit cities in several ways. First, they help lower air temperatures in summer. In fact, regular black rooftops collect heat by day and release it again in the evening. Instead, the plants on green rooftops prevent the heat from building up. Second, green roofs absorb a lot of rainwater during storms —up to 70 percent. This can make a big difference in cities where heavy water running off roofs can cause flooding and pollution.

Furthermore, with a green roof, a new green space is created. This can benefit both building owners and everyone in the city who lives or works nearby. Whether it is planted with vegetables, grasses, or trees, it can provide people in the middle of cities with a green place to go. Studies have shown, in fact, that spending time in green spaces helps reduce stress and lower blood pressure.

Finally, scientists have noticed that green roofs are also good for wildlife. The roofs provide a home for many kinds of birds and insects, and a much-needed resting place for birds or butterflies on their way north or south.

B. *Write your finishing time:* _____ *Then turn the page and answer the questions.*

Circle the best answers. Do not look back at the passage.

1. Why does the passage mention the cities of Toronto, Chicago, Tokyo, and Basel?

    a. Because they are all promoting green roofs.
    b. Because they are all planting vegetable gardens.
    c. Because they all have many new buildings.

2. Which country encourages green roofs the most?

    a. Canada
    b. United States
    c. Switzerland

3. Intensive green roofs have a deep layer of soil for _____.

    a. vegetables or flowers and trees
    b. small plants, such as grasses
    c. children to play in

4. Which of the following is NOT mentioned in the passage?

    a. Extensive green roofs have a thin layer of soil.
    b. Extensive green roofs have low-growing plants.
    c. Extensive green roofs need more care and watering.

5. On a summer day, a green roof _____.

    a. gets warmer than a black roof
    b. stays much cooler than a black roof
    c. keeps the building drier

6. Green roofs help building owners save money on _____.

    a. heat
    b. water
    c. air-conditioning

7. Which of the following is NOT mentioned in the passage?

    a. Green roofs reduce water runoff.
    b. Green roofs keep the city cleaner.
    c. Green roofs help cool the city.

8. Which of the following can you infer from the passage?

    a. Scientists have studied the people who use green roofs.
    b. Scientists have studied the wildlife found on green roofs.
    c. Scientists have studied the effects of green roofs in the winter.

D. **Read the passage again. Try to read faster this time. Then look at the questions again and change your answers if necessary.**

E. **Calculate your reading time: _____**
   Find your reading rate on page 233. Write it in the progress chart on page 236.

F. **Check your answers to the questions with your teacher. Write your comprehension score in the progress chart.**

A. *Write your starting time:* _____ *Preview and then read the passage.*

An Oceanful of Plastic

When he planned his trip, David de Rothschild knew there was a lot of plastic in the ocean. That was the whole point of the trip. He had studied the problem and wanted to bring attention to it. So he built a boat from 12,500 plastic bottles, named it the *Plastiki*, and sailed it across the Pacific Ocean.

5   Even though he was prepared, de Rothschild was shocked by what he saw. The route of the *Plastiki* took it through the "eastern garbage patch." This is a collection of floating garbage that covers an area of about 550,000 square miles—more than twice the size of Texas. Until 12 years ago, it was unknown to scientists because it is mostly invisible—millions of very small pieces of plastic floating just underwater, a kind of plastic soup.

10   According to scientists, the garbage patch may contain 100 million tons of plastic. It has been carried to this area by ocean currents and winds from all over the Pacific. Scientists used to think that plastic bags or bottles broke up into small pieces only after many years in cold water. However, studies have shown that it happens much more quickly. In about a year, plastic bottles, bags, or other plastic objects are broken down into 15   many small pieces, which may remain in the water for a hundred years.

Furthermore, when plastic breaks up, chemicals are released into the water, and these too remain for a long time. Researchers in Japan have studied water from the world's oceans and found that it contains chemicals from plastic. Two of these chemicals, polystyrene and bisphenol A, have also been found in fish. It is not known yet what effect 20   they may have on the fish or on other kinds of marine animals, but they are known to be harmful to human health.

The large pieces of plastic that have not yet broken down are also a problem. Scientists who study marine life say that marine animals often mistake larger pieces of plastic for food. The consequences can be deadly. According to the United Nations Environmental 25   Program, plastic causes the death of more than a million seabirds a year, as well as over 100,000 dolphins and whales, and thousands of sea turtles.

On his trip across the Pacific, de Rothschild was also shocked by the lack of marine life. He compared his experience with that of Thor Heyerdahl who sailed across in 1947. Heyerdahl saw all kinds of fish, dolphins, whales, and sea birds every day. There were 30   so many flying fish, for example, that he sometimes had to throw them off the boat. De Rothschild, on the other hand, saw very few fish or other marine animals. This confirms what scientists are now saying—that 80 percent of the fish in the world's oceans have disappeared. Plastic is not the only cause of this disappearance, but it is one of them.

To reduce the amount of plastic that ends up in the ocean, we need to reduce the 35   amount we use. Plastic grocery bags are the worst source of pollution mainly because there are so many. In 2005, about five trillion bags were produced worldwide. A number of cities and countries have taxed or banned them (made them illegal), including Dhaka, Mumbai, and San Francisco; and South Africa, Australia, Ireland, Greece, Italy, and China.

In places where measures have been taken, people are using many fewer bags. In 40   Ireland, for example, bag use dropped by 90 percent after the tax. In China, where people were using three billion bags daily before the new laws, bag use was reduced by about 70 percent.

B. *Write your finishing time:* _____ *Then turn the page and answer the questions.*

C. *Circle the best answers. Do not look back at the passage.*

1. Why did de Rothschild sail the *Plastiki* across the Pacific?
   a. He wanted to study the fish and marine animals in the ocean.
   b. He wanted people to know about the plastic in the ocean.
   c. He wanted to go to Japan by boat.

2. The "eastern garbage patch" is made up mostly of _____.
   a. whole plastic bags and bottles
   b. very small pieces of plastic
   c. floating pieces of boats

3. Which of the following is NOT mentioned in the passage?
   a. Pieces of plastic bottles can float for long distances.
   b. Plastic bottles last for a hundred years.
   c. Plastic bottles break down into small pieces.

4. Which of the following can you infer from the passage?
   a. Fish from the ocean might not be good to eat.
   b. Chemicals were found only in Japanese fish.
   c. The chemicals from plastic do not harm fish.

5. When marine animals see plastic, they _____.
   a. stay away from it
   b. do not notice it
   c. often try to eat it

6. What surprised de Rothschild on his way across the Pacific?
   a. The way the fish jumped up onto his boat.
   b. The fact that he did not see much marine life.
   c. The number of sea birds he saw every day.

7. According to scientists, there are _____.
   a. 100,000 fish in the ocean today
   b. 2,000,000 tons of fish in the ocean today
   c. 80 percent fewer fish in the ocean today

8. Which of the following is NOT mentioned in the passage?
   a. taxes on plastic bags
   b. banning plastic bags
   c. recycling plastic bags

D. *Read the passage again. Try to read faster this time. Then look at the questions again and change your answers if necessary.*

E. *Calculate your reading time: _____*
Find your reading rate on page 233. Write it in the progress chart on page 236.

F. *Check your answers to the questions with your teacher. Write your comprehension score in the progress chart.*

A. *Write your starting time:* _____ *Preview and then read the passage.*

Energy from an Exploding Lake

An exploding lake is a strange phenomenon (thing that happens). There are three of them in the world, all in Africa: Lakes Monoun and Nyos in Cameroon and Lake Kivu between Rwanda and Congo.

5   These lakes were formed when water collected in deep craters (large holes) left by old volcanoes. Though those volcanoes are no longer active, there is still volcanic activity in the mountains nearby. Because of this, gases such as methane and carbon dioxide are released from deep under the earth into the lake waters.

This happens in other crater lakes around the world. However, in those lakes the gases are not dangerous because the water "turns over" regularly. That is, the water from the
10   bottom of the lake rises and mixes with the water at the top, allowing the gases to escape slowly.

In the African lakes, however, the water does not turn over, so most of the gases remain trapped at the bottom. Small amounts of carbon dioxide are sometimes are released and form pockets on the water near the shore. These "evil winds," as they are known, are most common
15   on the Congo side of Lake Kivu, where every year a number of people die from the gas.

But another, far more serious problem for people living on Lake Kivu is the risk of explosion. The other two lakes have exploded quite recently: Lake Monoun in 1984, killing 47 people, and Lake Nyos in 1986, killing 1,700 people. Those explosions released the gases from the lakes, so another explosion is not likely soon.

20   However, scientists fear for Lake Kivu. This is the largest and deepest of the lakes. The layer of gas lies under 1,500 feet of water. However, as gas builds up on the lake bottom, the danger increases. One day, a storm or a landslide could cause the water to turn over suddenly. Then all the gases would escape at once in a violent explosion.

The consequences of an explosion would be devastating. Over two million people live
25   along the lakeshore. Since scientists cannot tell when an explosion might happen, it would be impossible to warn people and send them away. According to the scientists, the only way to prevent an explosion is to remove the gases from the lake. This is possible, but difficult and dangerous.

At the same time, however, the methane from the lake could be put to good use. Both
30   Rwanda and Congo have no other source of cheap energy. The methane from the lake could reduce energy costs and help development in Rwanda and Congo. Many areas of these countries are now without electricity. In Rwanda, for example, only 1 in 14 homes has electricity. This means that no one can use computers or other machines, and that children cannot study in the evening.

35   Working with American scientists, the Rwandan government has started removing methane from the lake. A tall barge (flat boat) now sits out in the middle of Lake Kivu. Workers pipe the gas up from the bottom and across to the Kibuye Power plant, which produces about 50 megawatts of power. By 2010, the government was getting a third of all its electricity from the lake.

40   So far, the project is entirely controlled by the Rwandan government. In the future, several foreign companies will become involved, and the project will be expanded. The government of Rwanda is also holding talks with the government of Congo, which has rights to half of the methane. The two countries plan to work together to build a much larger power plant that will produce 200 megawatts of power.

B. *Write your finishing time:* _____ *Then turn the page and answer the questions.*

C. *Circle the best answers. Do not look back at the passage.*

1. Exploding lakes form in areas with _____.

   a. a warm climate
   b. volcanic activity
   c. lots of lakes

2. In most crater lakes, _____.

   a. the gases are released slowly
   b. there are no gases
   c. the gases remain at the bottom

3. Which of the following is NOT mentioned in the passage?

   a. People sometimes die from carbon dioxide at Lake Kivu.
   b. People died in explosions at Lakes Monoun and Nyos.
   c. People were killed by an explosion at Lake Kivu.

4. At the lakes in Cameroon, _____.

   a. there has never been an explosion
   b. there will soon be another explosion
   c. there will probably not be another explosion

5. Which of the following is NOT true about Lake Kivu?

   a. It is very deep.
   b. It has not exploded recently.
   c. It is not at risk of explosion.

6. Scientists know all of the following facts EXCEPT _____.

   a. how much gas is in the lake
   b. when the gases might explode
   c. what gases cause the explosions

7. Which of the following can you infer from the passage?

   a. Scientists did not know about the explosions at the lakes in Cameroon.
   b. Scientists could not study Lake Kivu because it is too deep.
   c. Nothing was done to prevent explosions at the lakes in Cameroon.

8. The government of Rwanda _____.

   a. is already using methane from the lake
   b. does not plan to use methane from the lake
   c. is selling the methane to foreign companies

D. *Read the passage again. Try to read faster this time. Then look at the questions again and change your answers if necessary.*

E. *Calculate your reading time:* _____
Find your reading rate on page 233. Write it in the progress chart on page 236.

F. *Check your answers to the questions with your teacher. Write your comprehension score in the progress chart.*

A. *Write your starting time:* _____ *Preview and then read the passage.*

Blowing in the Wind

What small northern European country is known for its windmills? In the past, it was Holland. But these days, the country with the most wind turbines, as they are now called, is Denmark. The largest producer of wind turbines in the world is Vesta, a Danish company. Denmark is also the country with the highest percentage of energy coming from wind power—20 percent in 2010. If you travel through Denmark you see wind turbines everywhere—small ones near houses and farms, and groups of enormous turbines just off the coast.

It all started in 1973, with the oil crisis. At that time, Denmark, like many other developed countries, was mostly dependent on foreign petroleum (oil) for energy. With the crisis, the price of oil rose steeply. Many governments then decided to try to reduce their dependence on foreign oil. There were two ways to do this. One was to reduce energy use, and the other was to develop other sources of energy.

The Danish government did both. It improved energy standards for buildings, had car-free Sundays, and encouraged people and businesses to turn off lights and turn down heat. Unlike many other countries, Denmark also raised taxes on energy and used the money from these taxes to pay for research into other ways of producing energy. With the country's frequent cloudy weather, solar energy was not practical, but there was plenty of wind.

When oil prices went down again in the 1980s, most countries gave up their energy-saving programs and stopped research into solar and wind power. In the United States, for example, many companies working in these fields had to close down. But not in Denmark. The Danish government continued to invest in energy reduction and in wind power.

At that time, the Danes mainly feared another oil crisis, but they also were concerned about the environment and the air pollution in their cities. Then, as scientists began to learn more about global warming, they began to worry about its effects on the climate. Reducing the amount of petroleum they used would reduce the amount of global-warming gases they produced.

The Danes also saw wind power as an important economic opportunity. At first, with government investments, that opportunity was mainly inside Denmark. However, by the 1990s, demand was growing outside of Denmark as well. With their experience and their advanced technology, Danish companies were ready to meet that demand. Today, many of the largest wind farms around the world use Danish wind turbines.

Thus, the key to Denmark's success with wind power was partly long-term thinking. The government was willing to spend money on something that was not immediately necessary or profitable, but was important in the long term.

Another important factor was the support of the Danish people. From the beginning, there was a strong wind power movement. The first wind turbines were in small communities, with people sharing in the building costs and then in the energy savings. These examples helped convince other communities that wind power was practical, and also that the turbines were not noisy or ugly, as many had feared. In fact, modern turbines make very little noise and are quite beautiful—like modernist sculptures.

Furthermore, when planning large wind farms, the government and companies invited everyone living or working in the area—including fishermen—to take part in the planning. Those who might lose their homes or jobs because of the wind farms were compensated (paid), and everyone had an opportunity to buy shares of the project. Thus, wind power became something that belonged to everyone and would benefit everyone.

B. *Write your finishing time:* _____ *Then turn the page and answer the questions.*

Circle the best answers. Do not look back at the passage.

1. Which of the following is NOT mentioned in the passage?

    a. Denmark had a lot of windmills in the past.
    b. Denmark gets more of its energy from wind than any other country.
    c. The largest wind power company is Danish.

2. In the 1970s, many developed countries _____.

    a. stopped buying oil from foreign countries
    b. used only wind and solar power for energy
    c. tried to reduce the amount of foreign oil they used

3. What did the Danish government do in the 1970s?

    a. It decided to develop wind power.
    b. It started using only electric cars.
    c. It began developing solar power.

4. How was Denmark different from most countries after the oil crisis ended?

    a. It stopped investing in wind power.
    b. It continued to work for energy independence.
    c. It gave up energy-saving programs.

5. Which of the following is NOT mentioned in the passage?

    a. The Danes were concerned about global warming.
    b. The Danes were afraid of another oil crisis.
    c. The Danes were worried about their taxes.

6. Which of the following can we infer from the passage?

    a. Wind power helped Danish companies become strong worldwide.
    b. The government kept companies from other countries out of Denmark.
    c. The government subsidies made no difference for Danish companies.

7. The first wind turbines many Danes saw were built by _____.

    a. the government
    b. small communities
    c. artists

8. Which of the following did not help wind power grow in Denmark?

    a. long-term thinking by the government
    b. the involvement of people on all levels
    c. the cost of land and materials in Denmark

D. **Read the passage again. Try to read faster this time. Then look at the questions again and change your answers if necessary.**

E. **Calculate your reading time: _____**
Find your reading rate on page 233. Write it in the progress chart on page 236.

F. **Check your answers to the questions with your teacher. Write your comprehension score in the progress chart.**

A. *Write your starting time*: _____ *Preview and then read the passage.*

Warming up with Computers

If you have ever sat with a computer on your lap, you know how warm it can get. It's not hard to imagine what happens in a data center where there are many computers. The whole room heats up, and the computers crash if nothing is done to cool them down. Cooling systems are essential for data centers, but since they use a lot of energy, they are also very expensive to run. This has always been viewed as a necessary expense by universities and businesses that run large data centers.

However, that view is changing. Data centers are becoming larger and more numerous. At the same time, the cost of energy is rising. As a result, scientists have begun to rethink computer cooling systems. Until now, their only concern was to remove the heat. But now they are beginning to think about what they could *do* with the heat. After all, in colder climates, heat is valuable. People, companies, cities, and universities pay large amounts of money for energy to heat buildings in winter. Why not make use of the heat from computers instead?

This is now happening in Finland. In the center of Helsinki, a technology company called Academica has built a new data center that recycles the heat from its computers. This is made easier by Helsinki's centralized heating system with underground tunnels that bring hot water from central heaters to many buildings. The data center has become one of the city's sources of heat. First, cold water is brought in from the Baltic Sea to the data center. When this water has been warmed up by the computers, it flows out from the data center and enters the city's heating system.

By recycling heat this way, Academica saves about $240,000 in cooling costs. At the same time, Helsingin Energia, the city's energy company, has gained a cheap source of energy. Enough heat is produced by the Academica data center to heat 500 houses or 1,000 apartments through the long, cold Finnish winter. After the success of this first project, several other companies are planning similar heating/cooling systems for their data centers in Finland.

In the United States, one of the leading researchers into heat recycling is Paul Brenner, a computer scientist at Notre Dame University in Indiana. Brenner's interest in recycling started because the computers were running very slowly. The reason was the high cost of cooling them, so Brenner decided to look for ways to reduce cooling costs.

Unlike the Finnish system, which used water to heat and cool, he used the computers themselves. First he experimented with a small set of computers placed in an office, but connected with the university's data center. When the office was cold, work was sent to these computers and the room soon warmed up. When it was warm enough, the computers stopped working.

Brenner then tried out his system in a larger space—the nearby Botanical Conservatory (place to keep plants), which was owned by the city. He placed a large set of computers in the area with cactuses, which need to stay warm in the winter. The system worked just as well as it did in the office and greatly reduced the amount of energy used. The city saved about $70,000 a year in heating costs, and the university saved $100,000 in cooling costs.

Savings is one important reason to develop heat recycling from computer servers. Another reason is to reduce pollution and global-warming gases. Traditional cooling systems, in fact, require a lot of energy, and most of the energy comes from burning gas, coal, or petroleum.

B. *Write your finishing time*: _____ *Then turn the page and answer the questions.*

C. **Circle the best answers. Do not look back at the passage.**

1. Why do places with data centers spend a lot of money on energy?
    a. to keep the computers cool
    b. to warm up the computers
    c. to turn on the computers

2. Which of the following is NOT mentioned in the passage?
    a. There are more data centers than in the past.
    b. Computers crash more often these days.
    c. The cost of energy has increased.

3. Which of the following can you infer from the passage?
    a. Scientists in countries with warm climates are studying heat recycling.
    b. Cooling systems are not necessary in countries with cold climates.
    c. Heat recycling has been studied most in countries with cold climates.

4. What happens to the warm water from the Helsinki data center?
    a. It is used to run the computers.
    b. It is sent back to the Baltic Sea.
    c. It is used to heat homes in the city.

5. Other companies in Finland are planning to recycle heat _____.
    a. because it will help them save money
    b. because they want to keep their houses warmer
    c. because the Academica project did not work

6. Why did Paul Brenner start research on heat recycling?
    a. Because the university computers were running too slowly.
    b. Because he heard about the projects in Finland.
    c. Because the university wanted to build a new data center.

7. In Brenner's system, the computers _____.
    a. used cool water to keep from overheating
    b. were placed outside in the winter to cool off
    c. turned on and off according to the need for heat

8. Recycling heat reduces all of the following EXCEPT _____.
    a. global-warming gases
    b. problems relating to viruses
    c. heating and cooling costs

D. **Read the passage again. Try to read faster this time. Then look at the questions again and change your answers if necessary.**

E. **Calculate your reading time: _____**
Find your reading rate on page 233. Write it in the progress chart on page 236.

F. **Check your answers to the questions with your teacher. Write your comprehension score in the progress chart.**

A. *Write your starting time*: _____ *Preview and then read the passage.*

Ushahidi—Software that Saves Lives

The idea came to her in 2008 when violence broke out in Nairobi after the Kenyan elections. Ory Okolloh, a young Kenyan, wrote a popular blog. Many people were in touch with her around the city by email or by SMS. At the same time, because of the violence, even the news reporters were afraid to move around the city. No one knew what
5   was happening outside of their neighborhood.

So Okolloh began to post the messages she received on her blog. Some described what they were seeing and experiencing. Others were from people who needed help. As more and more people contacted her, she realized that she needed something better than her blog. She needed a way to gather all the information and put it on a map. That would
10   make the overall situation much clearer, and it would also make it easier to get help for people.

Okolloh was not a technology expert (she had a law degree), so she asked for help. In two days, some young technical friends gave her what she needed. It was a program that uploaded information from text messages, phone calls, emails, and videos and placed
15   it on a map of the area. Okolloh decided to call it *Ushahidi*, a word from Swahili, the main language spoken in Kenya. It means evidence or testimony (showing or proving something clearly).

Ushahidi was not the first crisis-mapping program, but earlier ones had been much less accurate and less user friendly. Furthermore, unlike those programs, Ushahidi was web
20   based and open-source, so anyone with an Internet connection and server space could use it for free. Okolloh realized at once how valuable it could be. She left her consulting job to work full time raising money to maintain and improve Ushahidi. Very soon, people were using it in crisis situations around the world.

Haiti was the big test. On January 12, 2009, an earthquake caused massive destruction
25   and thousands of deaths in the capital city, Port-au-Prince. Within two hours after the earthquake struck, a group of volunteers had set up Ushahidi-Haiti. The volunteers were students at Tufts University in Boston, Massachusetts. Their job was to receive information, mostly text messages, from Port-au-Prince, and put it on a map.

Many messages were in Creole, the language spoken in Haiti. These messages were
30   sent to Haitian Americans around the country who translated them quickly and sent them back. A special short code was set up to make it easier for people to send text messages. Radio stations in Haiti and the United States helped spread and gather information.

Some of the messages that came to Ushahidi-Haiti were from relatives or passersby who knew about people trapped in buildings. Others were from trapped people
35   themselves to say that they were alive. The location of trapped people was put on a map, using GPS, and then sent to rescue teams in Port-au-Prince. The messages and the maps helped rescue organizations like the Red Cross to understand the situation better. They also made it possible to get aid where it was needed and to save many lives.

Since the Haitian earthquake, Ushahidi has been used in other rescue operations, after
40   the earthquake in Chile, forest fires in Russia, and floods in Pakistan and China. It has kept the outside world informed about violence in Afghanistan, Gaza, and South Africa.

Okolloh is also exploring other ways that the Ushahidi software could help people in developing countries. For example, in Africa it helps doctors and aid workers keep track of medical supplies and keep in contact with people who need medical treatment.

B. *Write your finishing time*: _____ *Then turn the page and answer the questions.*

C. *Circle the best answers. Do not look back at the passage.*

1. During the violence in Kenya, Okolloh _____.

   a. wrote articles for the newspaper
   b. traveled around Nairobi to talk with people
   c. wrote a blog that many people followed

2. Which of the following can you infer from the passage?

   a. Okolloh started Ushahidi because she wanted to help people.
   b. Okolloh started Ushahidi because she wanted to make money.
   c. Okolloh started Ushahidi so more people would follow her blog.

3. The software for Ushahidi was invented by _____.

   a. friends of Okolloh
   b. Okolloh herself
   c. American students

4. Which of the following is NOT mentioned in the passage?

   a. Ushahidi is open-source, so anyone can use it.
   b. Ushahidi is user friendly, so it's easy to use.
   c. Ushahidi is a good way to make money.

5. What did Okolloh do after Ushahidi was created?

   a. She went back to her consulting job.
   b. She went to work full time for Ushahidi.
   c. She continued to write in her blog.

6. Which of the following was NOT true about Ushahidi-Haiti volunteers?

   a. They went to work in Port-au-Prince.
   b. They put information from Haiti on a map.
   c. They sent messages in Creole to be translated.

7. After the earthquake in Haiti, Ushahidi helped _____.

   a. Haitian Americans find out about relatives
   b. rescuers save the lives of people under buildings
   c. make a better map of Port-au-Prince

8. Ushahidi has been used during all of the following EXCEPT _____.

   a. floods in Pakistan and China
   b. violence in Afghanistan, Gaza, and South Africa
   c. storms in the Midwestern United States

D. *Read the passage again. Try to read faster this time. Then look at the questions again and change your answers if necessary.*

E. *Calculate your reading time: _____*
   Find your reading rate on page 233. Write it in the progress chart on page 236.

F. *Check your answers to the questions with your teacher. Write your comprehension score in the progress chart.*

Answers to Practice Exercises

Page 38, Practice 1

A. 1. verb (passive)   3. noun
   2. noun   4. adjective

B.

	Noun	Verb	Adjective	Adverb
1.	valued	valued	valuable	
2.	valued			

Page 41, Practice 2

A. 1. verb: to continue to happen or exist
   2. adjective: most recently before now
   3. adverb: after everything or everyone else
   4. noun: the person or thing that comes after all the others

Page 43, Practice 3

1. on   3. criminal
2. holds/broke 4. collection

Page 58, Practice 1

1. Part of speech: noun
   General meaning: the part of a pot that you can take off
2. Part of speech: verb + preposition (phrasal verb)
   General meaning: to connect things (a CD player, a TV) with electricity
3. Part of speech: adjective
   General meaning: having rules about what you can or cannot do

Page 65, Practice 2

Part of speech: noun
Possible word or meaning: a visa, something you have to get from a government before you can enter some countries.
Clues: is required, travelers, not allowed to enter, airport, border, officials, refuse entry, embassy

Page 85, Practice

A. 1. pointed out
   2. turn up
   3. ran into
B. 1. run into
   2. pointed out
   3. turned up

Page 94, Practice

S: Experiments   V: have shown;   S: The Monarch Butterfly   V: is;   S: The Monarch   V: is;   S: it V: is;   S: thousands of Monarchs   V: travel

Page 132, Practice

(These are possible responses to the questions. Some answers will vary.)
1. The people are on a street corner (at the corner of Garden and Somerset Streets).
2. One person is asking another person for directions.
3. A is visiting or moving to the area from someplace else. He/She has a suitcase and will be staying in a nearby house or apartment.
4. B lives in the area. B is a kind, helpful person.
5. B will help A find where he/she is going. A will thank B.

Page 147, Practice 1

A. 1. Topic: *Famous physicists*
   Famous scientists is too general. That topic could also include scientists who were famous in other fields, such as biology or chemistry.
   Famous astronomers is too specific. Only some of the scientists were astronomers.
   2. Topic: *Kinds of software/applications/programs*
   Computers is too general. The list does not include words about the hardware on a computer or about use of the computer.
   Internet programs is too specific. A media player and a photo editor also function without the Internet.

Page 150, Exercise 1

B. Paragraph B:

    Doing the laundry is not difficult. Some of us have done it hundreds of times, but if it is your first time, don't worry. It really is very simple. First, you sort all the clothes into piles. It is best to separate dark clothes and light clothes. When you have enough clothes to fill the washing machine, turn it on. Be sure to follow the directions. You can ruin your clothes if you make a mistake. When the washing machine is done, you can put your clothes in the dryer, if you have one. If not, you will have to use old-fashioned methods and hang up the clothes outside. When they are dry, you need to fold all the clothes, sort them out, and put them away. Then you are done—for now. Soon the time will come to do it again.

Page 152, Practice 2

A. **Topic:** *b. materials used for houses.* All the sentences in the paragraph relate to that topic.
    a. *Houses around the world* is too general. The paragraph talks only about one aspect of houses (materials). It does not talk about other aspects, such as the size, color, or design.
    c. *The wooden houses of North America* is too specific. Not all the sentences talk about that topic. Some sentences talk about other materials for houses in other places.

B. 1. in the first sentence
    2. houses and materials

C. **Topic:** *materials used for houses*
    1. *North America—houses of wood*
    2. *Mediterranean—houses of stone and brick*
    3. *tropical Asia and Africa—houses of bamboo and plants*
    4. *northern Canada and Alaska—houses of blocks of ice*

Page 154, Practice 3

A. **Topic:** *People's interest in bees.* All the sentences are about that topic.
    Bees is too general. A paragraph with this topic can be about other aspects of bees, for example, the kinds of bees or how they make honey.
    How bees communicate is too specific. Not all the sentences are about this topic. There are also sentences about other reasons why people have been interested in bees.

B. **Topic:** *people's interest in bees*
    1. *ancient people ate honey*
    2. *in more recent past people observed bees*
    3. *today scientists interested in the way they communicate*

Page 156, Practice 4

A. **Main idea:** *c. Television has negative effects on family life.* All the sentences in the paragraph talk about the negative effects.
    a. *Children who watch a lot of television may have problems at school* is too specific. This fact is mentioned, but it is not the writer's main idea in the paragraph.
    b. *Some people today watch a lot of television every day* is too general. A paragraph with this main idea could include sentences about many other things, such as the number of hours they watch television, or the kind of people who watch a lot of television.

B. **Main idea:** *negative effects of television on families*
    1. *stop communication*
    2. *do not talk about events, problems, or feelings*
    3. *no interaction*
    4. *serious problems: conflict, difficulty at school, divorce*

Page 158, Practice 5

A. **Main idea:** *Honey bees have several ways that they can communicate with each other.*

B. **Main idea:** *Honey bees have several ways that they can communicate with each other.*
    1. *by smell—to protect the hive from outsiders*
    2. *through movement—to tell other bees where to find food*

Page 161, Practice 5

    1. Choice *a* is not possible. There are many words in the paragraph that refer to dogs positively—*help, protect, good company, pets, best friend.*
    Choice *b* is also not possible. We do not know about any other possible "friends." The paragraph does not mention any other animals.
    Choice *c* is not possible. The word *latest* refers to something recent, but the paragraph refers to early human history.
    Choice *d* is the answer. The paragraph refers to dogs as *the first domesticated animals.*

2. Choice *a* is not possible because it makes no sense. You cannot avoid accidents by driving faster.

Choice *b* is the answer because it is the most logical. If you cannot see ahead, you do not have time to do anything if you see something in the road (turn away, put on the brakes) and so are more likely to have an accident.

Choice *c* is not possible because in fact you have less time, not *more time*.

Choice *d* is not possible because it makes no sense. If you cannot see far ahead, you will have less time to see things in the road, but that makes it more (not less) likely that you will have an accident.

Page 195, Practice 1

B. 1. sequence
   2. problem/solution
   3. comparison

Page 197, Practice 2

Introduction:
  Overall idea: Cinema grew out of earlier forms of entertainment at the end of the 19th century.

Development:
1. Main idea: Peep shows were popular in many American cities.
   1. film was viewed in a peep show
   2. Thomas Edison invented a peep show machine
   3. Edison opened special peep show shops
2. Main idea: Inventors began to work on film projectors.
   1. limit to peep show machines—one person at a time
   2. improved technology so could show films to more people
   3. in 1895, film projectors in use
3. Main idea: From the point of view of the producers, cinema had advantages over theatre and musical hall productions, as well as peep shows.
   1. recorded material, so no need to pay people
   2. no limits to size of audience
Conclusion:
  Audiences enthusiastic about cinema—the beginning of mass entertainment

Page 231, Practice

C. 1. c
   2. a
   3. c
   4. c
   5. b
   6. a
   7. b
   8. a

APPENDIX 1
Pronunciation Key

Vowels		Consonants	
Symbol	**Key Word**	**Symbol**	**Key Word**
i	beat, feed	p	pack, happy
ɪ	bit, did	b	back, rubber
eɪ	date, paid	t	tie
ɛ	bet, bed	d	die
æ	bat, bad	k	came, key, quick
a	box, odd, father	g	game, guest
ɔ	bought, dog	tʃ	church, nature, watch
oʊ	boat , road	dʒ	judge, general, major
ʊ	book, good	f	fan, photograph
u	boot, food, student	v	van
ʌ	but, mud, mother	θ	thing, breath
ə	banana, among	ð	then, breathe
ɚ	shirt, murder	s	sip, city, psychology
aɪ	bite, cry, buy, eye	z	zip, please, goes
aʊ	about, how	ʃ	ship, machine, station special, discussion
ɔɪ	voice, boy	ʒ	measure, vision
ɪr	beer	h	hot, who
ɛr	bare	m	men, some
ɑr	bar	n	sun, know, pneumonia
ɔr	door	ŋ	sung, ringing
ʊr	tour	w	wet, white
		l	light, long
		r	right, wrong
		y	yes, use, music
		t̬	butter, bottle
		t̚	button

APPENDIX 2
Frequently Used Words in English

This list was compiled from the Pearson International Corpus of Academic English. It contains the top 3,000 words in the corpus ranked by raw frequency. The Pearson International Corpus of Academic English, Version 1.2010 was developed and is owned by Pearson Language Tests, London, UK, a division of Edexcel Ltd (http://www.pearsonpte.com/).

a	adapt	alien	apparent	asset	band
abandon	adaptation	alike	apparently	assign	bank
ability	add	alive	appeal	assignment	bar
able	addition	all	appear	assist	barrier
about	additional	allocate	appearance	assistance	base
above	address	allow	applicable	assistant	basic
abroad	adequate	ally	applicant	associate	basically
absence	adequately	almost	application	association	basis
absent	adjacent	alone	apply	assume	battle
absolute	adjust	along	appoint	assumption	be
absolutely	adjustment	alongside	appointment	assure	bear
absorb	administer	already	appreciate	at	beat
abstract	administration	also	appreciation	atmosphere	beautiful
abuse	administrative	alter	approach	atom	beauty
academic	admission	alternative	appropriate	attach	because
accelerate	admit	alternatively	appropriately	attachment	become
accept	adopt	although	approval	attack	bed
acceptable	adoption	altogether	approve	attain	before
acceptance	adult	always	approximately	attempt	begin
access	advance	amazing	arbitrary	attend	beginning
accessible	advanced	ambiguity	architecture	attention	behalf
accident	advantage	ambiguous	area	attitude	behave
accommodate	advertising	among	arena	attract	behavior
accommodation	advice	amongst	argue	attraction	behind
accompany	advise	amount	argument	attractive	being
accomplish	advocate	an	arise	attribute	belief
accord	aesthetic	analogy	arm	audience	believe
accordance	affair	analysis	army	author	belong
accordingly	affect	analyst	around	authority	below
account	afford	analytical	arrange	automatic	beneficial
accumulate	afraid	analyze	arrangement	automatically	benefit
accuracy	after	ancient	array	autonomous	besides
accurate	afternoon	and	arrest	autonomy	between
accurately	again	anger	arrival	availability	beyond
accuse	against	angle	arrive	available	bias
achieve	age	angry	art	average	big
achievement	agency	animal	article	avoid	bill
acid	agenda	announce	articulate	award	billion
acknowledge	agent	annual	artificial	aware	binary
acquire	aggressive	another	artist	awareness	bind
acquisition	ago	answer	artistic	away	biological
across	agree	anticipate	as	baby	biology
act	agreement	anxiety	aside	back	bird
action	agricultural	any	ask	background	birth
active	ahead	anybody	aspect	bad	bit
actively	aid	anyone	aspiration	bag	black
activity	aim	anything	assemble	balance	blame
actor	air	anyway	assert	ball	blind
actual	albeit	anywhere	assertion	assessment	block
actually	alcohol	apart	assess	ban	blood

blow	case	closed	completely	consultation	creativity
blue	cash	closely	completion	consume	credit
board	cast	closer	complex	consumer	crime
body	catch	clothes	complexity	consumption	criminal
bond	category	clothing	complicate	contact	crisis
bone	cause	cloud	complicated	contain	criterion
book	caution	club	component	contemporary	critic
border	cease	clue	compose	content	critical
borrow	celebrate	cluster	composition	contest	critically
both	celebrity	coast	compound	context	criticism
bottom	cell	code	comprehensive	continually	criticize
boundary	cent	coffee	comprise	continue	critique
box	center	cognitive	compromise	continued	crop
boy	central	coherent	computer	continuity	cross
brain	centre	coin	conceive	continuous	crowd
branch	century	coincide	concentrate	contract	crucial
brand	ceremony	cold	concentration	contradiction	cry
break	certain	collaboration	concept	contrary	cultural
breakdown	certainly	collapse	conception	contrast	culture
bridge	chain	colleague	conceptual	contribute	curious
brief	chair	collect	concern	contribution	current
briefly	challenge	collection	concerned	control	currently
bright	chance	collective	conclude	controversial	curriculum
brilliant	change	college	conclusion	controversy	curve
bring	channel	color	concrete	convenient	custom
broad	chapter	column	condition	convention	customer
broaden	character	com	conduct	conventional	cut
broadly	characterize	combat	conference	conversation	cycle
brother	characteristic	combination	confidence	conversely	daily
budget	characterize	combine	confident	conversion	damage
build	charge	combined	configuration	convert	dance
building	chart	come	confine	convey	danger
burden	cheap	comfort	confirm	conviction	dangerous
burn	check	comfortable	conflict	convince	dark
bus	chemical	command	conform	cool	data
business	chemistry	comment	confront	cooperation	database
busy	chief	commentary	confuse	coordinate	date
but	child	commentator	confusion	cope	datum
buy	childhood	commercial	conjunction	copy	daughter
by	choice	commission	connect	core	day
calculate	choose	commit	connection	corner	dead
calculation	church	commitment	conscious	corporate	deal
call	circle	committee	consciousness	corporation	death
camera	circuit	commodity	consensus	correct	debate
camp	circumstance	common	consent	correctly	debt
campaign	cite	commonly	consequence	correlation	decade
campus	citizen	communicate	consequently	correspond	decide
can	city	communication	conservative	correspondence	decision
cancer	civil	community	consider	corresponding	declare
candidate	claim	company	considerable	cost	decline
capability	clarify	comparable	considerably	could	decrease
capable	clarity	comparative	consideration	council	dedicate
capacity	class	compare	consist	counsel	deem
capital	classic	comparison	consistency	count	deep
capitalism	classical	compatible	consistent	counter	deeply
capitalist	classification	compensate	consistently	counterpart	defeat
capture	classify	compensation	constant	country	defense
car	classroom	compete	constantly	couple	defend
carbon	clean	competence	constituent	course	define
card	clear	competition	constitute	court	definitely
care	clearly	competitive	constrain	cover	definition
career	client	complain	constraint	coverage	degree
careful	climate	complaint	construct	create	delay
carefully	clinical	complement	construction	creation	deliberately
carry	close	complete	consult	creative	deliver

delivery	disagree	duration	employment	ever	exposure
demand	disagreement	during	empty	every	express
democracy	disappear	duty	enable	everybody	expression
democratic	disaster	dynamic	enact	everyday	extend
demonstrate	discipline	dynamics	encompass	everyone	extended
demonstration	discourse	each	encounter	everything	extension
denote	discover	ear	encourage	everywhere	extensive
density	discovery	earlier	end	evidence	extent
deny	discrete	early	endorse	evident	external
department	discrimination	earn	enemy	evil	extra
departure	discuss	earth	energy	evolution	extract
depend	discussion	ease	enforce	evolve	extraordinary
dependence	disease	easily	engage	exact	extreme
dependent	dismiss	eastern	engagement	exactly	extremely
depict	disorder	easy	engine	exam	eye
deposit	displace	eat	engineer	examination	face
depression	display	echo	engineering	examine	facilitate
depth	dispute	economic	enhance	example	facility
derive	dissolve	economics	enjoy	exceed	fact
describe	distance	economy	enormous	excellent	factor
description	distant	edge	enough	except	factory
deserve	distinct	edit	ensure	exception	faculty
design	distinction	edition	entail	exceptional	fail
designate	distinctive	editor	enter	excess	failure
desirable	distinguish	educate	enterprise	excessive	fair
desire	distribute	education	entertainment	exchange	fairly
despite	distribution	educational	enthusiasm	excite	faith
destination	district	effect	entire	exciting	fall
destroy	diverse	effective	entirely	exclude	familiar
destruction	diversity	effectively	entitle	exclusion	family
detail	divide	effectiveness	entity	exclusive	famous
detailed	division	efficiency	entry	exclusively	fan
detect	divorce	efficient	environment	excuse	fantastic
determination	do	effort	environmental	executive	fantasy
determine	doctor	eight	episode	exemplify	far
develop	doctrine	either	equal	exercise	farm
development	document	elaborate	equality	exert	farmer
device	dog	elect	equally	exhibit	fascinating
devise	dollar	election	equation	exhibition	fashion
devote	domain	electric	equilibrium	exist	fast
diagram	domestic	electrical	equip	existence	faster
dialogue	dominance	electron	equipment	existing	fat
dictate	dominant	electronic	equivalent	expand	fate
die	dominate	element	era	expansion	father
diet	door	eligible	error	expect	fault
differ	double	eliminate	escape	expectation	favor
difference	doubt	elite	especially	expenditure	fear
different	down	else	essay	expense	feature
differential	dozen	elsewhere	essence	expensive	federal
differentiate	draft	email	essential	experience	fee
differently	drama	embed	essentially	experienced	feed
difficult	dramatic	embody	establish	experiment	feedback
difficulty	dramatically	embrace	established	experimental	feel
digital	draw	emerge	establishment	expert	feeling
dilemma	drawing	emergence	estate	expertise	fellow
dimension	dream	emergency	estimate	explain	female
diminish	dress	emission	ethic	explanation	feminist
dinner	drink	emotion	ethical	explicit	few
direct	drinking	emotional	ethnic	explicitly	fiction
direction	drive	emphasis	evaluate	exploit	field
directly	driver	emphasize	evaluation	exploitation	fifth
director	drop	empirical	even	exploration	fifty
dirt	drug	employ	evening	explore	fight
disability	dry	employee	event	export	figure
disadvantage	due	employer	eventually	expose	file

fill	freedom	graph	history	improvement	integrate
film	freely	grasp	hit	impulse	integrated
filter	frequency	great	hold	in	integration
final	frequent	greatly	hole	inability	integrity
finally	frequently	green	holiday	inadequate	intellectual
finance	fresh	gross	home	inappropriate	intelligence
financial	friend	ground	honest	incentive	intend
find	friendly	group	hope	incident	intense
finding	friendship	grow	hopefully	include	intensity
fine	from	growth	horse	inclusion	intensive
finger	front	guarantee	hospital	income	intent
finish	fruit	guard	host	incorporate	intention
fire	fuel	guess	hot	increase	interact
firm	fulfill	guest	hour	increasingly	interaction
firmly	full	guidance	house	indeed	interactive
first	fully	guide	household	independence	interest
firstly	fun	guideline	housing	independent	interested
fish	function	guilty	how	independently	interesting
fit	functional	guy	however	index	interfere
five	fund	habit	huge	indicate	intermediate
fix	fundamental	hair	human	indication	internal
flat	fundamentally	half	humanity	indicator	international
flexibility	funding	hall	hundred	indigenous	interpret
flexible	funny	hand	hurt	indirect	interpretation
flight	further	handle	husband	individual	interrupt
flood	furthermore	hang	hybrid	individually	interval
floor	future	happen	hypothesis	induce	intervene
flow	gain	happy	ice	industrial	intervention
fluid	game	hard	idea	industry	interview
fly	gap	hardly	ideal	inequality	intimate
focus	garden	harm	identical	inevitable	into
folk	gas	hate	identification	inevitably	introduce
follow	gather	have	identify	infant	introduction
following	gay	he	identity	influence	invent
food	gender	head	ideological	influential	invest
foot	general	health	ideology	inform	investigate
football	generally	healthy	if	informal	investigation
for	generate	hear	ignore	information	investment
force	generation	hearing	ill	infrastructure	invite
foreign	generic	heart	illegal	inherent	invoke
forest	genetic	heat	illness	inherit	involve
forget	genre	heavily	illustrate	initial	involvement
form	genuine	heavy	illustration	initially	ion
formal	geographical	height	image	initiate	iron
formally	geography	help	imagination	initiative	irrelevant
format	gesture	helpful	imagine	injury	island
formation	get	hence	immediate	inner	isolate
former	giant	her	immediately	innovation	isolated
formula	gift	here	impact	innovative	isolation
formulate	girl	hero	imperative	input	issue
formulation	give	herself	implement	inquiry	it
forth	glass	hidden	implementation	insert	item
forum	global	hide	implication	inside	its
forward	go	hierarchy	implicit	insight	itself
foster	goal	high	imply	insist	job
found	god	highlight	import	inspiration	join
foundation	gold	highly	importance	inspire	joint
founder	good	him	important	instance	joke
four	govern	himself	importantly	instead	journal
fourth	government	hint	impose	institution	journalist
fraction	grade	hire	impossible	institutional	journey
fragment	gradually	his	impress	instruction	judge
frame	graduate	historian	impression	instrument	judgment
framework	grand	historical	impressive	insurance	jump
free	grant	historically	improve	integral	just

justice	like	many	miss	necessity	occurrence
justification	likelihood	map	mission	need	ocean
justify	likely	margin	mistake	negative	odd
keen	likewise	mark	mix	neglect	of
keep	limit	market	mixed	negotiate	off
key	limitation	marketing	mixture	negotiation	offer
kick	limited	marriage	mobile	neither	office
kid	line	marry	mobility	nervous	officer
kill	linear	mass	mode	net	official
kind	linguistic	massive	model	network	often
know	link	master	moderate	neutral	oil
knowledge	liquid	match	modern	never	okay
label	list	material	modest	nevertheless	old
labor	listen	mathematical	modification	new	on
laboratory	literally	matrix	modify	newly	once
lack	literary	matter	molecular	news	one
lady	literature	mature	molecule	newspaper	ongoing
land	little	maximum	moment	next	online
landscape	live	may	money	nice	only
language	living	maybe	monitor	night	onto
large	load	me	month	nine	open
largely	loan	meal	mood	nineteenth	opening
last	local	mean	moral	no	operate
late	locate	meaning	more	nobody	operation
later	location	meaningful	moreover	noise	operator
latter	lock	means	morning	none	opinion
laugh	log	measure	most	nonetheless	opponent
launch	logic	measurement	mostly	nor	opportunity
law	logical	mechanical	mother	norm	oppose
lawyer	long	mechanism	motion	normal	opposite
lay	longer	medical	motivate	normally	opposition
layer	look	medicine	motivation	north	optical
lead	loose	medium	motive	northern	option
leader	lose	meet	motor	not	or
leadership	loss	meeting	mount	notable	oral
learn	lot	member	mountain	notably	order
learning	love	membership	mouth	note	ordinary
least	low	memory	move	nothing	organ
leave	lower	mental	movement	notice	organic
lecture	machine	mention	movie	notion	organization
lecturer	magazine	mere	much	novel	organize
left	magnitude	merely	multiple	now	orient
leg	main	merge	multiply	nowhere	orientation
legacy	mainly	merit	murder	nuclear	origin
legal	mainstream	message	music	number	original
legislation	maintain	metal	musical	numerous	originally
legitimate	maintenance	metaphor	must	nurse	originate
leisure	major	method	mutual	object	other
lend	majority	methodology	my	objection	otherwise
length	make	middle	myself	objective	ought
less	maker	might	myth	obligation	our
lesser	making	migration	name	obscure	ourselves
lesson	male	mile	namely	observation	out
let	man	military	narrative	observe	outcome
letter	manage	million	narrow	observer	outline
level	management	mind	nation	obstacle	output
liberal	manager	mine	national	obtain	outside
liberty	manifest	minimal	native	obvious	outstanding
library	manifestation	minimum	natural	obviously	over
lie	manipulate	minister	naturally	occasion	overall
life	manipulation	minor	nature	occasional	overcome
lifestyle	manner	minority	near	occasionally	overlap
lifetime	manual	minute	nearly	occupation	overlook
lift	manufacture	mirror	necessarily	occupy	overseas
light	manufacturing	mislead	necessary	occur	overview

overwhelming
owe
own
owner
ownership
pace
pack
package
page
pain
paint
painting
pair
panel
paper
paradigm
paragraph
parallel
parameter
parent
park
part
partial
partially
participant
participate
participation
particle
particular
particularly
partly
partner
partnership
party
pass
passage
passion
passive
past
path
pathway
patient
pattern
pay
payment
peace
peak
peer
penalty
people
per
perceive
percent
percentage
perception
perfect
perfectly
perform
performance
perhaps
period
permanent
permission
permit
persist

person
personal
personality
personally
personnel
perspective
persuade
phase
phenomenon
philosopher
philosophical
philosophy
phone
photo
photograph
phrase
physical
physically
pick
picture
piece
pioneer
place
placement
plain
plan
plane
planet
planning
plant
plastic
plate
platform
play
player
please
pleasure
plenty
plot
plus
poem
poet
poetry
point
police
policy
political
politically
politician
politics
pollution
pool
poor
poorly
pop
popular
popularity
population
portion
portray
pose
position
positive
positively
possess

possession
possibility
possible
possibly
post
potential
potentially
pound
poverty
power
powerful
practical
practice
practitioner
praise
precede
precise
precisely
predict
prediction
predominantly
prefer
preference
preferred
prejudice
preliminary
premise
preparation
prepare
presence
present
presentation
preserve
president
press
pressure
presumably
pretend
pretty
prevail
prevent
previous
previously
price
pride
primarily
primary
prime
principal
principle
print
prior
priority
prise
prison
private
privilege
probability
probably
problem
problematic
procedure
proceed
proceeding
process

processing
produce
producer
product
production
productive
productivity
profession
professional
professor
profile
profit
profound
program
progress
progressive
prohibit
project
prominent
promise
promote
promotion
prompt
proof
proper
properly
property
proportion
proposal
propose
proposition
prospect
protect
protection
protest
proud
prove
provide
provider
provision
provoke
psychological
psychologist
psychology
public
publication
publicly
publish
publishing
pull
punishment
purchase
pure
purely
purpose
pursue
pursuit
push
put
qualification
qualify
qualitative
quality
quantitative
quantity

quarter
question
quick
quickly
quiet
quite
quote
race
racial
racism
radical
radically
radio
rain
raise
random
range
rank
rapid
rapidly
rare
rarely
rate
rather
rating
ratio
rational
raw
reach
react
reaction
read
reader
readily
reading
ready
real
realistic
reality
realize
really
realm
reason
reasonable
reasonably
reasoning
recall
receive
recent
recently
reception
recipient
recognition
recognize
recommend
recommendation
record
recording
recover
recovery
recruit
red
reduce
reduction
refer

reference
reflect
reflection
reform
refuse
regard
regardless
regime
region
regional
register
regular
regularly
regulate
regulation
reinforce
reject
relate
related
relation
relationship
relative
relatively
relax
release
relevance
relevant
reliable
relief
religion
religious
rely
remain
remainder
remark
remarkable
remember
remind
remote
removal
remove
render
rent
repair
repeat
repeated
repeatedly
replace
replacement
reply
report
represent
representation
representative
reproduce
reputation
request
require
requirement
research
researcher
resemble
reserve
reside
residence

resident	sample	set	slowly	spread	study
resist	sanction	setting	small	spring	stuff
resistance	satellite	settle	smile	square	style
resolution	satisfaction	settlement	smoke	stability	subject
resolve	satisfactory	seven	smooth	stable	subjective
resort	satisfy	several	so	staff	submit
resource	save	severe	social	stage	subordinate
respect	say	sex	socially	stake	subsequent
respective	scale	sexual	society	stance	subsequently
respectively	scenario	sexuality	sociology	stand	substance
respond	scene	shake	soft	standard	substantial
response	schedule	shall	software	standing	substantially
responsibility	scheme	shape	soil	star	substitute
responsible	scholar	share	soldier	start	subtle
rest	scholarship	sharp	sole	state	succeed
restore	school	she	solely	statement	success
restrict	science	sheet	solid	static	successful
restriction	scientific	shift	solution	station	successfully
result	scientist	ship	solve	statistic	successive
retain	scope	shock	some	statistical	such
return	score	shoot	somebody	status	sudden
reveal	screen	shop	somehow	stay	suddenly
revenue	script	short	someone	steady	suffer
reverse	sea	shortly	something	steal	sufficient
review	search	shot	sometimes	stem	sufficiently
revise	season	should	somewhat	step	suggest
revision	seat	show	somewhere	stereotype	suggestion
revolution	second	shut	son	stick	suit
revolutionary	secondary	sick	song	still	suitable
reward	secondly	side	soon	stimulate	sum
rhetoric	secret	sight	sophisticated	stimulus	summarize
rich	section	sign	sorry	stock	summary
ride	sector	signal	sort	stone	summer
right	secure	significance	soul	stop	sun
ring	security	significant	sound	storage	superior
rise	see	significantly	source	store	supplement
risk	seed	signify	south	storey	supply
ritual	seek	silence	southern	storm	support
rival	seem	similar	space	story	supporter
river	seemingly	similarity	span	straight	supportive
road	segment	similarly	spatial	straightforward	suppose
rock	select	simple	speak	strain	suppress
role	selected	simplify	speaker	strand	sure
roll	selection	simply	special	strange	surely
romantic	selective	simultaneously	specialist	strategic	surface
room	self	since	specie	strategy	surprise
root	sell	sing	species	stream	surprising
rough	semester	single	specific	street	surprisingly
roughly	seminar	sister	specifically	strength	surround
round	send	sit	specify	strengthen	survey
route	senior	site	spectrum	stress	survival
routine	sense	situate	speech	stretch	survive
row	sensitive	situation	speed	strict	suspect
rule	sensitivity	six	spell	strictly	suspend
run	sentence	size	spend	strike	sweet
rural	separate	sketch	spending	striking	switch
rush	separately	skill	sphere	string	symbol
sacrifice	separation	skilled	spin	strip	symbolic
sad	sequence	skin	spirit	strive	symptom
safe	series	sleep	spiritual	strong	synthesis
safety	serious	slide	spite	strongly	system
sake	seriously	slight	split	structural	systematic
sale	serve	slightly	sponsor	structure	table
salt	service	slip	sport	struggle	tackle
same	session	slow	spot	student	take

tale	third	transmission	until	voice	why
talent	thirty	transmit	unusual	volume	wide
talk	this	transport	up	voluntary	widely
tape	thoroughly	trap	update	volunteer	widespread
target	those	travel	upon	vote	wife
task	though	treat	upper	vulnerable	wild
taste	thought	treatment	upset	wage	will
tax	thousand	tree	urban	wait	willing
teach	threat	trend	urge	wake	win
teacher	threaten	trial	us	walk	wind
teaching	three	trigger	usage	wall	window
team	threshold	trip	use	want	winner
tear	through	trouble	useful	war	winter
technical	throughout	truly	user	warm	wire
technique	throw	trust	usual	warn	wisdom
technological	thus	truth	usually	warning	wish
technology	ticket	try	utility	wash	with
telephone	tie	tune	valid	waste	withdraw
television	tight	turn	validity	watch	within
tell	time	tutor	valuable	water	without
temperature	timing	twelve	value	wave	witness
temporary	tiny	twentieth	van	way	woman
ten	tip	twenty	variable	we	wonder
tend	title	twice	variation	weak	wonderful
tendency	to	two	varied	weakness	wood
tension	today	type	variety	wealth	word
term	together	typical	various	weapon	work
terminology	tomorrow	typically	vary	wear	worker
territory	tone	ultimate	vast	weather	working
test	tonight	ultimately	vehicle	web	workplace
testing	too	unable	venture	website	workshop
text	tool	uncertain	verbal	week	world
textbook	top	uncertainty	version	weekend	worldwide
than	topic	under	versus	weekly	worry
thank	total	undergo	vertical	weigh	worth
that	totally	undergraduate	very	weight	worthy
the	touch	underlie	via	welcome	would
theatre	tough	undermine	vice	welfare	write
their	tour	understand	victim	well	writer
them	toward	understanding	victory	west	writing
theme	towards	undertake	video	western	written
themselves	town	undoubtedly	view	what	wrong
then	trace	unexpected	viewer	whatever	year
theoretical	track	unfortunately	viewpoint	when	yes
theorist	trade	uniform	village	whenever	yet
theory	tradition	union	violate	where	yield
therapy	traditional	unique	violence	whereas	you
there	traditionally	unit	violent	whereby	young
thereby	traffic	unite	virtual	wherever	your
therefore	train	unity	virtually	whether	yourself
these	training	universal	virtue	which	youth
thesis	trait	universe	visible	while	zero
they	transfer	university	vision	whilst	zone
thick	transform	unknown	visit	white	
thin	transformation	unless	visitor	who	
thing	transition	unlike	visual	whole	
think	translate	unlikely	vital	whom	
thinking	translation	unnecessary	vocabulary	whose	

Credits

TEXT CREDITS

Page 8, Copyright holder unknown. Every effort has been made to contact the copyright holder of this work. **Page 17,** Back Cover Copy from THE OUTSIDERS by S.E. Hinton. Used by permission of Viking Penguin, A Division of Penguin Young Readers Group, A Member of Penguin Group (USA) Inc., 345 Hudson Street, New York, NY 10014. All rights reserved. **Page 18,** Back cover copy from THE ISLAND OF THE BLUE DOLPHINS by Scott O'Dell, Houghton Mifflin Harcourt Publishing, copyright © 1960. Used by permission. **Pages 63–64,** From THE OUTSIDERS by S.E. Hinton, copyright © 1967 by S.E. Hinton. Used by permission of Viking Penguin, A Division of Penguin Young Readers Group, A Member of Penguin Group (USA) Inc., 345 Hudson Street, New York, NY 10014. All rights reserved. And, by permission of Curtis Brown, Ltd. All rights reserved. And, by permission of Penguin Books, Ltd. Copyright © 2010 Guardian News and Media Ltd. Used by permission. **Pages 64–65,** From THE DIARY OF A YOUNG GIRL: THE DEFINITIVE EDITION by Anne Frank, edited by Otto H. Frank and Mirjam Pressler, translated by Susan Massotty, translation copyright © 1995 by Doubleday, a division of Random House, Inc. Used by permission of Doubleday, a division of Random House, Inc., Penguin Group (UK), and Liepman AG. **Page 115,** From "Surge in Teeth Grinding Linked to Recession" by Dennis Campbell and Janet Hardy-Gould, Guardian Weekly, April 9, 2010. Copyright © 2010 Guardian News and Media Ltd. Used by permission. **Page 134,** Copyright holder unknown. Every effort has been made to contact the copyright holder of this work. **Page 135,** "The Standard of Living," copyright 1941 by Dorothy Parker, renewed © 1969 by Lillian Hellman, from THE PORTABLE DOROTHY PARKER by Dorothy Parker, edited by Marion Meade. Used by permission of Viking Penguin, a division of Penguin Group (USA) Inc. and by Gerald Duckworth and Co., Ltd. **Page 189,** Adapted from "The Language of Online Love" by Lucy Tobin, Guardian Weekly, June 25, 2010.

PHOTO/ILLUSTRATION CREDITS

Page 1, iStockphoto.com. **Page 3,** Moodboard/Alamy. **Page 31,** Shutterstock.com. **Page 105,** Shutterstock.com. **Page 117,** Shutterstock.com. **Page 227,** Shutterstock.com.